The Oil Cris

CW00406322

Turning Points Series List

TURNING POINTS
General Editor: Keith Robbins
Vice-Chancellor, University of Wales Lampeter

THE FALL OF FRANCE, 1940
Andrew Shennan

THE OIL CRISIS
Fiona Venn

THE FALL OF CONSTANTINOPLE, 1453
Michael Angold

ENDING APARTHEID
Jack Spence

THE INDIAN MUTINY
Rudrangshu Mukherjee

NUREMBERG TRIALS
Michael Biddiss

SLAVE EMANCIPATION AND AFTER
David Turley

GERMAN UNIFICATION
Lothar Kettenacker

EASTER RISING
Charles Townshend

The Oil Crisis

Fiona Venn

An imprint of **Pearson Education**

London · New York · Toronto · Sydney · Tokyo · Singapore · Hong Kong · Cape Town
New Delhi · Madrid · Paris · Amsterdam · Munich · Milan · Stockholm

PEARSON EDUCATION LIMITED

Head Office:
Edinburgh Gate
Harlow CM20 2JE
Tel: +44 (0)1279 623623
Fax: +44 (0)1279 431059

London Office:
128 Long Acre
London WC2E 9AN
Tel: +44 (0)20 7447 2000
Fax: +44 (0)20 7240 5771
Website: www.history-minds.com

First published in Great Britain in 2002

© Pearson Education Limited 2002

The right of Fiona Venn to be identified as Author
of this Work has been asserted by her in accordance
with the Copyright, Designs and Patents Act 1988.

ISBN 0 582 30809 7

British Library Cataloguing in Publication Data
A CIP catalogue record for this book can be obtained from the British Library

Library of Congress Cataloging in Publication Data
A CIP catalog record for this book can be obtained from the Library of Congress

10 9 8 7 6 5 4 3 2 1

Typeset by Fakenham Photosetting Ltd in Bembo 11.5/13
Printed and bound in Great Britain by Ashford Colour Press Ltd, Gosport

The Publishers' policy is to use paper manufactured from sustainable forests.

CONTENTS

LIST OF TABLES AND MAPS

LIST OF ABBREVIATIONS

ARAMCO	Arabian American Oil Company
AWACS	Airborne Warning and Control System
BNOC	British National Oil Corporation
BP	British Petroleum
CFP	Compagnie Française des Pétroles
CIA	Central Intelligence Agency
CIEC	Conference on International Economic Cooperation
ERAP	Enterprise des Recherches et d'Activités Pétrolières
GDP	gross domestic product
GNP	gross national product
ISI	import substitution industrialization
IMF	International Monetary Fund
IPC	Iraq Petroleum Company
KOC	Kuwait Oil Company
LDCs	less-developed countries
mbd	million barrels per day
NIEO	New International Economic Order
OECD	Organization for Economic Cooperation and Development
OPEC	Organization of Petroleum Exporting Countries
OAPEC	Organization of Arab Petroleum Exporting Countries
PLO	Palestine Liberation Organization
SALT	Strategic Arms Limitation Treaty
UAE	United Arab Emirates
UN	United Nations
UNCTAD	United Nations Conference on Trade and Development
USSR	Union of Soviet Socialist Republics (Soviet Union)

PREFACE

In October 1973, the Organization of Petroleum Exporting Countries (OPEC) decided unilaterally to end the oil corporations' monopoly over crude oil prices and production levels, and immediately set a price considerably in excess of the prevailing norm. In the same month, a war broke out between Israel and the neighbouring Arab states: in order to support the Arab cause, a number of leading Arab oil producers announced a selective boycott of oil supplies, coupled with a progressive cut in production levels. In the aftermath of these two separate decisions, oil prices soared, the traditional role of companies within the international oil industry changed, and the incomes of the major oil-exporting states increased severalfold. The petrodollar became an important element in the world economy, and Western companies competed for the contracts available for the rapid further development and modernization of the newly affluent oil states. Meanwhile, the vast rise in the price of oil caused further problems for the economies of the industrialized world, already suffering from inflation. Even when the real price of oil began to decline later in the 1970s, the power over pricing and production decisions still remained with the producer governments rather than the oil companies. In 1979 the Iranian Revolution triggered a worldwide panic about oil supplies that again pushed up prices severalfold and dealt a further blow to the developed economies.

Although both crises had a transforming effect upon the international political economy, it is the first, in 1973, whose date is commonly used as a shorthand reference point for a moment of transformation. In histories of the world economy, the Middle East and the oil industry, '1973' is used as a synonym for a moment of crisis and change. Many commentators and politicians at the time regarded this apparently massive upset in traditional sources of power within the world economy and the oil industry as heralding an irreversible – and regrettable – change. In examining elements of both continuity and change in a number of different political and economic spheres, this study will cast doubt upon some of the more exaggerated conclusions and predictions of contemporaries, and emphasize the many aspects of the international political economy that have remained remarkably unchanged since 1973. Nonetheless, the magnitude of the perceived changes suggests, rightly, that while the oil crisis might not have had the degree of influence and change that some maintained at the time, nonetheless it accelerated existing forces for change and acted as a catalyst to such an extent that the use of the term 'turning point' is indeed justified.

In a personal respect, also, the 1973 oil crisis was indeed a significant turning point. In October 1973, as a fledging doctoral student, I was struggling to find a topic within Anglo–American relations upon which to base my research and thesis. Fascinated by the turn of events during that eventful month, I began to examine the historical antecedents of the petroleum industry in the Middle East, and soon came to realize that its history provided, in microcosm, an ideal case study for the protracted process by which the United States replaced the United Kingdom as the world's leading capitalist power. The eventual consequence was my PhD thesis on 'Anglo–American relations and Middle Eastern Oil, 1918–34'. My entire career as a historian of oil diplomacy dates from the October 1973 oil crisis. It is a salutary thought to realize that those turbulent events, which I recall so well (including the subsequent economic difficulties and high British inflation rate, which had a devastating impact upon a postgraduate student seeking to subsist upon a Department of Education studentship), have now passed into the historical domain. Yet many of the issues are still alive today: for that reason, while this discussion centres on the decade of the 1970s, it also addresses developments until the current day.

ACKNOWLEDGEMENTS

We are grateful to the following for permission to reproduce copyright material:
Map 1 redrawn from *The Dent Atlas of the Arab-Israeli Conflict, 6th Edition* published by J.M. Dent and reprinted by permission of Routledge (Gilbert, M. 1993); Map 2 redrawn from *The Making of the Modern Gulf States: Kuwait, Bahrain, Qatar, The United Arab Emirates and Oman*, published by Unwin Hyman and reprinted by permission of Routledge (Said Zahlan, R. 1989); Tables 2.1, 2.2, 4.2 and 4.3 adapted from *BP Statistical Review of World Energy 2001*, reprinted by permmission of BP Plc.
In some instances we have been unable to trace the owners of copyright material, and we would appreciate any information that would enable us to do so.

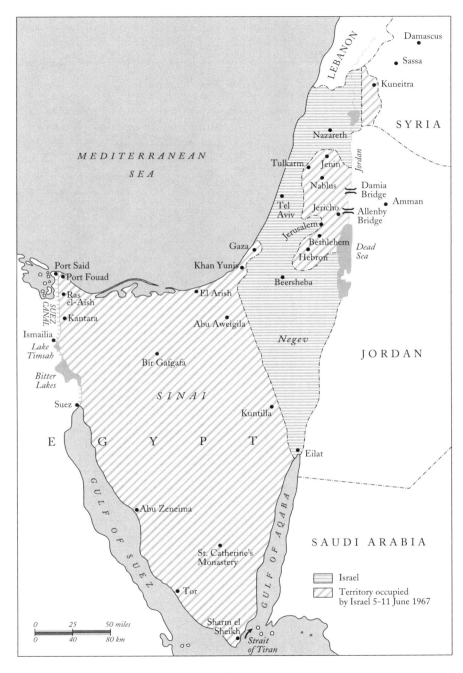

Map 1   Israel and the Occupied Territories, 1967

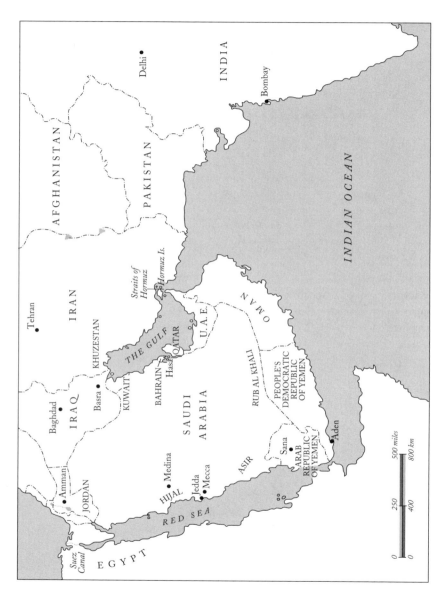

Map 2   The Arabian Peninsula and the Gulf

INTRODUCTION

At the heart of the two oil crises of the 1970s – the causes and consequences of which are discussed in the following chapters – was the multi-faceted impact of sudden, unexpected and substantial increases in the price of crude petroleum. In addition to materially affecting events in the Middle East and within the oil industry – the two areas in which they both had their origins – the crises had immediate and undoubted impacts on the world economy. The 1973 crisis in particular caused a rift between the United States and its trans-Atlantic allies, caused Japan to depart from American foreign policy for the first time since the Second World War, and provoked considerable debate within the recently enlarged European Economic Community about not just energy but also wider foreign policy issues. The fourfold increase in oil prices in the space of three months in 1973, followed in 1979 by an equally rapid, if less sustained threefold increase, directly affected the domestic economy of every country in the world: for the apparently fortunate oil producers it produced a dramatic increase in oil revenues twice in a single decade; and for oil consumers, whether industrialized nations or less-developed countries (LDCs), it increased the cost of imports severalfold. The oil-exporting nations used their new influence in world affairs to press for a substantial revision of the traditional relationships between the developed and the developing nations, in particular a New International Economic Order. The global economic institutions sought to absorb the flood of petrodollars into an unstable world economy and meetings of OPEC, hitherto virtually overlooked by the world's press, became leading items in news reports. To comprehend why, during a period of rising inflation and in a world economy dominated by the industrialized countries, an increase in the price of one commodity should have had such an impact, it is necessary to explain a little about the role played by petroleum and its derivatives in the world economy.

Although the uses of petroleum are many and varied, there are three main categories of use which, between them, did much to explain the dramatic increase in petroleum production and consumption in the years following the Second World War. These are: transportation; energy generation; and the petrochemical industry. By 1945 the importance of the combustion engine had been long recognized; the automobile, already a stalwart of daily life for millions of Americans, became increasingly important within Europe too.[1] Petroleum fuelled much of the vast transportation network which spanned the globe by rail, road, sea and air as part of the increasing integration of the world economy. By the second half of the twentieth century, even such commodities as basic foodstuffs were frequently produced far from their place of consumption. Cheap supplies of petroleum made this possible; but contingent in this dependency was that a sharp rise in the price of petroleum would necessarily have an impact on the price of any commodity transported even over a short distance.

Petroleum did not just power the transportation of the world, however; it played a growing role in the generation of energy, both in the direct heating of buildings and also the production of electricity. Until 1945 Europe had still depended predominantly on coal for its energy generation but, prompted by the Americans and encouraged by falling real prices, oil from the Middle East challenged the predominance of coal, even though, for most European nations, it meant replacing indigenous sources of coal with imported petroleum. The resultant cheap energy transformed the lifestyles of those living in industrialized nations, making electrical household appliances more affordable and transforming leisure activities. It accelerated the spread of mechanization and improved productivity in manufacturing. Meanwhile, improved refining techniques allowed the growth of a sophisticated petrochemical industry producing lubricants, cheap textiles, plastics and other goods which were rapidly integrated into the affluent lifestyle of the West.

The rapid rise in the consumption of petroleum was accompanied by a dramatic change in the main areas of production. The modern oil industry had begun in the United States in 1859, and until the Second World War North America was, for most of the period, the leading producer of petroleum. Despite the energy-hungry lifestyle of Americans, the United States was still able to export large quantities of oil to other countries. However, this was to change. American production could not keep pace with rapidly growing consumption and was in any event undercut by cheaper foreign oil. In 1948, the United States became a net importer of petroleum, although in 1958 oil import quotas were introduced to protect domestic producers and prevent an over-reliance on foreign supplies. Meanwhile, new areas of production were discovered. First in Latin America, in the first thirty years of the century, then the Middle East, and later North Africa, prolific new sources of petroleum were steadily exploited, in such amounts as to undercut rival sources of energy such as coal. These new areas of production shared certain characteristics. First, they were generally in areas outside the developed, industrialized nations. Second, in many cases, petroleum rapidly became the main source of government revenue (although not necessarily of employment, as the labour required in the oil industry is both comparatively small and highly skilled). Third, many of the new oil-producing regions were within either the formal or informal empires of the major Western powers. Finally, because of very low domestic demand, virtually all of the petroleum produced could be directed towards the export market.

The companies responsible for discovering, and exploiting these new supplies of petroleum were, at least in the first half of the twentieth century, predominantly the large multinational oil companies referred to as 'majors' or – more pejoratively – the 'Seven Sisters'.[2] These companies – Texaco (The Texas Oil Company), Exxon (Standard Oil of New Jersey), Mobil (Standard Oil Company of New York), Chevron (Standard Oil of California), Gulf Oil, British Petroleum and Royal Dutch Shell – either independently or in combination held concessions in most of the major oilfields in Latin America and the Middle East as well as some of those in North Africa. Through informal agreements and formal contracts, these companies acted in concert to set prices, control production and generally police the smooth functioning of the oil industry. Conscious of the vital economic and strategic importance of petroleum, parent governments generally accepted this interlocking of interests and policies. Even before 1973 the oil companies were an important part of the American and British economies. The oil companies both needed government support in their overseas dealings and often lobbied for particular policies to be pursued. They were not always successful in the latter; for example, the British Government decided, during the interwar period, that retaining American friendship was more important than bowing to the pressure for British companies to retain control over the Iraq oilfields.[3] However, neither governments nor companies were averse to seeking the support and cooperation of each other. This does not imply that the parent governments were controlled or manipulated by the companies, but rather that there was, in most instances, a very close identification of interests and outlook between the oil companies on the one hand and the government on the other; this frequently meant that their desired policies were similar, even if the reasons underlying them were different. Liaison and discussion on matters of shared concern was to be expected, given the financial importance of the companies, and the fact that they operated in so many different countries, many of them politically sensitive.

3

The relationships between the companies and the host governments were also close, but for different reasons. Because of the pattern of subsoil ownership in most countries, it was the government which negotiated oil concessions (often with only one company or consortium for the whole country) and received the payments for the petroleum that was produced. Where those payments constituted the main source of government revenue, then decisions regarding the price and production level – both firmly in the domain of the company, not the host government – were critical to economic prosperity and planning. Governments routinely sought to persuade the companies to increase revenue, whether by higher prices, higher production levels, or improved concessionary terms. Dissatisfaction with the original concessionary agreements, often signed by a government or ruler with little or no experience of modern industrial practices or financial training, was widespread. Companies also played other important functions which affected governments, whether by the provision of infrastructure and employment, or by less formal arrangements concerning political influence, the provision of advice and education and welfare services. More and more, host governments put pressure on companies to provide training for nationals, to improve employment opportunities, and even to modify or completely replace the original concessions.

Petroleum was not only a vital commodity in the world economy, and in the individual economies of producing and consuming countries, but was also an important factor in the conduct of foreign policy and the pattern of international relations. The host governments relied upon predominantly foreign companies – many of which were closely linked to some of the most powerful Western governments – to maximize their revenue and exploit their main resource. For many consuming countries, access to a commodity crucial to their economic well-being depended upon oil companies (sometimes foreign oil companies) bringing oil sources from foreign oilfields ostensibly owned by foreign governments. As I have argued elsewhere, when the main consumers of petroleum are not its main producers, petroleum must inevitably form an important part of their diplomacy.[4]

In the early stages of development in any oil-producing country, particularly those in the developing world, the government relied heavily upon the expertise, international facilities and capital of the oil companies. However, once the initial stage of development was past, host governments increasingly resented and challenged the companies' total control over their resources. Oil nationalism – an assertion of national rights over petroleum – developed first in Latin America (particularly in Mexico in the 1920s) and then in the Middle East, with the first major producer in that region, Iran, challenging the rights of British Petroleum (then known as the Anglo-Iranian Oil Company) in 1933.[5] By the 1950s links between the Latin American and Middle Eastern producers had been fostered by Venezuela and Saudi Arabia in particular and, following the companies' unilateral cuts in the price they paid host governments for their oil, the decision was taken to formalize the links. In September 1960, at the invitation of the Government of Iraq, representatives of Venezuela, Iran, Iraq, Kuwait and Saudi Arabia met in Baghdad, and decided to form the Organization of Petroleum Exporting Countries (OPEC).[6] Although few realized it at the time, this was a very important development within the oil industry, and was ultimately to change fundamentally the relationships between host governments and the multinational oil companies.

As will be discussed in more detail in later chapters, the six years leading up to the 1973 oil crisis saw major developments in a number of key areas. In 1968 OPEC set out its agenda for change; its members agreed a common set of goals, set out in the Declaratory Statement of Petroleum Policy in Member Countries,[7] in which the Organization identified its future priorities as securing for host governments the right to influence and direct their oil industries. Three years later, in 1971, the major oil companies negotiated collectively with a group of host governments (the Persian Gulf states within OPEC) for the first time. In 1967 war broke out between Israel and a number of Arab states, resulting in Israel's victory and its occupation of very substantial additional territory. During this six-year period, the American economy experienced difficulties which led to the devaluation of the dollar, and the subsequent undermining of the world's financial structure. As the United States was dragged deeper into the mire of Vietnam, its authority as leader of the free world was undermined, while at the same time the European Economic Community expanded not only in terms of numbers of members but also in economic growth. Essentially, the period 1967–73 was a period of transition and change in the Middle East, in the oil industry, in the world economy and in the international political scene. Following this era of transition, all the different contexts outlined above were to come to a head during the autumn and winter of 1973 and, in interrelated ways, brought about fundamental changes in the world's international political economy.

Notes

1. Fiona Venn, *Oil Diplomacy in the Twentieth Century*. Macmillan, London, 1986, Table 1.1, p. 5.
2. Anthony Sampson, *The Seven Sisters: The Great Oil Companies and the World They Made*. Hodder & Stoughton, London, 1975.
3. Fiona Venn, 'Anglo-American Relations and Middle East Oil, 1918–1934', *Diplomacy and Statecraft* 1 (1990), pp. 165–84.
4. Venn, *Oil Diplomacy*, esp. p. 169.
5. George Philip, *Oil and Politics in Latin America: Nationalist Movements and State Companies*. Cambridge University Press, Cambridge, 1982; J.H. Bamberg, *The History of the British Petroleum Company: Volume II, The Anglo-Iranian Years, 1928–1954*. Cambridge University Press, Cambridge, 1994; Venn, *Oil Diplomacy*, pp. 54–82.
6. Ian Seymour, *OPEC: Instrument of Change*. Macmillan, London, 1980, pp. 36–8.
7. Seymour, *OPEC*, pp. 63–5.

1

A DECADE OF CRISIS:
1973 AND 1979

During the 1970s, in the course of six years, the world experienced two major oil shocks; in both cases, sudden and dramatic increases in the price of oil accompanied political turmoil in the Middle East. There were, however, marked differences as well as similarities between the two: while the first, in October 1973, combined a new outbreak of violence in the long-standing Arab–Israeli conflict with a real shortage of supply in the oil market, the second revolved around domestic revolution in Iran on the one hand, and an anticipated shortage of oil on the other. Both, however, caused consternation among consumers, and had wide-reaching, and often unanticipated, consequences. This chapter looks in turn at how each crisis unfolded.

October 1973

The October 1973 'oil crisis' was really the conjuncture of four separate crises which intersected with each other over a short space of time in the turbulent month of October 1973. The first was an independent decision by the major oil exporters, expressed through the Organization of Petroleum Exporting Countries (OPEC) to wrest control of oil prices from the major oil companies, and thereafter to decide production and price levels independently of the corporate interests that had traditionally dominated their oil industries. The second was the long-standing Arab–Israeli dispute, which in 1967 had resulted in a short, decisive and – for the Arabs – humiliating war, at the end of which Israel had occupied territories in the Sinai Peninsula, the West Bank and the Gaza Strip, which increased considerably the area under its control (Map 1). The third, interrelated, crisis was the decision by a group of Arab oil-producing states, linked through the Organization of Arab Petroleum Exporting Countries (OAPEC), to impose an oil boycott on selected countries regarded as sympathetic to Israel, and also to implement cuts in production in an attempt to persuade the West, particularly the United States, to moderate their support for Israel. At the same time as responding to each of these three crises during the critical month of October 1973, the American President Richard Nixon was also facing a number of critical domestic problems, including the resignation of Vice President Spiro Agnew and escalating pressure upon the White House as a consequence of the Watergate investigations into the President's own conduct during the 1972 Presidential election. Each of these crises is described separately below: the key dates are also outlined in the selective chronology (Appendix Three).

The first factor listed above was the decision by the members of OPEC — many of which were not Arab and had no particular commitment to the Arab cause — to address the oil price issue. Despite company concessions in 1971, by 1973 the real price paid to the governments of the main oil-exporting countries had been eroded by problems in the world economy, which led to the devaluation of the dollar and worldwide inflation. By September 1973 the member governments of OPEC were keen to renegotiate the arrangements on price and agreed on a target posted price of 6 dollars for oil from the Persian Gulf. On 8 October 1973, negotiations between the Gulf states of OPEC and the oil companies opened in Vienna, but while the companies initially offered an increase of 45 cents, and their negotiators were authorized to offer up to 60 cents extra, the producers demanded a doubling of the posted price, representing an increase of around 3 dollars per barrel, as well as an automatic mechanism for adjusting posted prices in line with market prices and an inflation index. The companies consulted the governments of the main consuming countries, but found no support for substantial concessions to the OPEC position. It soon became apparent that rapid agreement was unlikely, and hence on 12 October the companies asked for an adjournment. However, only four days later the main Persian Gulf producers met in Kuwait, where they were attending an OAPEC meeting, and decided to act unilaterally, setting the price of Arabian light crude at 5.12 dollars, an increase of over 70 per cent on the prevailing 3.01 dollars. The individual producer governments' share of the price was also increased, from 1.99 dollars per barrel to 3.44 dollars.[1] These increases were for purely economic, not political, reasons and were made possible by the prevailing tight market in oil supply. While the accompanying

Arab–Israeli War may have been a factor in increasing the willingness of OPEC members to challenge the companies and, indirectly, the leading consuming nations of the world. Ian Skeet[2] concludes that 'the writing was already on the wall'.

The oil boycott imposed the following day by Arab producers, and discussed below, further tightened supplies, and by December 1973 the producer governments were receiving bids for their so-called 'participation oil' far in excess of the set price, even as high as 20 dollars or more per barrel for crude from the Mediterranean producers. Led by Iran, which was neither an Arab country nor a participant in the boycott, and supported by Kuwait and Iraq, some OPEC members argued for a much higher price to be set – a position opposed by Saudi Arabia, which had taken the initiative in implementing the oil boycott but was now concerned *inter alia* that excessively high oil prices could trigger a major economic depression in West Europe and Japan.[3] It was finally agreed that from January 1974 the posted price would be 11.65 dollars per barrel, including a government take of 7 dollars.[4]

Two days before the members of OPEC first began discussions on price with the oil companies, events in the Middle East had reached flash point. On 6 October 1973 (the Jewish religious festival of Yom Kippur), two Arab states, Egypt and Syria, launched an attack on Israeli troops on the Golan Heights and the Sinai Peninsula in an attempt to recapture territory occupied by Israeli forces as a result of the 1967 war. This was the most visible, and potentially serious aspect of the complex month of crisis. Although the combined attacks of the two front-line Arab states apparently took the Israelis by surprise, and indeed the West too, there had been indications for some time that a resumption of war between Israel and its hostile neighbours was likely. Egyptian President Anwar Sadat had planned for a military solution to the Arab–Israeli conflict since he had succeeded to the Presidency following the death of President Nasser in October 1970. Preparations for a military Arab response had already begun: on 27–29 January 1973 there was a meeting of the Arab League Defence Council, suggesting that unified planning was in hand.[5] The Defence Council agreed that the Arabs would be justified in using military means to regain the occupied territories. As part of Sadat's preparations, he had sought (unsuccessfully) to obtain advanced offensive Soviet weaponry; but in the early part of 1973 he apparently decided to launch an attack against Israeli positions in the Sinai Peninsula at some point during that year. To increase pressure upon Israel, Sadat and President Hafiz al-Assad of Syria agreed on a two-fronted, coordinated plan of attack. Meanwhile the Soviets, while still denying Egyptian requests for MIG-23s did provide SCUD surface-to-surface missiles and resumed regular shipments of military equipment and spare parts. The Syrians were also supplied with more SAMs and MIG-21s, although the MIG-23s were denied to them too.[6] Sadat may have originally planned to attack in May, but changed his mind because of delays in the promised Soviet arms deliveries, and also to avoid taking action during the planned Soviet–American summit scheduled to begin at the end of that month. Nonetheless, there was sufficient evidence of a possible attack that Israel put a partial mobilization in place, and the following month held military exercises in Sinai.

By now, it was clearly a matter of time before war began. The Soviets, however, continued to urge the Egyptians to accept their own preferred solution, a negotiated peace settlement. The Arab–Israeli conflict was now more than just a matter of regional politics, as the consolidation of the 'special relationship' between Israel and the United States, mirrored by the strong links between the Soviet Union and a number of radical Arab regimes (Egypt, Syria and Iraq) had turned a regional conflict into superpower conflict by proxy. Aware of the Egyptian plans for a military solution, as early as June 1973 General Secretary Leonid Brezhnev of the Soviet Union had issued a warning to President Nixon at their summit meeting in California, and similar warnings were relayed by Foreign Minister Andrei Gromyko in his address to the United Nations General Assembly on 23 September 1973 and in a meeting with Nixon in the White House on 28 September. Kissinger, however, dismissed the warnings in the belief that if fighting broke out Israel would win a quick and decisive victory.[7] The Administration also ignored warnings from the Saudi Arabians of a possible oil boycott should war result. However, the Egyptians and the Syrians were moving closer to war. There was a joint command meeting from 22 to 26 August 1973, and at the end of August an October date was finally agreed. On 3 October, the Egyptians informed the Soviets that the attack was imminent; on 4 October the Syrians told them the exact timing. On the same day the Soviets began to evacuate their civilians from Egypt, an operation carried out without secrecy over the next two days. On 5 October the Soviets also moved their ships out of Egyptian ports.[8] However, despite these signals, which had been picked up by the Americans, the outbreak of war took the United States by surprise; only the previous day the CIA had reported that war in the Middle East was unlikely.[9]

On 6 October 1973 the Egyptian and Syrian forces launched a co-ordinated attack on Israeli positions on the Golan Heights and in the

Sinai Peninsula. Although Israel was able to consolidate its position on the Golan Heights, the Egyptians managed to cross the Suez Canal and establish a strong position on the East Bank. At this point, Egypt indicated to the United States that their intention was to wage a limited war, aimed not at the annihilation of Israel, but the return of the Occupied Territories and a negotiated peace settlement.[10] Both countries had specific territorial goals: for Egypt, this was to reoccupy Sinai, or at least to occupy both banks of the Canal, and then trust that international pressure, particularly from the United States, might bring the Israelis to the negotiating table, with the ultimate Egyptian goal being a peace treaty in which Israel would surrender the rest of the Sinai area. Syria's President Assad, on the other hand, hoped to retake the whole of the Golan Heights and, if possible, to occupy the bridges across the River Jordan. However, if the Syrian Army was unable to take and secure this area, Assad planned to call upon the Soviet Union to mediate a ceasefire, along with the United States, to halt hostilities between Syria and Israel.[11] These war aims had a number of important elements. First, neither major belligerent envisaged or even aimed at the ultimate defeat of Israel, but rather the return of the Occupied Territories; both hoped to make initial military gains, but then looked to the possibility of superpower intervention to achieve their ultimate ends; however, while Sadat's policy was to look primarily to the United States as the power with the most direct influence on Israel, Assad still relied on the Soviet Union. Since both main belligerents had individual specific interests, this meant that their military tactics would not necessarily coordinate with each other, and this turned out to be the case. In the Sinai Peninsula, Egypt made an operational pause from 7 to 14 October, which allowed the Israelis to concentrate their efforts on the Golan Heights, where they made substantial gains.[12]

Initially the Arab attack proved successful, surprising many (including Kissinger and the rest of the Nixon Administration)[13] whose judgement of the comparative strength of the two sides was related to the rapid outcome of the 1967 war. Within the first couple of days the Syrians made sizeable gains in the Golan Heights, while the Egyptians broke through the Israeli defences near the Suez Canal, the Bar-Lev line, within a few hours, crossing the Suez Canal in order to achieve this. As the war intensified, it became plain that questions of supply would be critical – in the first three days of the war Israel lost 60 aircraft.[14] Israel in particular had stockpiled consumables for only a few days of fighting, and not only was it clear that the war would be longer than many had anticipated, but the ferocity of the fighting meant that it was rapidly exhausting its supplies. According to his biographer, President Nixon decided at an early stage that Israel must be rearmed, but the implementation of that decision was delayed, although it is unclear whether that was at the instigation of Secretary of Defence Schlesinger or Secretary of State Kissinger. It has been suggested that Kissinger had a vested interest in delaying shipments to emphasize to the Israelis how important the United States was to their future security, and thus make its government more amenable to American plans after the war.[15]

Both superpowers acted quickly to contain the conflict. The Soviet Union moved its ships further away from the region, demonstrating that its intention was not to intervene directly, while it pressed Egypt to agree to a ceasefire at an early point. Galia Golan[16] concluded that the Soviet stance in 1973 was less bellicose than in 1967, and did not signal any intention to intervene. It seems probable that the Soviets wished to see an end to hostilities at a point where their clients were successful, and before any Israeli counter-attack could pose a sufficiently severe threat to Egypt and Syria that the Soviet Union would be under immense pressure to take action. The United States meantime tried to organize an urgent meeting of the Security Council, while maintaining contact with the Soviet Union. On 8 October the Council met; however, the Soviets were unwilling to support the American proposal for a ceasefire, which called for all belligerents to withdraw to the lines prevailing before October, thus negating any Arab gains. Instead they wished to link a ceasefire with an Israeli commitment to withdraw to the pre-1967 frontiers. Egypt had meanwhile rejected the Soviet pressure for a ceasefire. However, it soon became apparent that the Arabs' initial successes were not being maintained. On 8 October Israeli troops began to recapture their positions on the Golan Heights, and on 9 October Israeli planes bombed Damascus, not only demonstrating the extent of their threat to the Syrian capital but also destroying the Soviet cultural centre, prompting an official complaint by the USSR to the UN Security Council. By 10 October Israel announced that it had recaptured all of its previous positions in the Golan Heights. With Israel now reversing the tide of battle, the United States was less concerned to pursue a ceasefire, while the Soviet Union wished to see the war halted before the defeat of its protégés in the region.

It was now apparent that the war would not result in a speedy victory for either side, making the issue of resupplying the belligerents a critical one. On 9–10 October the Soviets began an air and sea lift of arms to Egypt and Syria[17]; on 12 October a Soviet ship was sunk in

Israeli raids on Syrian ports, prompting yet another complaint to the United Nations. On 9 October Israel urgently asked the United States for more arms, but although the Nixon Administration agreed to the request, the supplies were not immediately forthcoming. Both superpowers continued to work for a peace, individually and in conjunction with each other. Initial differences over where the ceasefire should draw the lines between combatants gradually gave way to a general acceptance that the ceasefire should be 'in place' – in other words, that troops should continue to occupy the territory of which they were in control at the moment of the ceasefire. This eased political difficulties, but meant that all belligerents had a vested interest in ensuring that the ceasefire took hold at a point most advantageous to them. By now the Israeli counter-offensive was in full swing in Syria, with the Israeli troops advancing towards Damascus.

On 13 October the first American arms lift to Israel began, and over the next week both superpowers maintained a constant resupply operation. The United States alone flew 550 missions in that week, American deliveries greatly exceeding Soviet supplies to the Arab belligerents.[18] On 14 October the Egyptians launched a heavy offensive, resulting in a massive tank battle in the Sinai Peninsula. However, Egypt's manoeuvre was unsuccessful, and two days later, Israeli troops began to cross the Suez Canal, posing a threat to its West Bank. On the same day, 16 October, King Feisal of Saudi Arabia requested the United States Government, both directly and through ARAMCO, to halt all arms shipments to Israel. By now, the Soviet airlift of supplies to Egypt had tripled in size, although the superpower continued to press for Egyptian agreement to the ceasefire, especially during a visit to Cairo by Alexei Kosygin.[19] The Soviet proposal for a ceasefire included a halt to hostilities, with the rival armies to remain in place; a (possibly phased) Israeli withdrawal to the pre-June 1967 borders; and the use of international forces, including contingents from the two superpowers, to guarantee the frontiers and the ceasefire. However, at the same time the Soviet Union was increasing its troop carriers in the Mediterranean, and on 18 October American Secretary of Defence Schlesinger warned that if Soviet troops became involved in the Middle Eastern war, the position of American forces would be reconsidered. Nonetheless, throughout Kosygin's visit to Cairo the two superpowers remained in contact.

On 17 October OAPEC members met and decided to impose destination restrictions on their oil, together with production cutbacks; on the same day, President Nixon met with the Ambassadors of Saudi Arabia, Algeria, Kuwait and Morocco who asked him to mediate in the conflict. By now events were moving swiftly, with Egyptian troops facing encirclement in the Sinai, while Israel's need for further supplies of arms continued. While on 19 October Sadat indicated his willingness to agree to a ceasefire on the terms presented by the Soviet Union, on the same day the United States reinforced its support for Israel, despite the OAPEC declaration, when Nixon asked Congress for over 2 billion dollars in additional aid for Israel.[20] The superpowers continued to discuss ceasefire proposals, but while the Soviets were keen to ease pressure on the Egyptians by negotiating an end to the fighting at the earliest possible point, Kissinger was prepared to stall in order to allow Israeli forces to capitalize upon their improving position. On 20 October Kissinger left for Moscow at the Soviets' invitation; talks began soon after his arrival and continued into the next day. On 21 October the two superpowers agreed on a proposal for a ceasefire resolution. Kissinger left Moscow for Tel Aviv, the capital of Israel, the following day, by which time Resolution 338 had been passed by the United Nations, calling for an immediate ceasefire in place, and the commencement of the implementation of Resolution 242 together with negotiations between the concerned parties with the aim of establishing a just and durable peace in the Middle East.

Notably lacking from the Resolution was any provision of machinery for the supervision of the ceasefire. This was to prove crucial. The ceasefire went into effect on the Egyptian front on the evening of 22 October (local time), but Syria did not agree until 24 October. However, with no supervision by impartial forces, it was tempting for the party then in the ascendant – Israel – to continue fighting in order to secure as advantageous a position as possible. Thus, within hours, the fragile ceasefire broke down, as Israel launched another major offensive against the Egyptian position. On 23 October the Security Council met and passed Resolution 339, calling for all parties to return to the lines held at the time of the first ceasefire. By now Egypt's 20,000 troops of the Third Army were virtually surrounded by Israeli forces and the main road from Suez to Cairo was cut off. The second ceasefire again broke down on 24 October, by which time the atmosphere in Egypt was at a stage of panic: the militia was mobilized, Cairo radio made an appeal for civil resistance, and President Sadat wrote to both General Secretary Brezhnev and President Nixon, asking the two superpowers to send troops to police the ceasefire.

It was at this stage that events became apparently critical. The tense period leading up to the implementation of a holding ceasefire was accompanied by superpower tension as well. Both superpowers had sought to avoid the regional conflict escalating into a direct Soviet–American confrontation, which would threaten the current *détente* between them. However, with their protégé states in the region in apparent disarray, the Soviet Union was placed in an awkward dilemma. Whereas the United States almost immediately rejected the appeal by Sadat to send troops to police the ceasefire, the Soviet Union was less prepared to dismiss the idea. During the rest of 24 October the two superpowers remained in constant contact with each other, but it became clear that the Soviet Union was not prepared to dismiss Sadat's proposal out of hand. In the late evening Nixon received a communication from Brezhnev suggesting that, if Israel did not observe the ceasefire, the Soviet Union would be prepared to send troops to guarantee it; if the United States was not prepared to cooperate, the Soviets would if necessary act unilaterally. Galia Golan suggests that given the limited level of Soviet military preparedness, at most the USSR was likely to send a symbolic force; she argues that the main aim of the Soviet leadership was to put pressure on the United States to compel Israel to abide by the ceasefire.[21] However, reluctant to see any Soviet military involvement, the American Government reacted swiftly; in the early hours of 25 October it declared a worldwide DEFCON 3 alert of its forces, including its nuclear capabilities. Kissinger's memoirs suggested that the tension was very real, and the potential for a direct superpower conflict in the Middle East was serious; others, more sceptical, suggested that President Nixon may have over-reacted in an effort to divert attention from the growing Watergate storm, or that Kissinger himself over-reacted to the scale of the threat.[22]

The period of overt superpower confrontation was brief, however. Late on 24 October, before deciding on the nuclear alert, the United States had already persuaded Israel to spare the Third Army by agreeing to the dispatch of vital supplies. The Soviets then agreed to the deployment of a United Nations force, excluding the superpowers, which was passed by the Security Council on 25 October. The Americans began easing off their alert on 26 October. However, even after the ceasefire was in place, the situation on the ground remained volatile, particularly around the Suez Canal, where the entrapped Third Army needed basic supplies. Although on 11 November 1973 Israel and Egypt reached an agreement by which supplies would be allowed in and United Nations checkpoints were set up, it was clear that a more lasting disengagement agreement was needed, a point which Henry Kissinger directly addressed by his shuttle diplomacy over the next few months. Those efforts are discussed in Chapter 3.

The United States played a major role in the unfolding crises, but it did so at a time of severe domestic political crisis within the American Government. In 1972 President Nixon was re-elected as President after a campaign managed by the Committee to Re-elect the President (CREP). Shortly after his re-election, however, investigations by two reporters on the *Washington Post*, Carl Bernstein and Bob Woodward, began to reveal a campaign of 'dirty tricks', which had included breaking into Democratic Party headquarters in the Watergate buildings. Moreover, other aspects of the Nixon Presidency, including his employment of the Internal Revenue Service to hound political enemies, his use of public funds to improve his personal private properties and his suspected tax evasion, began to emerge. The so-called Watergate affair, which was ultimately to force Nixon's resignation in August 1974, was at a critical stage in October 1973. During the first weeks of October, at a time when decisive and prompt action was required to deal with both the Middle Eastern and the energy crises, President Nixon was also fighting for his political life, which meant that Secretary of State Kissinger exercised a greater than usual autonomy in conducting foreign affairs. At the same time, however, the President was suspected of using the Middle Eastern crisis, first, to remind Americans of the area in which he had had his greatest successes, i.e. foreign policy, and, second, to divert attention away from concurrent political events in Washington, DC. Nor was Watergate the only political scandal rocking the American Government. On 10 October Vice President Spiro Agnew, who was facing a number of charges of fraud and tax evasion, resigned; over the next two days the President took soundings on whom to nominate as his successor, before eventually deciding upon Gerald Ford on 12 October. The latter date also saw an important court decision which ordered President Nixon to hand over seven tapes, rather than the transcripts, of conversations held in the Oval Office. On 20 October, while Kissinger was in Moscow discussing the possible ceasefire with the Soviets, Attorney General Elliott Richardson resigned, and the President fired the Watergate special prosecutor, Archibald Cox, also abolishing the post. By now, the President was beleaguered, and on 23 October no fewer than 21 resolutions for Nixon's impeachment were introduced in the House of Representatives.[23] On the same day, in the face of strong political and public pressure, Nixon agreed to hand over the subpoenaed tapes, which were ultimately to tarnish his reputation and reveal his links with the Watergate cover-up. Although Nixon was later blamed for triggering the nuclear alert as a device in his domestic political problems, there is some doubt as to whether he was even consulted about the decision. It is clear that Henry Kissinger retained a great deal of independence in conducting foreign policy at the time, delaying the rearming of Israel until President Nixon forcefully intervened to get it started, and ignoring Nixon's instructions to use the ceasefire as a way of moving towards a permanent peace in the region.[24] What is clear is that the American President, both during the crisis itself and in later initiatives aimed at ending the oil boycott, had also a pressing domestic agenda to bear in mind.

Yet another factor in shaping international reaction to the Middle Eastern crisis was the concurrent energy crisis, which combined the dramatic price increase announced by OPEC with fears of supply shortages subsequent upon the oil boycott and production cutbacks announced by OAPEC on 17 October. In making his preparations for war, Sadat had sought the backing of the major Arab producers, and in August 1973 Saudi Arabia, the most influential of the producers, had agreed in principle to use the oil weapon in furtherance of the Arab cause. Even before this, in 1972 Sheikh Yamani, the Saudi Oil Minister, had informed the American Government directly that Saudi Arabia was no longer willing to treat oil supply and Arab political interests as two distinct issues.[25] During the summer of 1973 King Feisal of Saudi Arabia tried to convince the United States Government that the threat of economic action was real, through private representations, using ARAMCO as the intermediary, and also publicly on American television. However, despite these efforts to warn the United States of the potential threat to Western oil supplies should they give aid to Israel in any future war, it was not taken particularly seriously, except by a few individuals such as James Akins, the State Department's petroleum expert. The United States and Europe still hoped, following the failure of the last politically motivated boycott in 1967 and the major political differences between the main front-line states, (i.e. Egypt and Syria on the one hand, and the major oil producers such as Saudi Arabia on the other) that there would not be a concerted Arab front against Israel. However, the use of the Arab oil weapon was likely to be more potent in 1973 than in 1967: while in 1970 the Americas had produced a third of the world's oil, by 1973 that share had fallen to a quarter. By 1970 Venezuela had already been overtaken as the world's leading exporter of oil by Saudi Arabia and Iran.[26]

In October 1973, there was an extra incentive towards the use of this weapon, as it became clear that Israel would be unable to win a swift victory, thus requiring – if the war developed into one of attrition –

fresh supplies from abroad, in particular spare parts for existing American weaponry. This would make the role of the United States, as the main source of armaments for Israel, critical to the outcome of the war. The Arab states hoped that, through the astute and orchestrated use of the oil weapon, they could force Western countries to reconsider re-arming Israel. On 17 October 1973 there was an OAPEC meeting in Kuwait which turned into a Conference of Arab Oil Ministers: this group decided to implement a programme of production cuts, starting at 5 per cent of the September figure, and increasing by a further 5 per cent per month until Israeli forces had been evacuated from all the territories occupied in the June 1967 war, and the legitimate rights of the Palestinians had been restored.[27] Saudi Arabia, Kuwait, Libya, Algeria, Egypt, Syria, the United Arab Emirates, Bahrain and Qatar all agreed with the policy: Iraq, although a member of OAPEC, chose instead to nationalize the American and Dutch holdings in the Basra Petroleum Company. Iraq also participated in the boycott of the United States, later extended to the Netherlands and Portugal, which was agreed by the Oil Ministers on 20 October. Any state designated as 'preferred' would continue to receive the same level of supplies as before the production cuts, which implied that other countries would see an even greater reduction. These cutbacks meant that in November the Arab OPEC states reduced their production by 4.5 million barrels per day (mbd) compared to September, although increases in production by other members brought the reduction to only 4.2 mbd. Nonetheless, this still represented 13 per cent of OPEC's September production.[28] This boycott was not imposed by OPEC, however, nor was it sponsored by that organization. Non-Arab OPEC members such as Venezuela and Iran had no reason to join the boycott, and indeed increased production.

Even after the ceasefire was in place, the use of the oil weapon continued in an effort to influence the subsequent negotiations for disengagement, and to secure the Israeli withdrawal from the Occupied Territories. Indeed, it was actually intensified; on 4 November the Arab oil ministers agreed that production that month would be reduced by 25 per cent from the level prevailing in September, with a further 5 per cent planned for December.[29] The boycott against the United States and the Netherlands would continue, and consumer countries previously exempted would be expected to demonstrate a positive attitude towards the Arab cause for their favourable position to continue. Over the next two months the boycott was further refined: (1) the most favoured countries would obtain as much oil as they required (this included the United Kingdom, France, Spain, the Arab importing countries, Islamic countries and African countries which had broken off diplomatic relations with Israel); (2) preferred countries, who had modified their policies in support of the Arab cause, including (after January 1974) Belgium and Japan, would receive supplies at the level prevailing in September; (3) supplies to neutral countries (originally including Belgium and Japan) would be cut in accordance with the general level of production cuts; and (4) hostile countries, which in addition to the United States and the Netherlands, included Portugal, South Africa and Rhodesia, would face a total embargo on oil from the member states of OAPEC.[30] Officially decisions on production levels from individual oilfields and countries rested with the oil companies but it is a measure of the extent to which the balance of power had shifted towards the producer governments that the companies were prepared to cooperate and implement the production cutbacks and the strict letter of the boycott, not least because of threats of sanctions should they fail to comply.[31]

Reaction to the hostilities and the boycott in the main Western oil-consuming nations varied. The boycott, however, ensured that countries that would otherwise have played only a minor role, if any, in the resolution of the Arab–Israeli war became directly involved; moreover, it created tension within the Western alliance. On 6 November the European Community published a declaration in which both parties in the Arab–Israeli conflict were urged to withdraw to the positions occupied on 22 October, and called for a peace settlement on the lines of UN Security Council Resolution 242.[32] On 22 November Japan also called for Israel's withdrawal from all territories occupied in 1967. Several European powers refused to allow their bases to be used for the resupply of Israel (or, in the case of the British Government, removed the need for an actual refusal, by letting it be known that it would be unwise to ask). On 23 October, after the collapse of the first ceasefire, West Germany used the opportunity to formalize their opposition to the American use of their bases in West Germany for resupplying Israel, and called on the United States to stop. The American response, which was to claim that West Germany's sovereignty over the bases was limited and that therefore the American Government would use them as they saw fit, annoyed the Germans. Meanwhile, the Europeans generally were deeply perturbed at the red alert declared by the United States on 25 October, as this included some 7,000 nuclear weapons located at over 100 sites in West Europe. This directly involved the West European governments in any possible confrontation with the Soviet Union, despite their not having been consulted, and their concerns at American foreign policy in the Middle East.[33]

The boycott of the United States continued throughout the ceasefire and mediation attempts, with a temporary lifting of its conditions in March 1974 following the negotiation of the Egyptian/Israeli disengagement agreement under American auspices, before being finally terminated in June and July 1974. The potential impact of this boycott should not be taken lightly. Prior to October 1973 the United States had been importing 1.2 million barrels of Arab oil a day, and five months later that had fallen to just 18,000 barrels per day, while the Netherlands drew over 70 per cent of its oil from Arab sources.[34] In world terms, the situation never became critical as many oil producers, both within and outside OPEC, continued to produce as required, and oil companies were able to honour the letter of the boycott while redistributing supplies to ensure that no customer was disproportionately denied oil. However, even if the potentially damaging consequences of the boycott were averted, it demonstrated categorically that supplies of oil to the West were no longer simply a matter of economics, but were intimately entwined with politics as well. Moreover, when two major consuming countries, France and the United Kingdom, attempted to put pressure upon oil companies domiciled in their states, particularly those in which the respective governments held equity – British Petroleum (BP), the Compagnie Française des Pétroles (CFP) and the Enterprise des Recherches et d'Activités Pétrolières (Elf-ERAP) – they were officially unsuccessful, although it has recently been revealed that British Petroleum did bend the rules privately to assist the United Kingdom.[35] The position had now been reversed: rather than wishing to court the parent governments in order to win diplomatic backing, the companies were anxious not to alienate the producer governments.[36] Yet other governments remained suspicious of the close relationship some companies had with their parent governments, the Japanese in particular were convinced that the oil majors were giving preferential treatment to their own governments.[37]

For a beleaguered President Nixon, the domestic impact of a prolonged boycott was serious, and it is clear from Kissinger's memoirs that, even if during the immediate crisis the first priority was Soviet relations and Cold War considerations, in the aftermath the question of oil supplies for the American domestic market was accorded a high priority by the President.[38] The difficulty was knowing what strategy to adopt. The Administration therefore adopted a complex policy, or rather set of policies. At the same time as trying to broker peace, in

December 1973 President Nixon twice wrote to King Feisal suggesting that the oil embargo and production restrictions were more likely to cause the United States to withdraw from its role in the Middle East than persuade it to pursue peace,[39] while on 7 January 1974 Defence Secretary Schlesinger appeared to threaten retaliatory action against the countries implementing the boycott, including, implicitly, the use of force.[40] However, Kissinger's shuttle diplomacy, to be discussed in more detail in Chapter 3, was both more even-handed in its dealings with the respective belligerents than was expected by the Israeli Prime Minister, Golda Meir, and was also a startling departure from normal practice in the 'hands-on' approach adopted by the Secretary of State, which entailed spending long periods of time out of the United States.

By the end of 1973, the main part of the crisis was over, although peace in the Middle East was still precarious, and the consuming nations were reeling at the likely impact of a fourfold increase in the price of oil in only three months. OPEC and OAPEC had both contributed to the cause of that increase: OAPEC through its boycott, as opposed to the oil price decisions which remained entirely within OPEC's jurisdiction. In the discussions on the appropriate price level for oil, particularly in the December 1973 OPEC meeting that agreed on a new official price of over 11 dollars per barrel, one of the leading hawks was the Shah of Iran, leader of a non-Arab state which at that time provided Israel with the majority of its oil needs. The country taking the lead in implementing the oil boycott, Saudi Arabia, pressed for moderation on price, and argued forcibly against setting an official price close to the highest spot market levels. However, this potent combination – a Middle Eastern crisis and a feeling on the part of the oil producers that a price rise was appropriate and overdue – also coincided in the second major oil crisis of the decade in 1978–9.

The second oil crisis: 1979

The gloomy prognostications of many commentators in the immediate aftermath of 1973 proved to be erroneous.[41] Although the cash price of petroleum remained high, the escalating rates of inflation in the industrialized world eroded its impact upon their economies, while increasing the prices of manufactured goods to the developing world (including the members of OPEC). While the position of oil companies in the international oil industry had been affected by the unilateral decision by OPEC to take total control of oil price and production levels, changes had already been in train before 1973, and in many respects the shift towards a more managerial and technical role reduced political pressures upon the companies, while doing little to affect their profit levels. By the end of the 1970s, therefore, there was a real sense within the industrialized West that the worst of the oil crisis had definitely passed. However, towards the end of the decade, the international atmosphere once again became one of crisis, and yet again events in the Middle East, coupled with the desire of the oil producers to secure an increase in the real price of their oil, were to produce a dramatic and rapid increase in oil prices, and catapult the energy crisis back on to the international agenda.

As in 1973, a number of different factors contributed to the genesis of the crisis. Of these trends, perhaps the most striking initially was the escalation of tension within the Cold War. The early 1970s had witnessed a slackening of some Cold War tensions, encouraged by the Nixon Administration, which had made friendly overtures towards the Soviet Union and China and encouraged *détente*. The Nixon Doctrine of encouraging other countries and regions to take more responsibility for their own defence reduced the likelihood of a direct superpower conflict, while also contributing to the enhanced role of Iran as a regional policeman. Moreover, the downplaying of the arms race was regarded by both superpowers as an important element in their own domestic economic policies. Hence, the two superpowers negotiated agreements on the limitation of strategic arms, and the path seemed set for even further reductions in due course. This mood of complacency was rudely shattered during the course of 1979. The Cold War abruptly worsened, as the Soviet Union invaded Afghanistan, posing a threat, even if only indirectly, to the stability of the Northern Tier and hence the Middle East more generally. There was a distinct hardening of rhetoric, accompanied by increasing problems within the SALT II talks. President Carter was notably tougher in his stance towards the Soviet Union, pressing his European allies to accept Cruise and Pershing missiles in their territory.

Moreover, there was an additional threat to Middle Eastern oil as trouble flared in Iran. Since his restoration to the Peacock Throne in 1953 as a result of a CIA-orchestrated coup, the Shah, although a hawk on matters of oil price, had been strongly pro-Western. With the upsurge in oil revenues after 1973 (in the year 1975–6 alone, Iran's oil revenue was 20 billion dollars)[42] he had pursued policies of economic modernization, development and military spending. However, he had also sought to undermine any possible internal threat to the stability of his regime: he did not wish to be forced once again to flee his country. He had therefore strengthened his regime in a number of ways during the 1970s, including an end to genuine two-party politics (a formal one-party system was introduced in 1975): in addition, he tried to undermine the position of religion within the country, emphasizing the secular nature of his regime and questioning the impact of Islam on everyday life. Economically he pursued a policy of modernization and industrialization, hoping to use oil as a base for a major industrial economy able to compete internationally, although inefficiency undermined progress towards this goal. However, Iran had undergone in a very short period of time the destabilizing forces of very rapid modernization, major land reform, massive urbanization and internal migration from the land to the cities, industrialization, and the secularization and rapid expansion of education. With an emphasis on large Western style industries requiring foreign technology and skills, the Shah turned Iran into one of the fastest industrializing third world countries. However, he also accompanied this pattern of modernization with the construction and consolidation of the machinery of repression, including a massive army and police, particularly after the popular disturbances of 1963, which led to the exile of Ayatollah Khomeini.[43] By 1976 Iran had the fifth largest military force in the world, armed with up-to-date Western equipment.[44] The Shah specifically sought to weaken two traditional sources of opposition or discontent, the bazaar merchants (through the emphasis on large-scale Western enterprise) and the Islamic clergy (by a programme of secularization).

Ironically, President Carter of the United States, in pressing the Shah to liberalize the regime in order to minimize human rights infringements, simply led to an escalation of opposition among the population. Moreover, by that time the fall in the real price of oil and lessening demand for Iranian production meant that the Shah had to reduce many of his ambitious development plans. By the late 1970s, a wide range of groups within Iranian society questioned the Shah's regime, including Western-educated professionals, the students from secular universities, the traditional sectors of urban society such as bazaar merchants and students from theological colleges, the National Front which sought a constitutional monarchy along the lines of the 1906 constitution, and a religious faction led by the Ayatollah Khomeini, demanding the overthrow of the Shah and the creation of an Islamic Republic.

Thus, when in 1978 the Shah tried to repress the religious opposition to his regime, this caused considerable unrest, which was enhanced when, later that year, the Shah's economic policies, intended to address inflationary pressures, caused recession. Protests first broke out in Qum, in response to an attack on Khomeini in an official government newspaper; this led to further repression, which in turn was seized upon, particularly by religious groups, to further question the Shah's regime. Demonstrations were met with violence: in keeping with the traditions of Shia Islam the funerals of those killed were themselves turned into further protests, thus further emphasizing the religious dimension of the revolution. The Iranian Revolution brought together modern and traditional groups in Iranian society, and was caused both by modernizing impulses – the demands of oil workers for greater rewards and the desire of urban groups for a freer economy – and the disquiet with modernization among traditional groups such as the bazaar merchants, theology students and the clergy. It was from this latter group that the strongest vision of an alternative Iranian society emerged.[45] From October 1978 onwards strikes, particularly in the oil industry, brought further economic crisis. However, the radical elements in the revolution, typified by the strikes of the economically powerful oil workers, were gradually overwhelmed by the religious dimension, as students and mullahs combined.

On 16 January 1979 the Shah bowed to the inevitable and fled from Iran. Twenty-six years earlier, when he had then left his country in the face of popular protest, he had been returned to the Peacock Throne in short order, courtesy of a CIA coup. However, there was no Kim Roosevelt waiting in the wings in 1979; instead, the leading religious critic of his regime, Ayatollah Khomeini, returned triumphant from his own period of exile (some sixteen years in all), to steer the Iranian revolution resolutely towards a religious, Islamic republic. This outcome – and indeed the revolution which had preceded it – took Western observers by surprise. Even when the strength of opposition to the Shah became apparent during 1978, the well-known commentator on Iranian affairs, James Bill, suggested that while the Shah might not be able to retain power, the most likely successor regime would be either a modified Pahlavi rule, under the Crown Prince, or a government led by a radical-progressive military group.[46]

Inevitably, the strikes in the oil industry rapidly had an impact upon Iranian production. In September 1978 Iran had been producing at close to its maximum capacity, at around 6 mbd, but strikes by oil workers saw production decline steeply for the rest of the year and at the end of December 1978 oil exports were effectively suspended; production was only 500,000 barrels per day in January and 700,000 in February, although in March it reached 2.4 mbd.[47] Its high point was only 4.1 mbd in May and overall the average production for 1979 was 3.1 mbd, compared with 5.7 mbd in 1977.[48] However, the potential threat to oil supplies went beyond merely this dip in Iranian production. Inevitably, upheaval in so important an oil producer – upheaval which threatened to spill over into other oil states, especially those with Shia populations such as Iraq and many of the Persian Gulf states, or even to prompt the escalation of Cold War tensions – raised fears about the stability and security of oil supplies. The vulnerability of oil tankers going through the Straits of Hormuz was widely recognized. Consumers were concerned not only at the actual disruption to supplies, but by the fear that other major producers might, at some point in the future, themselves succumb to political turmoil.

Although other producers in fact helped to compensate for disruptions to Iranian supplies by stepping up their own production, supplies were still affected, a situation not aided by the increase in world demand during 1978. Unlike 1973, there was no attempt to use oil as a weapon in international relations, as opposed to domestic Iranian politics. There was no politically-inspired boycott this time, and indeed there was no real shortage of supply. However, the main consumers were still heavily dependent upon imported oil: the United States for over a third of its requirements, and Japan for virtually 100 per cent.[49] Fears of potential shortages led companies and governments to build up stocks in anticipation of high winter demand. These fears had a self-fulfilling effect, as some OPEC producers diverted contracted oil to the spot markets, which in turn caused oil companies to use the spot markets for their own needs and, where possible, to reduce deliveries to their customers, who in turn had recourse to the spot markets. Moreover, there was a natural but unfortunate tendency to buy more than was needed to safeguard against not only future supply shortages but also possible additional increases in prices. The main industrialized countries, particularly West Germany and Japan, were unwilling to agree to suggestions that they avoid over-reliance on the spot markets.

Because the problem was not one of overall supply shortage, but rather over-buying and sharp price increases, the emergency measures elaborately constructed after the 1973 crisis were irrelevant to this second crisis, and were not implemented. Assisted by the fact that the market in oil was less structured, as a consequence of the end of the concession system, and the growth in the importance of 'spot markets' such as Rotterdam, market forces pushed the price of petroleum well above its official price. Similarly, yet again there were calls for the West to engage in a campaign for conservation and the exploitation of alternative sources, as well as pursue cooperation between the main exporters and importers.[50] Nonetheless, prices shot upwards, and the lack of consumer control over the market was graphically demonstrated. In the event, no serious actual shortage was experienced. The crisis happened in the winter, and although demand was of course high, so too were stocks in anticipation of the heavier demand. Moreover, Saudi Arabia increased production, albeit only by 1 mbd for the period January–March 1979, which was not as much as was required to compensate for all the Iranian production. Nonetheless, the increase in prices paid by consumers was largely self-inflicted in the first instance.

At first, OPEC did not put up prices, but as panic buying rapidly pushed up prices severalfold, there was a growing discrepancy between the official prices on the one hand, and the prevailing market prices paid on the spot market on the other. On 31 December 1978 the oil marker price was 12.70 dollars, and OPEC had agreed a series of price increases through 1979 which would create a new base by the end of the year of 14.55 dollars. As against that, during the height of the panic buying, prices on the spot market at times exceeded 40 dollars, and although this was not sustained, the price per barrel in early 1982 was still high, at 30 dollars. For the OPEC producers, who had seen their real revenue from oil fall as a result of reduced demand and the effect of high inflation on the purchasing power of the dollar, this seemed an ideal opportunity to use the impact of Middle Eastern events on the oil market to increase prices as they had done in 1973. A number of OPEC members began to charge surcharges on their oil – an action condoned by the organization. OPEC member states met in Geneva in March 1979, and officially agreed that they would bring forward the price increase planned by the end of the year, but also authorizing each individual member country to add whatever premium it felt appropriate. With the exception of Saudi Arabia, most OPEC members did charge a premium. In June OPEC met again; while it agreed upon a price of 18 dollars for marker crude, it also allowed members to charge a market premium over and above their normal differential, subject to a ceiling price of 23.50 dollars. However, in effect what emerged was a free-for-all, in which members were free to charge whatever price they deemed appropriate; while Saudi Arabia pegged its price at 18 dollars, other producers charged a premium, and still found buyers.

As stated above, in terms of overall supply and demand, the situation was not particularly strained. Ian Skeet, an oil company executive of many years' experience, attributed the crisis in the oil market to a number of factors: first and foremost, uncertainty, not only about the course of the Iranian Revolution, but also whether it might spread to other producers, including the prolific states in the Arabian peninsula. Moreover, the cuts in the Iranian production affected particular consumers and companies (notably Japan, British Petroleum and Shell) worse than others, while the increase in Saudi production gave more oil to the companies within the ARAMCO consortium, which were relatively unaffected by the Iranian cuts. Thus, BP and Shell had to compete in the spot market to meet their contracts and, in some cases, were forced to renege on those. Moreover, OPEC oil was now effectively priced on a two-tier system, with the cheaper Saudi oil largely available to ARAMCO, while the other producers charged additional premiums on their oil. Even after the Iranian oilfields recommenced production, it remained the case that companies and customers – with the winter of 1979/80 to prepare for and with uncertainty about the future supplies of oil – sought to build up their stock levels.[51] That uncertainty was exacerbated by the lengthy Iranian hostage crisis. On 4 November 1979 the American Embassy in Teheran was seized by students, protesting at the entry of the Shah into the United States for medical treatment. Later in the month it appeared as though contagion might be spreading elsewhere in the Middle East when the Grand Mosque in Mecca was seized by religious extremists. The United States Government not only halted all imports of Iranian oil, but also froze all Iranian assets held by United States banks. To no avail: the hostages were held for 444 days, only released by their captors on the day of President Reagan's inauguration. The disastrous failure of an attempted military rescue undermined the Carter Presidency.[52] This meant, however, that for well over a year political uncertainty in the Middle East offered oil producers the opportunity to capitalize upon demand for their oil and adjust prices accordingly.

Because of the nature of the crisis, which was one of price rather than supply, the emergency arrangements agreed by the consuming nations in the aftermath of 1973 were irrelevant, and the International Energy Agency, set up largely to coordinate those arrangements, could do little in the face of the crisis other than to counsel restraint. The IEA monitored the position, and encouraged its members to reduce demand by 5 per cent while at the same time urging them to keep up and replenish stock levels. However, as no effective action was taken collectively by the leading oil consumers to control the escalating panic and price increases, it was therefore left to the individual governments and consumers to decide upon their own policy. The United States faced the difficulty that while in 1973–8 oil consumption in the European Community had dropped, American consumption had actually risen over the same period at an annual average growth rate of 1.7 per cent.[53] In July the American Government used its political influence with Saudi Arabia to persuade it once again to increase production (which had returned to normal levels in April), by 1 mbd; it did so on the understanding that no petroleum would be added to the Strategic Petroleum Reserve until the crisis was over.[54] However, as in 1973, the United States combined diplomatic methods with more belligerent signals. In the same month the American Government announced the creation of a Rapid Deployment Force, specifically to give it the capacity to intervene in the Gulf if necessary to keep oil routes open. In December 1979 Russian troops invaded Afghanistan, and the following month the Carter Doctrine reinforced the threat of American intervention. Once again Japan, very conscious of its vulnerability on oil supplies, followed an assertive, independent policy designed to serve national interest rather than international co-operation. It bought on the spot market at high prices in 1979, bought oil from Iran in the face of American requests for an international boycott following the hostage crisis, and tried to build up government to government contacts for the supply of oil, often by links with development projects. In addition, Japan also followed a policy of direct investment in the Middle East, particularly in the petrochemical industry.[55] This reflected the common assumption that effective action would be unilateral rather than collective. In the 1979 Tokyo summit of the seven leading Western industrialized nations, at which blame for the deepening recession was placed at OPEC's door, all countries agreed to set limits on oil imports roughly similar to the levels pertaining in 1978. However, in the panic buying which prevailed as the supply position worsened, countries continued to act individually, rather than collectively, in their search for petroleum security.

With political turmoil in the Middle East and the possibility that there might be a threat to the safe passage of oil through the Straits of Hormuz, and with winter fast approaching and a pervading sense of uncertainty in the oil markets, OPEC continued to leave prices, effectively, to market forces. When its members met in December 1979 it took no decision on price. Saudi Arabia had hoped to gain acceptance among at least some of the producers for its own new price of 24 dollars but this did not happen; instead, in the face of considerable debate, an agreement was reached: not to reach an agreement on a price. Over the following few months, individual producing countries, including Saudi Arabia, raised their prices on a number of occasions. In September, OPEC (including Saudi Arabia) decided to set the marker price at 30 dollars.[56]

The 1979 crisis showed that divisions still remained among the industrial countries, while the mechanisms set up after the previous crisis in 1973 proved inadequate to meet the changed nature of the problems. It also reinforced the potent effect of a Middle Eastern crisis coupled with the main exporters' desire to improve the oil price. Within a very short period of time, while prices were still high as a consequence of the Iranian Revolution, the outbreak of a major war between two of the Persian Gulf's leading producers, Iran and Iraq, threatened once again to trigger a dramatic upward price increase.

The crisis that did not happen: 1980

Although prices remained high, it is useful to consider the consequences when, a year later, war broke out between two of the leading Middle Eastern producers, Iran and Iraq. Not only did this threaten a reduction in oil exports from the two belligerents, but there was a distinct possibility that Iran would seek either to reduce Iraq's own exports or, in an attempt to reduce the support given to the Iraqi regime by other Middle Eastern oil producers, to block their exports from the Gulf through the Straits of Hormuz. This would affect, in particular, Kuwait. However, underlying factors made this third price crisis remarkably short-lived. First, the underlying pattern of demand was downwards, and as a consequence stocks, built up over the previous year and a half in response to the state of uncertainty, were high and remained so. Other producers, notably Saudi Arabia, increased their production. The IEA, although still not in a position to take mandatory action, urged its members to draw on stocks, and to abstain from abnormal purchases on the spot market. By mid-1981 the spot market price was roughly in accord with official prices. Thus, despite the undoubted political seriousness of this new crisis, there was only a short period of upward pressure on prices and, with increased supplies from producers outside the Gulf region, coupled with falling demand because of the recession affecting many industrial countries, stability soon returned. With high stocks levels, the panic buying which had marked the 1979 crisis was absent.

In the space of under ten years, events in the Middle East had triggered two massive oil price increases, had concentrated international attention on the political problems of the region and the threat posed thereby to oil supplies for the consuming nations, and brought about substantial economic and social transformations in many of the leading oil-exporting nations. Moreover, at the time many commentators predicted that the impact of the decade of crisis would go far beyond the Middle East and the oil industry. Blamed for the ills of a world economy beset by recession, heralded by the developing world as a new and powerful champion for their cause as against the industrialized nations, OPEC assumed an importance which few had envisaged when it had been formed, only thirteen years before the first crisis. The year 1973 is universally used as a shorthand for major changes in the international arena. To assess the extent to which the oil crises of the 1970s represented a turning point in history, and to evaluate their causes and consequences, the following chapters will look at each of the key issues in turn.

Notes

1. Ian Skeet, *Opec: Twenty-five Years of Prices and Politics*. Cambridge University Press, Cambridge, 1988, pp. 88–90.
2. Skeet, *Opec*, p. 91.
3. George Lencowski, 'The Oil Producing Countries', in Raymond Vernon (ed.), *The Oil Crisis*, Norton, New York, 1976, pp. 59–72, esp. pp. 69–70.
4. Skeet, *Opec*, p. 102.
5. Galia Golan, *Yom Kippur and After: The Soviet Union and the Middle East Crisis*. Cambridge University Press, Cambridge, 1977, pp. 38–9.
6. Golan, *Yom Kippur*, p. 47.
7. Henry Kissinger, *Years of Upheaval*. Weidenfeld & Nicolson, London, 1982, pp. 297–9.
8. Golan, *Yom Kippur*, pp. 66–9.
9. Stephen E. Ambrose, *Nixon: Volume Three. Ruin and Recovery 1973–1990*. Simon & Schuster, New York, 1991, p. 229.
10. T.G. Fraser, *The Arab–Israeli Conflict*. Macmillan, London, 1995, p. 99.
11. Erik L. Knudsen, 'The Syrian-Israeli Political Impasse: A Study in Conflict, War and Mistrust', *Diplomacy and Statecraft* 12 (2001), pp. 211–34, esp. pp. 220–1.
12. Knudsen, 'Syrian–Israeli Political Impasse', p. 221.

13. In his memoirs, Kissinger states that he originally expected Israel to win overwhelmingly, within a few days. Kissinger, *Years of Upheaval*, pp. 467–8.
14. Burton I. Kaufman, *The Arab Middle East and the United States: Inter-Arab Rivalry and Superpower Diplomacy*. Twayne Publishers, New York, 1996, p. 81.
15. Ambrose, *Nixon*, pp. 230–4.
16. Golan, *Yom Kippur*, pp. 78–9.
17. Galia Golan, *Soviet Policies in the Middle East from World War Two to Gorbachev*. Cambridge University Press, Cambridge, 1990, pp. 87–8.
18. Ambrose, *Nixon,* p. 240.
19. Golan, *Soviet Policies*, p. 88.
20. Kaufman, *Arab Middle East*, p. 84.
21. Golan, *Yom Kippur*, pp. 122–3.
22. Ambrose, *Nixon*, pp. 255–6.
23. Ambrose, *Nixon*, pp. 229–56.
24. Ambrose, *Nixon*, pp. 255–6.
25. Louis Turner, *Oil Companies in the International System* (3rd edn). Allen & Unwin, London, 1983, pp. 133–6; and Mordechai Abir, *Saudi Arabia in the Oil Era: Regimes and Elites: Conflict and Collaboration*. Croom Helm, London, 1988, p. 127.
26. Stephen G. Rabe, *The Road to OPEC: United States Relations with Venezuela 1919–1976*. University of Texas Press, Austin, Texas, 1982, pp. 179–82.
27. Seymour, *OPEC*, p. 117.
28. Skeet, *Opec*, p. 100.
29. Seymour, *OPEC*, p.117.
30. Seymour, *OPEC*, p. 118.
31. Robert B. Stobaugh, 'The Oil Companies in the Crisis', in Vernon, *The Oil Crisis*, pp. 179–202, esp. pp. 186–7.
32. Lencowski, 'Oil Producing Countries', p. 66.
33. Michael M. Harrison, *The Reluctant Ally: France and Atlantic Security*. The Johns Hopkins University Press, Baltimore, 1981, pp. 176–9.
34. Anthony Sampson, *The Seven Sisters: The Great Oil Companies and the World They Made*. Hodder & Stoughton, London, 1975, pp. 274–5.
35. James Bamberg, *History of the British Petroleum Company. British Petroleum and Global Oil, 1950–1975: The Challenge of Nationalism*. Cambridge University Press, Cambridge, 2000, pp. 480–3.
36. Stobaugh, 'Oil Companies', p. 179.
37. Turner, *Oil Companies*, pp. 176–85.
38. Kissinger, *Years of Upheaval*, p. 634.
39. Kissinger, *Years of Upheaval*, pp. 882 and 890.
40. Peter Mangold, *Superpower Intervention in the Middle East*. Croom Helm, London, 1978, pp. 72–6.
41. Influential journals and newspapers of the time, such as *Foreign Affairs*, *International Affairs* and *The Economist*, included many articles, on a range of subjects, predicting dire consequences for the 1973 crisis.
42. William L. Cleveland, *A History of the Modern Middle East*. Westview Press, Boulder, Colorado, 1994, p. 277.
43. James F. Goode, *The United States and Iran: In the Shadow of Musaddiq*. St Martin's Press, New York, 1997, pp. 179–81.
44. Cleveland, *Modern Middle East*, p. 277.
45. Fred Halliday, *Islam and the Myth of Confrontation: Religion and Politics in the Middle East*. I.B. Tauris, London, 1996, pp. 62–5.

46. James A. Bill, 'Iran and the Crisis of "78"', *Foreign Affairs* 57 (1978–9), pp. 323–42, esp. p. 341.
47. Skeet, *Opec*, p. 158.
48. Robert J. Lieber, *The Oil Decade: Conflict and Cooperation in the West*. Praeger, New York, 1983, Table 2.5, p. 27.
49. Walter J. Levy, 'Oil: An Agenda for the 1980s', *Foreign Affairs* 59 (1980-1), pp. 287–305.
50. For example, Levy, 'Agenda'; and André Bénard, 'World Oil and Cold Reality', *Harvard Business Review* 58 (1980), pp. 91–101.
51. Skeet, *Opec*, pp. 160–1.
52. David Patrick Houghton, *U.S. Foreign Policy and the Iran Hostage Crisis*. Cambridge University Press, Cambridge, 2001.
53. Fadhil J. Al-Chalabi, *OPEC and the International Oil Industry: A Changing Structure*. Oxford University Press, Oxford, 1980, n. 3, p. 4.
54. Skeet, *Opec*, p. 166.
55. Peter Odell, *Oil and World Power* (6th edn, London, 1981), pp. 104–5 and 157–62.
56. Skeet, *Opec*, p. 171.

2

A TURNING POINT FOR THE OIL INDUSTRY?

The company era

For the first fifteen years after the end of the Second World War, there was no reason to predict any upheaval within the international oil industry, dominated, although not monopolized, by American companies. The 'Seven Sisters' – the American majors, Texaco, Exxon, Mobil, Chevron and Gulf Oil, together with British Petroleum and Royal Dutch Shell – cooperated with each other to control the international oil market through a series of marketing agreements and interlocking ownership of many of the large oilfields of the Middle East. In the early 1950s, the Justice Department accumulated evidence of an international petroleum cartel, hoping to prove that oil companies cooperated in ways that were in restraint of trade. However, first the Truman then the Eisenhower administrations initially toned down and later completely dismissed the investigations. They argued that such an investigation was against the interests of national security; oil was so critical to the economy and defence of the United States that nothing should be done which might potentially harm the oil companies.[1] With political support, and a dominating position in the prolific oilfields of the developing world, the position of the Seven Sisters appeared unassailable. Ultimately the extent of the majors' power was to be whittled down, first by increased competition from other oil companies, and later by the producing governments, but until 1960 they cooperated to provide a stable international oil order, which provided cheap oil not only to the United States but also to Western Europe and Japan.

In addition to the power and control of the oil companies, international political factors also contributed to the stability of the oil industry. The bulk of the industrialized countries' oil imports came from countries that were within the Americas (particularly Venezuela) and were susceptible to the influence of the United States, or were in the Middle East (Kuwait, Iran, Iraq and Saudi Arabia), whose governments were, for the most part, willing to cooperate with the oil companies and the Western governments. The main exception was Iran, which had a long tradition of conflict with both the British Government and the company which controlled the Iranian oil industry, British Petroleum.[2]

Such protest as was made was averted either by persuasion or coercion. In the case of Venezuela, and later Saudi Arabia and Kuwait, incipient discontent on the part of the host government was diverted by an immediate improvement in the financial terms available, through the so-called 'fifty–fifty' agreements. Under these agreements, which were first introduced in Venezuela in the late 1940s, instead of paying a fixed sum royalty per barrel of oil produced, which had hitherto been the main mechanism of payment, the profit on its production was split 50–50 between the host government and the oil company. This apparent benevolence on the part of the oil companies was accomplished by a sleight of hand on the part of parent governments, particularly that of the United States. By organizing the 50–50 split so that much of the host government's revenue was ostensibly a tax rather than a simple royalty, the payment ceased to be an expense against profits, but was instead a tax payment. As the Internal Revenue Service declared that a company could not be taxed twice on the same income, the taxes paid to the host government could be offset against taxes owed to the United States Government. This policy enabled the United States to promote stability, economic prosperity and, ideally, pro-Western conservative regimes in the key producing states: while tax incentives muted company opposition to higher costs. The impact was immediate and dramatic. In 1950 ARAMCO paid the United States Government 50 million dollars in taxes, as opposed to 66 million to the Saudi Arabian Government. Just one year later there had been a sharp reversal: it gave the American Treasury only 6 million dollars while Saudi Arabia was paid 100 million. During the 1960s the large multinational oil companies' foreign tax credits actually exceeded their American tax liabilities every year.[3]

Less accommodating was the firm stand taken by the oil companies when Iran decided to nationalize the holdings of British Petroleum (then known as the Anglo-Iranian Oil Company) in 1951. When the

Iranian Government tried to sell the oil produced from the nationalized oilfields, they found it impossible. Potential purchasers were threatened with legal action if they bought the oil; and in order to compensate for the loss of Iranian oil on the market, the oil companies increased production in Saudi Arabia and Kuwait. Eventually, following a CIA-orchestrated coup to restore the overthrown Shah, Iranian oil returned to the world market, produced and distributed by a new multinational consortium which took the place of the Anglo-Iranian company. This apparently demonstrated the futility of immediate nationalization: oil companies now controlled vast oil supplies in the Middle Eastern oil-fields, where production could easily be varied, allowing the manipulation of the oil market to meet commercial criteria. The Western governments, particularly the two main parent governments (the United States and the United Kingdom), were content to allow the oil companies to utilize their vast commercial power in return for their control over and guarantee of oil supplies. In compensation for their service to the perceived national interest, oil companies were given considerable advantages, not least in tax incentives and freedom from monopoly investigation. It was widely assumed that the existing system of company-directed oil diplomacy would continue to serve the objectives of the industrial West for the foreseeable future.

Thus, during the 1950s oil prices fell in real terms, the West benefited from cheap energy, American and European consumption rocketed, and the oil companies gathered vast profits. In an era of cheap oil, petroleum replaced coal as the most important source of energy and by 1970 every country in Western Europe, with the exception of the United Kingdom, relied more on oil than on coal. In the world as a whole, oil's share of commercial energy consumption rose from just under a quarter in 1950 to over 45 per cent in 1973.[4] The industry appeared to be very orderly, and controlled by an elaborate network of marketing agreements, production agreements and inter-company deals. Many of the most prolific concessions were for very long periods of time, and, particularly in the Middle East, the very large reserves and comparatively low cost of production enabled the oil companies to adjust production to demand, which, for the three decades after the Second World War, essentially meant upwards adjustments as the demand for oil roughly doubled every decade.[5] The low cost and prolific nature of Middle Eastern oil outweighed any political instability in the region, particularly as the main producers in the Arabian Peninsula were ruled by conservative monarchies, and Iran and (until 1958) Iraq were pro-Western.

The control exercised by the oil majors meant that there was very little 'market' in the oil industry: most of the oil was either controlled by the majors from production to the eventual distribution of refined products, or was sold through long-term contracts. The price used to calculate the host governments' share of production profits, the so-called 'posted price', was an artificial price set by the companies and rarely tested in the marketplace. However, it was only a matter of time before the oil-producing governments realized that the West was obtaining its oil at an unduly low price.[6] Even then, it was difficult to see what effective action they could take as they had no access to distribution facilities and often no local refining capacity. While the oil majors controlled geographically diverse reserves of petroleum, enabling them to switch production if required, any host government taking the route of nationalization faced an uncertain future, as the cases of Mexico (1938) and Iran (1951–3) apparently demonstrated.

However, the oil producers of the developing world, although more often controlled by informal than formal empires, were nonetheless susceptible to the forces of Third World nationalism. In the fifteen years after the end of the Second World War, there was a tide of decolonization as the weakened empires of Europe were no longer able to maintain their imperial possessions. Rejection of Western influence extended beyond the throwing off of imperial rule. Third World countries, in seeking to control their own economies, frequently regarded Western companies with suspicion and sought greater state control over their economies. Moreover, the ambitions of the oil-producing governments were becoming more sophisticated and expensive. For more conservative regimes, the judicious use of oil wealth might succeed in diverting potential social unrest and provide political stability. For some producing governments – particularly those whose oilfields had been among the first to be exploited, such as Iran and Venezuela – development plans did not simply exploit oil revenues, they also sought to address the issue of alternative sources of income when the oil wells eventually ran dry. In short, while in the early days of many concessions, rulers or governments had seen oil revenues as an unexpected bonus, by the late 1950s they sought a predictable and guaranteed oil income from which they could fund long-term development programmes. Thus, while companies resisted any suggestions that levels of production and price should reflect the revenue needs of host governments, rather than their own commercial judgement, the producing countries were clear that they wanted greater involvement in, and influence over, managerial decisions which had a crucial impact on their income. It soon became apparent that improvements in the terms and conditions of one concession would be demanded by other host governments. This is evident in the speed with which the so-called 50–50 agreements spread from Latin America to the Middle East. As circumstances altered in the oil market, the oil-producing states were able to improve their terms and conditions, although companies still retained control over prices and production levels.

Development policy was further emphasized by the new generations of leaders, often educated in the West or advised by those who were – for example, the Saudi Petroleum Minister at the time of the formation of OPEC, Sheikh Tariki, was a geology graduate from the University of Texas. The host governments were increasingly aware of their lack of control over both the prices and the production levels of their oil. This had been conclusively demonstrated at the time of the Iranian oil boycott, when companies had been able to meet demand through extra production from Saudi Arabia and Kuwait, thus keeping prices stable. The desire for greater control over oil united both radical regimes and conservative monarchies of the Arabian Peninsula, and extended across continents to bring together Venezuela and the Middle East. This strengthening oil nationalism came to a head in the late 1950s. The Venezuelan Government wanted to promote a policy of expensive oil and lower production, to extend the economic life of their oil-fields. However, during the 1950s the market price for oil tended to move downwards, in the face of increased competition from Soviet oil. Rather than adjust supply to cope with this added competition, the large oil producers were determined to retain market share by cutting prices. This infuriated the host governments, not least because the oil consumer countries took considerably more in taxes, both direct and indirect, on refined petroleum products than the producing governments received for the crude oil from which these had been derived. Leading oil exporters, notably Venezuela, Saudi Arabia, Iraq, Kuwait and Iran, had been in contact with each other to coordinate policy during 1959.[7] Annoyance at the level of control exercised by the companies came to a head when Exxon decided unilaterally to reduce the posted price on Arabian Light Crude by 14 cents a barrel in August 1960, breaking the customary link between crude oil prices in the United States (protected against international competition by oil import quotas) and international prices. In the immediate aftermath, five governments – those of Iran, Iraq, Kuwait and the two main instigators, Saudi Arabia and Venezuela – came together in Baghdad to form the Organization of Petroleum Exporting Countries.

Initially, there seemed to be little scope for the new organization to take effective action, as oil supplies were plentiful. Nonetheless, it was able, albeit mainly through the individual actions of its members, to make certain limited gains in its first few years of existence. In that historic first meeting, OPEC members demanded that the oil companies should maintain steady prices, and that any future modifications in the posted price should only be introduced after negotiations with the host governments. Indeed, 1960 was the last occasion when the companies unilaterally imposed a price cut. The members of this new organization also agreed to use their best efforts to restore the old level of posted prices and to formulate a system to ensure price stabilization. With the comparatively recent Iranian crisis in mind, it was also agreed that if companies adopted sanctions against a member country, the others would not accept a compensating increase in exports.[8] Although these were aspirations rather than achievements, nonetheless as other major exporters emerged on to the world market they joined OPEC, including not only Latin American (Ecuador) and Middle Eastern (Qatar) states, but also Indonesia, and the new producers in North and West Africa, where in 1960–61 commercial exports began from Algeria, Libya and Nigeria.[9] As a consequence, OPEC's share of free world oil exports remained steady throughout the 1960s, at between 82 and 84 per cent.[10] In 1968 the organization agreed upon a Declaration of Principles, which called for host government participation in the companies exploiting their resources, an improvement in concession terms and, above all else, control over prices. Its members were also able to secure a steady improvement of terms for host governments. By 1970 the profits on crude oil were divided roughly 70:30 in the host government's favour,[11] a position which was accepted by the oil companies as many of the extra costs were simply offset against their domestic tax liability.

In addition to seeking a greater share of the money profits, the host governments also began to argue that their stake in their natural resources should be formally represented by a percentage share, or participation, in the company exploiting those resources. In December 1961 the Iraqi Government enacted Law No. 80, which expropriated all of the Iraq Petroleum Company area not currently in production, although this was contested by the company for the next decade. In June 1971 OPEC agreed that their individual governments should demand an immediate 20 per cent share in the companies, eventually rising to 51 per cent, with due provision for compensation.[12] In the following year OPEC began participation negotiations with the

companies. Eventually an agreement was reached by which participation was to start at 25 per cent and rise to 52 per cent by 1982, with
provision for compensation and company 'buy back' of government
oil. The Shah of Iran reached an agreement with the Consortium
which, with the proviso that the government already owned the oil,
contained similar financial terms to those negotiated by Sheikh
Yamani.[13] However, this agreement was overtaken by events. Even
before 1973 some host governments rejected the gradualist approach.
In 1971 Algeria nationalized 51 per cent of all French interest in its oil
and Libya nationalized BP's assets, while on 1 June 1972 Iraq nationalized IPC's holdings in the north of Iraq, with agreement on an
appropriate level of compensation, finally reached in early 1973.[14] In
July 1971 Venezuela announced that concessions, which were due for
expiry in 1983–5, would revert to the state, complete with plant and
equipment, without compensation, although that was later superseded
by total nationalization in January 1976.[15]

These successes should not hide the fact, however, that in other ways
OPEC was less successful. Indeed, even where the organization was
able to achieve its goals or improve the financial terms of its members,
that was more often the consequence of the actions of an individual
member rather than the efforts of OPEC as a whole. There were considerable political divisions in the organization, particularly as some,
but of course by no means all, of the members were Arab states united
against Israel, to which Iran exported considerable quantities of oil.
Even among the Arab states, there was dissension: Iraq threatened to
attack Kuwait, which it maintained was legally part of Iraq, after
Kuwait declared independence of British protection in 1961. The
threat was only diverted by strong American and British protests, the
landing of 5,000 British troops as a symbol of Britain's continued commitment to protect Kuwait, and the pledge of the Arab League to protect Kuwait.[16] The Shah of Iran often acted alone rather than through
OPEC; by placing pressure directly on the oil companies and the
United States Government, rather than by working through OPEC to
harmonize terms and conditions, the Shah was able to secure concessions in Iran's favour. Such unilateral action undermined the authority
of OPEC to speak on behalf of its members.

The turning point in the organization's influence came in 1971,
when the oil companies agreed to negotiate with the host governments
collectively. Moreover, while the companies wished to link the Gulf
and Mediterranean producers in a single set of negotiations, the host
governments were not prepared to countenance this. On 14 February

1971, 23 oil companies signed the Teheran Agreement with six Persian Gulf producers, Abu Dhabi, Iran, Iraq, Kuwait, Qatar and Saudi Arabia. This provided for a general increase in the posted price of 35 cents, with an annual escalation of 2.5 per cent to cover inflation and confirmation of a 55 per cent tax rate. The agreement was to run for five years, but an agreement with Mediterranean producers was still to be formulated. Although the Tripoli Agreement, signed later in the year, was officially with Libya only, the other Mediterranean producers were able to achieve similar terms, which offered a different posted price increase to reflect the market advantages of the Mediterranean producers, but otherwise contained similar provisions to the Teheran Agreement.[17]

There were a number of reasons for this change in attitude, but the two most significant were, first, the increased complexity of the oil industry and, second, the vastly increased significance of OPEC's oil on the world market. In 1960, the international oil industry had been dominated by a small group of multinational oil majors. Although in 1971 the so-called 'Seven Sisters' still dominated the industry by reason of their size and their close cooperation, many other companies emerged to join the oil business. In the late 1950s, worried by the competitive risk posed by cheaper foreign oil, and keen to protect and expand their share of the domestic market, a number of American 'independents', which had hitherto operated only within the United States, began to venture into foreign exploration. Some, such as the Continental Oil Company and the Getty Oil Company, became important foreign operators. At the same time, a number of oil-consuming countries encouraged the formation of oil companies, some with state participation, in order to seek foreign concessions: Italian and Japanese companies now joined France's CFP as important bidders for concessions. These newcomers to the oil scene moved into new areas of exploration, such as the Neutral Zones and offshore concessions in the Middle East, and in particular the North African oilfields. Libya, for example, decided against a policy of awarding one large concession and instead negotiated some 55 different concessions, with some owned by the large majors (which of course had access to widespread markets) but others controlled by independents.[18] In order to gain a foothold in the lucrative and prolific areas of the Middle East and North Africa, these companies were often willing to give more generous terms than those offered by the established companies. Moreover, by the early 1970s, and in some cases before, host governments in the Middle East were beginning to control a share of the oil produced in their territories through participation oil, which could be in the form of autonomous companies, such as the National Iranian Oil Corporation. Faced with a tightening market for crude oil, refiners and distributors, anxious to loosen their dependence upon the major oil companies, began a process of 'outbidding', with the producer government's participation crude particularly attractive to the spot markets in such places as Rotterdam – one of the few opportunities to buy crude oil on the open market. This reinforced the opinion of these producer governments that the prevailing price was too low, and also increased the temptation to demand greater participation in the concessionary companies. Thus, the control of the oil majors was already being undermined.

This is not to imply that the oil company majors had lost their power. They still mainly owned the most prolific concessions of the Middle East, and their control over transportation, refining and distribution facilities still gave them a predominant position. Their close cooperation still underpinned the pricing regime. Nonetheless, their control over prices was partially undermined by the Teheran and Tripoli agreements. In addition, in their dealings with OPEC, the majors had to take account of the growing importance of its oil in the world oil market. The Soviet Union had aggressively marketed its oil during the 1950s, at cheap prices, in order to maximize the acquisition of hard currency, but in the 1960s, the oil was used closer to home and sold at higher prices to satellite states. The United States was importing more oil, and by the early 1970s was producing at maximum capacity. Europe had made a decisive shift to the use of cheap oil for energy generation and space heating. Market forces had swung in favour of the OPEC members, whose oil was now literally essential for the West. Although the companies still retained the power to set production levels and to negotiate prices, they could not now contemplate the possibility of a major disruption in supply, such as had occurred at the time of the Iranian crisis. There was no spare capacity readily available to compensate for any shortfall, particularly as an attempt to boycott a single producer would not succeed in the face of OPEC solidarity. This was in marked contrast to the position that had prevailed since 1945, in which oil companies had managed production from the prolific fields of the Middle East in order to keep prices low and supplies high. The new power of the oil producers was clearly demonstrated in the case of Libya, where in 1970 the new, and more radical regime of Colonel Gaddafy demanded, and obtained, better terms from the oil companies, triggering a process of leapfrogging as other producers demanded similar terms, only to be followed by further Libyan advances.

The oil company majors also faced hostile investigations into their activities. Although the oil companies had come to play an important role in their parent governments' foreign and national security policies, their reputation and standing among the general public, and in the academic and journalistic world, was not high. In the 1960s and early 1970s there was a spate of hostile journalistic reports into the dealings of the oil companies, published in books with titles such as *The Control of Oil*, *The Politics of Oil* and *The Empire of Oil*.[19] Oil companies were criticized, *inter alia*, at home for using political influence to gain privileged access to land, for exercising monopoly power in restraint of trade, for manipulating prices, and causing pollution: abroad they were criticized for undue influence over both host and parent governments, for excessive profits and for operating a cartel which excluded other, generally smaller, oil companies. As criticism grew in the United States in 1973, the Senate Foreign Relations Committee set up a subcommittee on multinational corporations under Senator Frank Church. This conducted a wide-ranging investigation into the multinational oil industry.[20] The hearings and report revealed a great deal about the way the oil companies operated, not only in cooperating with one another, but also how, through the 50–50 deals, the companies had been subsidized by the American taxpayer, how the price of oil was fixed in complex ways, and how production was shared out among the oil companies. These disclosures were used by a number of writers on the oil industry[21] and showed the extent to which the oil industry was a tight world in which erstwhile competitors often worked closely together. The complex interlocking relationships between the major oil companies, together with the small amount of oil which actually found its way onto the free market, allowed price fixing. By implication, the suggestion was that oil companies had distorted the oil market in ways that artificially kept prices high. Thus, while host governments were accusing oil companies of keeping down prices to levels that were too low by overproduction, the consuming governments saw things very differently. In April 1973 the United States ended mandatory oil import quotas which had been used both to control US reliance on foreign oil and to protect domestic independents. This was seen by many consumers as opening the way for further excessive profits on the part of the oil companies. However, by the time that the Church report was published, the oil crisis of 1973, together with the actions of OPEC and the host governments to seize control over the price of oil and to move rapidly towards 100 per cent participation, had altered the oil industry out of all recognition.

OPEC in control

Although the oil-consuming nations might have expected a period of stability in the industry following the Teheran and Tripoli agreements, both of which made provision for the next five years, developments in the world economy undermined this. The agreements had stipulated price increases of 2.5 per cent each year for five years, to take account of inflation: however, this agreed escalator for prices was eroded by rising inflation in the world economy and the devaluation of the dollar – the currency in which oil was priced. Although two supplementary agreements were reached to compensate for these unforeseen problems, it was nonetheless apparent that the Teheran and Tripoli agreements were being superseded by events. At the same time, the tightening oil market strengthened the hand of the oil exporters. The decision by OPEC unilaterally to set prices surprised the oil companies, but it remained unchallenged, while the 1973 oil crisis generally appeared to demonstrate the extent to which the oil companies had lost their control over the industry. They no longer set prices; although ostensibly still with majority management responsibility in most concessions, they were effectively powerless to halt the cuts in production imposed as part of the OAPEC boycott. It was the governments of Iran and Iraq, rather than the oil companies, which decided to increase production from those oilfields to compensate for the shortfall. Even after the oil had been produced and sold, the companies were solicitous of host government requirements, and refused to break the terms of the boycott (thus, no Saudi oil went to the United States for example), although, by adroit shifting of shipments of petroleum, they were able on the whole to meet the demands of customers. This shift of power and control away from the companies and towards OPEC raised additional concerns among consuming countries. Although in 1973 the oil companies succeeded in managing the available supplies to avoid any really serious shortfall even for those countries officially boycotted by OAPEC, it was apparent that consumer governments could no longer assume that the major oil companies would automatically serve their interests.

Although there had been a redistribution of power within the oil industry, the consequences for the large oil companies were mixed. For many companies the immediate effect was very positive, as their stocks of oil suddenly increased dramatically in price. As a consequence, they reported exceptional profits in early 1974 with the American majors registering an increase in their net profits of over 68 per cent for the first half of 1974 compared to the previous half year.[22] Moreover, the companies were no longer as subject to – often contradictory – political pressure from parent, consumer and producing governments. They still had a crucial role to play, partly for their technical and managerial expertise but also for their worldwide network of transportation, refining and distribution facilities. With managerial contracts rather than concessions, companies had fewer rights to make decisions but, on the other hand, neither could they be put under sustained pressure; for example, in the 1960s the Shah of Iran would if necessary seek the support of the American State Department for his demands that the level of production from Iran be increased. Moreover, in certain key areas – for example, in refining – the oil companies still retained an overwhelming position. There have been few signs, with such exceptions as Q8,[23] of host governments entering the world of distribution worldwide, although they have sold oil directly to consumer state companies. Moreover, despite attempts by consumer countries to build up stocks of petroleum, company stocks remained important in weathering short-term crises, such as that at the time of the Iran–Iraq War. OPEC did not use its power to undermine the market price by, for example, offering low-cost oil to other developing countries. The oil companies continued to wield considerable power in the world economy: in 1983 the five American majors and Standard Oil of Indiana were in the top ten American industrial corporations, and the five majors accounted for roughly the same share of the profits of the Fortune 500 as before the 1973 oil crisis (around a seventh).[24] The oil companies also retained an important interest in non-OPEC oilfields, such as those in the North Sea and Alaska. Moreover, many oil companies diversified into alternative sources of energy, including coal, nuclear fuel, and renewable energy sources, although this was not always entirely successful.

The fact, nonetheless, remains that as a result of the 1973 oil crisis, control over two important variables in the oil market, production levels and prices, now rested in the hands of OPEC and the oil-producing governments rather than with the companies. By proceeding rapidly towards '100 per cent participation', the producing governments effectively terminated the concessions regime and imposed national ownership and control over their petroleum resources. Excluding the communist world and North America, in 1970 the national companies of the host governments held on average 10 per cent of production; by 1979 that had reached 79 per cent. The major oil companies' share dropped from 72 per cent to 17 per cent. With this development, the role of the oil companies changed; in particular, they tended to fulfil technical and managerial functions only, with decisions on price and production levels firmly in the hands of the producer governments. In effect, this marked the end of the concession system, many years ahead of schedule (the ARAMCO concession was not due for reversion until 1999, and the KOC not until 2026).[25] Thus, rather than having a secure long-term supply of crude under their own control, companies had to meet a third or more of their needs from short-term sources.[26] This transformation in the structure of the oil industry, and the changes that it brought in the pricing regime for petroleum, represented a major shift. For companies accustomed to absolute control over the oil within their concessions, first the introduction and then the acceleration of the process of participation had very serious consequences, not least on their ability to manage supply to meet demand. Moreover, as both the price of oil and the tax and royalty rates were now effectively being set by OPEC, even financial planning was fraught with difficulties. It was not even certain that all OPEC members would abide by the commonly agreed price.

Thus, OPEC transformed its role in the course of 1973, obtaining for itself power over prices and production, and this had both advantages and disadvantages. OPEC was able to keep up prices during the mid-1970s by retaining a large gap between the maximum production available and the actual level of production, but when market conditions changed following a downturn in demand, it was OPEC, not the oil companies, that had to take hard decisions and impose production quotas. One marked feature of the period after 1973 is that the producing governments' greater control over their oil resources allowed the development of a much more active oil diplomacy between oil-producing and oil-consuming governments, in which oil could be used as a bargaining counter. The oil companies were increasingly relegated to the sidelines, where hitherto they had played an important role in oil diplomacy.[27] Indeed, some parent governments saw the companies as increasingly acting in the interests of OPEC rather than their own.[28] Instead, producer governments were able to use their control over their own resources to serve their goals in international relations. Opportunities for the overt use of oil diplomacy were enhanced by the desire of industrialized nations to conclude bilateral, government-level agreements with the leading oil producers, and there are many instances in which this occurred. Special relationships between governments have been sought by, *inter alia*, France with Iraq and the United States with Saudi Arabia. During 1974 a number of agreements were signed between the latter two countries, including a Technical Cooperation Agreement, an agreement on military and economic cooperation and American modernization of the National Guard. While this could be seen as an ongoing reaction to the security vacuum that was left in the Persian Gulf by the withdrawal of the United Kingdom, it was also clearly an attempt to build up a strong relationship with Saudi Arabia. The potential use of oil as a bargaining counter waxes and wanes depending upon the particular circumstances of the world oil market. While Iraq, for example, used its oil to reward its friends, especially France, oil diplomacy was only really effective when oil supplies were tight and production was heavily concentrated in a small number of states with clear political goals.

One of the most striking effects of the 1973 oil crisis was that it changed irrevocably the price-setting mechanism within the industry. Hitherto, there had only been a limited 'free' market in petroleum; now, the price was officially set by regular meetings of OPEC Petroleum Ministers although, as we shall see later in the chapter, even during the period of OPEC supremacy, market forces still played their part. However, this change in price regime signalled dramatically the degree to which the buyers' market had become a sellers' market. While oil consumers had become accustomed to a steady supply of cheap oil geared to the need of their economies, and expected that to continue, the producers' needs were not necessarily compatible with this. Their priority was high prices and, for many, an extension of the period during which they could expect to receive oil revenue. The control over prices was accompanied by a very rapid shift to 100 per cent participation, with even the moderates within OPEC, such as Kuwait and Saudi Arabia, taking total control of their oilfields.

The first OPEC decision on the price of oil came in October 1973, as a mark of frustration at the lack of company concessions, and in an atmosphere of political as well as economic tension. In December 1973 OPEC met again to fix prices and, as described in Chapter 1, agreed on a posted price of 11.65 dollars, with a government take of 7 dollars per barrel. For the first time, it was agreed that Arabian Light 34 API would be the marker crude – a base from which to calculate differential values for other crudes. A complex structure was set up to govern company payments of tax and royalties for their equity oil – still at that point 75 per cent for most companies and concessions – as well as the prevailing price of any government oil that the companies bought back. In this meeting, in an important precursor of later debates on price, Saudi

Arabia argued for a more moderate price, at around 7.50 dollars, but it was overruled by the other members, particularly Iran.[29]

However, the fact that OPEC rather than the oil companies was now in charge of setting prices would not necessarily mean a sustained programme of large price increases, as had been feared in 1973–4. Indeed, it was not even clear whether OPEC members would retain price discipline. There were a number of other factors that would determine how the oil industry developed over the succeeding decades. First, it remained to be seen whether OPEC could retain a cohesive approach to oil prices, given the tremendous differences between its various members. The political interests of the Arab producers of the Middle East and North Africa were different from those of its Latin American members and Iran. Countries with large populations and comparatively small future reserves would have different economic goals from the sparsely populated, reserve-rich states in the Arabian Peninsula. There was also a battle for leadership of OPEC, in particular between Saudi Arabia and Iran. Second, the significance of OPEC rested to a large extent upon its dominance in the world oil trade. Should other sources of crude petroleum become available in countries which chose not to enter OPEC, this might undermine OPEC's power. Third, OPEC had only become powerful when the supply of oil became tight; for a decade before that, it had been virtually impotent. Should the oil market change, either because of greater supplies of oil or a reduction in demand – or a mixture of both – the control of prices would pass to the market place rather than the regular OPEC meetings. Fourth, even if the oil consumers could not easily agree upon a common policy, each could individually adopt conservation policies and reduce demand, which could have a profound effect upon the oil market. In the three decades since the 1973 crisis, the oil market, and the role of OPEC within it, has changed in a number of ways.

Indeed, quite quickly, within the five years after the 1973 crisis, conditions within the oil industry changed in all these areas. OPEC oil remained critical in the world oil market: in each of the years between 1973 and 1978 OPEC members produced over 58 per cent of the world crude oil output (excluding the Sino-Soviet area) and contributed over 90 per cent of the world's oil exports in the same period.[30] However, while OPEC still continued to set prices at its meetings, this did not imply a total cohesion among its members. The organization rapidly developed into two separate factions, united around specific economic rather than political aims. A number of countries, mostly those with fewer reserves and larger populations, were anxious to maximize revenues from oil, and demanded that prices should be pushed up as high as possible. The states of the Arabian Peninsula, however, with small populations, very high per capita incomes, and excess revenues to invest in the West, argued for a more moderate policy, which would prevent too abrupt an impact upon Western economies, with the possibility of a rapid descent into deep recession. Traditionally Iran was the leading price hawk, supported by Iraq and Libya, and often Nigeria, while Saudi Arabia, the UAE and often Qatar tended to be price moderates with Venezuela and Kuwait acting as facilitators in the path to compromise. In the period 1973–78, the moderates prevailed: although the cash price of oil remained high, in real terms the value was eroded by high inflation within the industrialized West. It should not be overlooked, however, that OPEC succeeded in defending the massive increase in oil price which it had secured in the three months between October and December 1973 (more than it was able to do for the next massive price hike in 1979).

Where necessary, Saudi Arabia was prepared to use its position as the country with the greatest capacity to increase production to persuade its fellow OPEC members to follow its pricing policy. In September 1975 Iran sought to push up prices by 15 per cent, while Saudi Arabia only wanted a 5 per cent increase. Saudi Arabia was able to force through a compromise, with a 10 per cent increase taking effect on 1 October, but coupled with a price freeze for nine months. If necessary, the Saudi Government was prepared to employ – or threaten to employ – its immense unused productive capacity, to increase production and hence force down prices.[31] However, the price increases agreed by OPEC were in cash terms, at a time when global inflation was high; at the end of 1978, the real price of oil was 10 per cent lower than in 1974.[32] This raises the question of why, at the very least, the price of oil was not increased to keep pace with inflation. One reason for this was the ability of Saudi Arabia, with its vast production capacity, to act as a 'swing producer', increasing or decreasing its production level in accordance with its own policy on price. However, in 1978 Sheikh Yamani suggested that oil prices should be explicitly linked to those of industrial goods produced by the West – a proposal also suggested by the Trilateral Commission report on energy, published the same year.[33] This proposal resurfaced in 1980, but was overtaken by the tumultuous movements in oil prices during the early 1980s.

The fact nonetheless remains that, had they so wished, OPEC members might have exercised additional upward pressure on prices by withholding production. Indeed, for a number of producers, the revenue from their production was difficult to absorb domestically, thus generating large surpluses at a time of high inflation. Both the buying power of the oil revenues, and the value of foreign assets, was seriously eroded by the depreciation of the dollar. It could legitimately be argued that a barrel of oil in the ground was more valuable than its cash value in the bank, while at the same time prolonging the economic life of oil reserves. Venezuela, for example, followed a policy of conservation for just that reason. Nonetheless, the leading producers still retained substantial unused productive capacity: in October 1977 this ranged from 44 per cent in Kuwait to 27 per cent in Saudi Arabia to 29 per cent in Iraq.[34] The cheapest producers in the Middle East had marginal production costs of between 15 cents and 1 dollar per barrel, and could easily have undercut the prices of many other exporters. However these producers did not engage in cut-throat competition; on the other hand, neither did OPEC as an organization curtail production to force up real prices, despite the argument advanced by some OPEC members that the non-renewable nature of petroleum reserves made a strategy of maximizing prices both justified and economically sensible.

Reasons as to why this strategy was adopted vary. While some of the Gulf producers were generating massive budget surpluses, elsewhere oil producers were anxious to utilize their new revenues to the full, with ambitious programmes of development. A planned programme of production levels could only work if all members of OPEC subscribed and adhered to it, as events in the 1980s were to show. Some governments, such as Kuwait and Saudi Arabia, with massive investments in the West or in the global financial institutions such as the International Monetary Fund (IMF), were concerned about the health of the world economy as a whole. For states with reserves of oil likely to last well into the future, such as Saudi Arabia, exceptionally high prices, which might encourage conservation and the development of alternatives to petroleum, were counter-productive. Moreover, many of the oil producers – of which Iran is a particularly good example – also had political reasons for not wishing to alienate the West, which promoted regional stability, resisted Soviet ambitions, and provided advanced military equipment. Ultimately, this proved to be to the benefit of the Western consumer.

In addition, however, other forces also came into play. As discussed in Chapter 4, one key issue would be the extent to which the various consuming nations addressed the issue of conservation and the development of alternative sources of energy. Meanwhile, during the 1970s, a number of new oilfields began commercial production, many of them outside the jurisdiction of OPEC members. Although in most cases the fields had been identified before 1973, the prevailing atmosphere of crisis and high prices accelerated or facilitated their development. In the United States, the 1973 crisis succeeded in overturning delays to the planned Alaskan pipeline caused by environmental protests. The increased cost of oil made sources of petroleum which were difficult to produce or transport more commercially viable: when the price of oil was 14 dollars, an oil field in the Arctic had to contain one billion barrels to be worth developing, while with the price at 24 dollars the minimum size dropped to only 100 million barrels.[35] Thus, a vast new area of production was opened up within the boundaries of the world's largest consumer of petroleum, the United States. In Europe, the exploitation of the North Sea, which had already begun in the 1960s, increased in extent, aided by the higher price of petroleum which offset the expenses of offshore drilling. In 1970 British Petroleum made the first great discovery in the British zone of the North Sea in the Forties field,[36] a development from which the governments of both Norway and the United Kingdom benefited. Meanwhile in Latin America, Mexico, which had been a major producer earlier in the century but whose industry had shrunk dramatically for a combination of geological and political reasons, discovered new reserves. Oil from these new, usually politically more stable regions came on stream in large volumes during the 1970s, and started to erode OPEC's domination of the free world market in oil (see Table 2.1).

None of these new areas chose to enter OPEC, although the prices of their crudes tended to follow that organization's norms. OPEC was essentially an organization of developing countries, in which petroleum

Table 2.1 Oil production by selected areas, 1971–1978 (mbd)

Year	1972	1973	1974	1975	1976	1977	1978
USA	11.19	10.95	10.49	10.01	9.74	9.87	10.27
Mexico	0.51	0.55	0.64	0.79	0.87	1.09	1.33
UK	–	–	–	0.03	0.24	0.77	1.01
W. Europe*	0.43	0.44	0.45	0.63	0.91	1.41	1.82
Saudi Arabia	5.79	7.44	8.35	6.97	8.53	9.24	8.32
Middle East†	18.08	21.27	21.93	19.72	22.55	22.95	21.43
USSR	8.11	8.69	9.29	9.34	10.53	11.01	11.56

Source: Adapted from *BP Statistical Review of World Energy 2001*. BP Plc.
* Total for Western Europe includes the United Kingdom.
† Total for Middle East includes Saudi Arabia.

accounted for a substantial proportion of exports and government revenue. The United States, Norway and the United Kingdom clearly did not fit either of those criteria, and could not be expected to join. The first British North Sea oil flowed ashore in 1975, and by 1978 it provided 75 per cent of British consumption. However in many respects the British Government continued to act more like a consumer than a producer state. Sixty per cent of North Sea oil from the British sector was controlled by foreign companies, encouraged by generous tax concessions. The Ministry of Power justified these generous terms with the argument that if the terms were too harsh, they might tempt OPEC producers to follow suit.[37] In its desire to remain identified with the OECD consumers, with which it was linked through the International Energy Agency, the British Government was anxious to eschew any tactics similar to those adopted by OPEC; rather than seeking to control production levels and prices, or influencing the scale of the exploration programme, the government appeared more concerned with ensuring that in any emergency, British oil would be used in accordance with British interests. This was achieved through the British National Oil Corporation (BNOC), a wholly state-owned oil company with the option to buy up to 51 per cent of North Sea oil at market prices.[38]

A more likely contender for OPEC membership was Mexico, yet its government decided not to join its fellow Latin American states, Venezuela and Ecuador, in the organization. As a country which had been a net importer since 1968, and which had focused its attention on industrialization rather than raw materials (its state oil company, Pemex, increasingly concentrated upon processing, including refining and petrochemicals), Mexico was ineligible to join OPEC before 1973. However, in 1973 Pemex made considerable new finds, by 1975 the country had ceased to be a net importer, and from 1976 to 1982 there was a massive growth in production. Throughout the 1970s production and estimated reserves rose sharply. By 1977 reserves had climbed to 16 billion barrels, and by 1980 had reached 60 billion. Production nearly doubled during that three-year period, and by 1984 had doubled yet again.[39] Yet despite this, Mexico did not join OPEC even when that organization was at the height of its powers.

The reasons for this are many and complex. Undoubtedly, the likely response of the United States to a Mexican move into OPEC played an important role. While Mexico was prepared to use its new found oil reserves as a bargaining counter in negotiations on outstanding issues between the two countries, such as migration and trade, and was also courted by a number of oil-consumer governments – including Japan, Canada, Spain, France and West Germany, all of whom sought bilateral deals – the natural customer for Mexico's oil, and particularly its vast supplies of natural gas, was the United States. The United States Trade Act of 1974 gave preferential tariff treatment to selected exports of less-developed countries, but explicitly excluded OPEC members from its provisions. Moreover, the United States dominated other aspects of the Mexican economy, including trade, capital investment and tourism. Unlike most OPEC members, oil was not the only source of Mexico's export earnings; indeed, in 1979 it accounted for only 43 per cent of the total.[40] Another, pragmatic reason was more intangible, but significant nonetheless: that is, Mexico's view of its own role in the world economy, set against the common perception of OPEC as an organization of less-developed countries. Although it was clearly not a fully developed economy, Mexico was not prepared to identify itself as a developing country. The government had pursued a programme of industrialization even before the new reserves were opened up, and it intended to use the promise of its oil revenues to embark on an ambitious development programme.

The development of large sources of new production, close to major markets, and outside OPEC, was clearly significant, although it should be noted that exploration, production and transport costs, in Alaska and the North Sea in particular, were very high. Consumers also took steps to control the demand side of the equation: however, the reasons underpinning their various initiatives (discussed in more detail in Chapter 4) owed more to short-term expediency than long-term planning, in that the goal was to reduce dependency upon OPEC. Initial indications suggested that consumption would indeed fall. Whereas during the period from 1960 until the end of 1973 the energy consumed by OECD countries had increased on average by 5.1 per cent per year, in 1974 and 1975 energy consumption actually fell. However, in 1976 it began to rise again.[41] This would suggest that the real reason for the drop in consumption reflected the concurrent recession rather than long-term adjustments to energy usage. Even so, signs of a drop in demand, coupled with the growth in non-OPEC production, led experts to predict that the 'energy crisis' had passed, and that oil supplies would remain readily available for the foreseeable future, even if they might go through tight periods. As new areas opened up, it was easy to assume that this would be a perpetual process; large areas of the world remained unexplored for petroleum. In other words, rather than regarding the energy crisis as a long-term problem of reliance on the two non-renewable resources of oil and coal, it was perceived as a short-term political and economic problem that only required action when supplies were short or prices were high. Thus, within a few years complacency had set in. Towards the end of the 1970s, concern at the monopoly power of OPEC, often referred to as a cartel, was replaced by mounting complacency that its control over the oil industry was being eroded by a combination of conservation in consuming nations, the development of alternative oilfields outside the boundaries of OPEC members and the increasing use of alternative sources of energy.

In a survey of a number of different models of the future world oil market, Dermot Gately[42] found that most analysts were in agreement that over the next few years real oil prices would remain fairly constant, although they disagreed on whether that period of stability would continue beyond the mid-1980s or be replaced by severe upward pressure on prices. Writing before the Iranian Revolution, Gately found it surprising that so few analysts gave attention to the possibility of major, abrupt price increases. One reason for that, as a representative of Venezuela's state oil company (Petroleos di Venezuela) pointed out, was that with the decline in real prices, the consumers saw oil purely in economic terms, and made predictions on the future based purely in economic factors within the oil industry. However, as he stressed, for oil producers the political dimension was very important, including their dependence upon the industrialized consumers for advanced technology and, in some cases, modern weaponry and security.[43]

However, Gately was proved right when, in 1979, hopes of a fall in oil prices triggered by an oil glut were dashed when the Iranian Revolution triggered another dramatic increase in petroleum prices, as outlined in Chapter 1. It has already been noted that not only did the consumers, for the most part, demonstrate similar characteristics to those that had been apparent in 1973, but also that the emergency allocation plans worked out by the IEA were irrelevant, given the nature of the crisis. In effect, however, the Iranian crisis, although apparently reinforcing OPEC's power yet again as a crucial area for oil supplies, also demonstrated the weakness of the organization's control over its members. As spot market prices soared, OPEC in effect abandoned the idea of fixed prices based around a 'marker crude' and instead tended to follow spot prices, allowing members to set their own price, to reflect the particular country's location and quality of crude. Thus, while at the end of 1978 all OPEC members charged between 12 and 14 dollars per barrel, at the end of 1980 the differentials ranged from 31 to 43 dollars. In average terms, prices rose from 13 dollars per barrel at the end of 1978 to 39 dollars at the end of 1979.[44] The OPEC meeting in December 1979 essentially left its members free to charge whatever prices the market would bear. As spot market prices soared, OPEC continued to increase its price: in June 1980 it was set at 32 dollars per barrel with differentials for other crudes of up to 5 dollars per barrel, and in October 1981 all members agreed to 34 dollars per barrel.[45] Once again, however, the market conditions rapidly changed away from the oil producers. Even when two members actually went to war with one another (Iran and Iraq), although prices rose sharply when war first broke out (as it did at the time of the Gulf War in 1990 and 1991), the spare capacity of other OPEC producers was rapidly harnessed to keep prices under control and, as discussed in Chapter 1, the predicted third oil price shock failed to happen. The consumers appeared to have decoupled the umbilical link between Middle Eastern crises and oil price rises.

Members of OPEC experienced severe fluctuations in oil revenues during the period 1978–83. Even before the second oil price shock, they had begun to consider a formula for oil prices, to ensure stability in the market, and in 1980 the organization prepared a long-term strategy plan. This presumed a basic floor price, probably 30 dollars, which would then be adjusted in accordance with an index based on a number of indicators for ten leading industrial countries, including the exchange rates of their currencies, an inflation index based on export and consumer prices and a GNP index reflecting the weighted average real rate of growth for the same ten countries.[46] This would have perhaps secured stability, but not only was it never introduced, it presumed a level of discipline and market control which OPEC did not possess. By 1981 there was a temporary oil glut which stabilized prices after the rapid escalation in the aftermath of the Iranian revolution, despite the tendency of both Iran and Iraq to aim their attacks against each other's oil installations. As early as May 1981, although OPEC left prices at the prevailing rate, all member states except Saudi Arabia, Iraq and Iran decided to cut their production by at least 10 per cent in order to address the imbalance between supply and demand. Even so, Nigeria (in competition with North Sea oil) reduced its price in the late summer of 1981 and other member governments offered special discounts. This marked the beginning of a shift in the pricing mechanism for oil. From that date, experts predicted the demise of OPEC, arguing that its members had sown the seeds of their own undoing, as the consequences of high prices would be the rapid development of alternatives to OPEC oil, whether in the form of new oilfields or different sources of energy. One expert went as far as to predict that, with cuts in consumption and full production in North America and the North Sea, by the 1990s 'little oil will be required from the rest of the world to meet Western needs'.[47] While few shared quite such optimism, it seemed reasonable to conclude that OPEC's power was in decline. Moreover, from 1979 until 1983 oil demand actually fell by 5 per cent per year, and this loss in production was essentially borne by the OPEC producers.[48] By 1982 non–OPEC producers had overtaken OPEC's output by 1 mbd.[49]

Others, however, counselled caution. The Vice President of Exxon, Stephen Stamas, pointed out that lower consumption might well reflect the recession that had hit the world economy in 1979, and that lower prices would simply undermine the competitiveness of alternatives to OPEC oil, many of which were very expensive and difficult to obtain.[50] His message was that the United States could not afford to disregard the importance of a good working relationship with the major oil exporters, while others stressed that the tendency to 'use OPEC as a convenient scapegoat'[51] had allowed Americans to ignore the need to address their own high energy usage – the United States consumed about three times as much energy and twice as much oil per capita as other nations with similar per capita incomes. Bruce Scott warned starkly that 'Excess US consumption is our basic problem, not OPEC'.[52] From the other side of the Atlantic, a managing director of the Royal Dutch Petroleum Company also issued a cautionary note, and called for urgent attention to be given to the need to improve

Table 2.2 Oil production by selected areas, 1979–1985 (mbd)

Area	1979	1980	1981	1982	1983	1984	1985
USA	10.14	10.17	10.18	10.02	10.24	10.51	10.54
Mexico	1.63	2.12	2.59	3.01	2.95	3.02	3.02
UK	1.60	1.65	1.84	2.13	2.36	2.58	2.64
W. Europe*	2.30	2.48	2.64	3.02	3.45	3.77	3.94
Saudi Arabia	9.56	9.99	9.99	6.70	5.23	4.76	3.60
Middle East†	21.91	18.76	16.02	13.28	12.11	11.86	10.87
OPEC	31.47	27.45	23.38	19.93	18.43	18.47	17.23

Source: Adapted from *BP Statistical Review of World Energy 2001*. BP Plc.
* Total for Western Europe includes the United Kingdom.
† Total for Middle East includes Saudi Arabia.

energy efficiency and discover new sources.[53] However, as the 1980s progressed, such dire prognostications seemed unjustified. The world-wide economic slump reduced demand for oil: whereas global demand had stood at 62.9 mbd, by 1982 it was only 53.5 mbd.[54] In the first half of the 1980s, OPEC production slumped, with the Middle East experiencing a particularly marked downturn (Table 2.2).

The market in charge

The downturn in demand came at a bad time for OPEC: two of its members, Iran and Iraq, were actually at war with one another; there was political uncertainty in other countries as a consequence; and alternative sources of energy, such as North Sea oil, were having a major impact on the market. A significant turning point came in that same year, 1983, when the New York Mercantile Exchange introduced oil futures contracts, signalling the new importance of market forces in formally setting the price of oil. The organization had already attempted to address its changed role in the oil market: in March 1982, for the first time, OPEC agreed to set a ceiling for production at 17.5 mbd, with individual quotas for its members, in an attempt to hold up prices at 34 dollars per barrel. This is the point at which many commentators, including Ian Skeet,[55] would argue that the organization had become in reality what it had often been accused of being, i.e. a cartel. Saudi Arabia became, in effect, the swing producer with no official quota, but instead setting a production level which represented the difference between the OPEC ceiling and the other members' quotas. This was rapidly challenged not only by Iran but, in July, by Venezuela, which could not afford a reduction in revenue in the face of falling revenues and budget crises.[56] The former began producing over quota, reinforced by its apparent successes in the war against Iraq, and other members emulated its example, thus putting pressure on Saudi production. As North Sea and Mexican oil was often sold at discount prices, this put pressure upon Nigerian prices in particular: after BNOC cut the price of North Sea oil in February 1983, Nigeria followed suit. On 14 March 1983 the official price of oil was cut for the first time, from 34 to 29 dollars. In addition, an overall ceiling for production was again set, this time at 17.4 mbd, with individual quotas for all the members except Saudi Arabia. Clearly such an agreement would not be viable if non–OPEC producers simply expanded their own production; by 1984 OPEC acknowledged the significance of non–OPEC production and called on the leading exporters outside the organization to cooperate in stabilizing the oil market. This encouraged further complacency as to the future of oil supplies, although some experts still counselled caution, pointing out that it was unclear how far the move towards a glut of supplies was due, at least in part, to reduced economic activity.[57] However, throughout the 1980s, attempts by OPEC to control production by allocating individual member quotas faltered, as individual self-interest prevailed over collective agreement. Saudi Arabia was no longer able to act as swing producer, as reductions in its production to the level required to keep prices stable would have severe detrimental effects on its own domestic economy. Moreover, there was little incentive to cut production in order to maintain an overall OPEC production ceiling, if the response from other countries was simply to raise their own production instead. Even so, very few predicted the degree to which oil prices would fall in the future: in 1983, introducing a seminar of experts speaking on the tenth anniversary of the 1973 crisis, David Hawton concluded that 'Only in the very long run is it possible to envisage any substantial fall in relative oil prices'.[58]

As the oil market became more complex, so the role of OPEC also became more complex, more difficult to sustain, and more difficult to agree. The vagaries of the world economy caused fluctuations in demand, and production outside the OPEC member states expanded, making the planning of production and price virtually impossible. Throughout the late 1970s and early 1980s Saudi Arabia had played an influential role in matching projected consumer demand for OPEC oil with its actual production levels. Initially, it had exercised this power to restrain the hawks calling for what were seen as excessive price increases. Thus, when in December 1976 many members of OPEC wanted to increase the price of oil by 15 per cent, Saudi Arabia increased production and eventually secured agreement on an increase of only 5 per cent.[59] However, increasingly its adjustments to production were downward ones, from around 10 mbd in 1981 to about 2 mbd in September 1985, intended to match OPEC production to the decline in demand. As a consequence, from 1981 to 1985 the Saudi Arabian share of the total OPEC output fell from over 40 per cent to around 20 per cent, and yet the decline in prices was not reversed. The Saudi policy became more difficult to maintain as oil prices also declined, forcing the government to draw upon its (admittedly large, at around 150 billion dollars) financial reserves in order to maintain its budget. The government had to halve its annual budget between 1982/3 and 1986.[60] However, when it abandoned its role of 'swing producer' at the end of 1985, and increased production hoping to force other OPEC members and non-OPEC producers into line, the initial result was disastrous, with further falls in the price of a barrel of oil from over 27 dollars at the beginning of the year to less than 9 dollars by the middle of the year.[61] The intention was to achieve for OPEC a 'fair' market share *vis-à-vis* non-OPEC producers and also a 'fair' price. The consequence, however, was to pass the role of price-setter to impersonal market forces. It was not just OPEC that relied more on the markets: in July 1985 BNOC was disbanded, and British prices for North Sea oil were henceforth solely market related.

Faced with such a catastrophic drop in prices, well below that prevailing in January 1974, in late 1986 OPEC again decided upon a ceiling production and allocated quotas, and in February 1987 set a target fixed price of 18 dollars.[62] For a short time this was successful, with production held below 15.8 mbd for the first half of 1987 and a price hovering around the 18 dollars a barrel level, although the drop in the value of the dollar eroded this price. However, setting target prices was one thing, achieving them was another. As members over-produced, OPEC tended to increase individual and total targets, so that by March 1990 the overall ceiling was set at 24 mbd. Prices continued to fluctuate, but by the end of 1993 a barrel of oil sold for less than 14 dollars.[63] It would be easy to see, in OPEC's declining ability to manage the world oil market, an indication that it had ceased to be effective in its goals of controlling prices to secure a just return for the resource which was, for most of its members, far and above the most important element in their national economies. However, despite some reduction in membership (both Ecuador and Gabon left the organization), OPEC still managed to remain in existence, even when two of its members were actually at war with one another, as happened between 1980 and 1988 and again in 1990–1 during the Gulf War. The end of the twentieth century saw a partial resumption of OPEC's power. One reason for this is that demand for oil again grew, as the industrial economies recovered. Until the mid-1980s, there was little change in world demand for oil: from 65 mbd in 1979 it had actually dropped slightly to 61 million by 1986.[64] However, as a consequence, with demand relatively static and supplies apparently plentiful, interest in energy conservation and alternative sources of energy declined. While some consumer countries showed a sustained determination to develop other sources – such as Japan which had reduced the share of oil in energy generation from nearly 80 per cent in 1973 to under 58 per cent in 1990, with 9 per cent of its energy from nuclear sources[65] – investment in research and development for renewable energy resources by IEA members generally tended to drop as prices fell. In 1979 they were spending over a billion dollars on renewable energy research and development, but by 1985 the figure had slumped to under half a billion.[66] Moreover, support for nuclear power as an alternative to petroleum diminished after the Three Mile Island melt down in 1979 and the Chernobyl disaster in 1986. However, given the very long lead in times required for most viable alternative sources of energy generation, such as solar, wind or water power, it is clear that without sustained research and development these technologies will not be in a position to provide energy in any emergency.

In effect, there have been three different oil-pricing regimes. The first, lasting until 1971 and in some respects until 1973, saw the power to set prices resting with the oil companies: although clearly subject to market forces, the major oil companies could control production levels from the very prolific oilfields within the major oil-exporting states and keep prices relatively stable. From 1973 to 1983 OPEC essentially set prices, although it, too, responded to market forces by dramatically increasing prices when market demand was high (as in late 1973, January 1979 and October 1980, the start of the Iran–Iraq War). This, however, suggested that if consumers could avoid undue panic in the face of political problems, the price of oil would remain more stable.[67] The third regime, after 1983, saw market forces in effective control. After 1986, Arabian Light 34 API no longer fulfilled the role of marker crude, with each producer setting differentials on that price depending upon quality and location. Instead, a small group of spot, forward and futures markets effectively set prices, with Brent crude from the North Sea playing a significant role.[68]

The position in the oil industry as a whole is volatile, as technological innovations in the exploration and exploitation of oil deposits have transformed the supply position. In 1972 the Club of Rome stated that only 550 billion barrels of oil remained and oil supplies would be exhausted by 1990, but in fact the world consumed 600 billion barrels of oil between 1970 and 1990 and there were still more than a trillion barrels of proven reserves by the end of the twentieth century. The IEA estimates that there are 2.3 trillion barrels in ultimate recoverable reserves, while current global consumption is 73 mbd. Technological advances have brought down the cost of finding new oil reserves: in the 1980s the average costs for finding a barrel of oil in the United States dropped from around 15 dollars to just 5 dollars by 1998.[69] Nonetheless, OPEC still controls many of the fields whose production can be easily and cheaply produced (and indeed its members control a substantial volume of unused production capacity).

The current position on prices is very complex. There are now three major international petroleum exchanges – New York, London and Singapore – and there is a strong futures market in the commodity. During 1997 and 1998 the financial crises in Asia reduced demand, and again the price of a barrel of oil fell below 10 dollars. However, in 1999 the combination of a reduction in production by both OPEC and non-OPEC members, amounting to 2 mbd, together with a resumption of demand from Asia, pushed the price up again,[70] but during the year 2000 prices began to return to levels of around 25 to 30 dollars. OPEC members have begun to exercise more self-discipline in controlling production, and non-OPEC producers have shown a willingness to discuss possible controls on their production in response to OPEC initiatives. As OPEC has once more secured greater control over oil prices at the end of the twentieth century and the beginning of the twenty-first, it has again been the subject of appeals or demands from the leading consumer countries to moderate prices in order to prevent triggering a world economic recession. In looking to the foreseeable future, it remains the case that OPEC members control a very substantial share of the world's known oil reserves: at 1992 levels of production, estimates vary, but are between 60 and 75 per cent. Certain individual members are particularly well placed: Saudi Arabia has a further 85 years of oil production, and Iraq, the United Arab Emirates and Kuwait have in excess of 100 years each.[71] The position of OPEC in terms of reserves is likely to strengthen; in 1994 it produced only 41 per cent of global oil production.[72]

There was an abrupt shift in 1973 from one oil market – dominated by private companies, with a price regime manipulated by those companies and far removed from free market forces – to another, this time ruled by OPEC. As Stephen Krasner argues, 'The postwar oil regime characterized by private corporate control (although hardly a free market) was shattered in the early 1970s.'[73] As OPEC lost control over the market and even its own members, its dominance was, in turn, replaced by a third price regime, set by the market. At the end of the twentieth century, there were, however, indications that OPEC may yet again be emerging as a powerful force in the setting of prices, but it is still only one player in a complex industry. Over the past thirty years, oil prices have fluctuated wildly, and it seems reasonable to surmise that they will continue to do so. For the major oil exporters in OPEC, the fluctuations in oil prices have brought periods of immense increases in oil revenues but, as will be discussed in Chapter 6, that has not necessarily had as beneficial an impact upon their domestic economies as one might expect, particularly as periods of plenty were rapidly succeeded by falling prices and hence revenues. However, even at the lowest prices prevailing in the past thirty years, for many OPEC members, particularly those in the Arabian Peninsula, the price per barrel has far exceeded the costs of production: there remains a very large differential in production costs between, say, the North Sea and the large prolific fields of Saudi Arabia and Kuwait. In the long term, while oil deposits will undoubtedly be discovered and exploited elsewhere, these are often still far removed from the main areas of consumption, may not be as prolific, and will certainly be more expensive to exploit, than the oil wealth of the Middle East.

In terms of the oil industry, therefore, 1973 did indeed mark a clear turning point, with the position of companies and the pricing mechanism abruptly changed. With the erosion of the concession system and the growth of 100 per cent participation, the companies' role in production, especially in OPEC members, became technical and managerial rather than representing an equity investment in the oilfield. Until 1973 OPEC, despite its members' many political and economic differences, had been united by a common cause against the companies; but after 1973 that was no longer the case, and divergences between the members became more acute. Once OPEC had the power to set prices, a clear difference rapidly emerged between the price hawks and the moderates, and in an era of falling demand for OPEC oil, disputes over which member should bear the cost of adapting production to market conditions caused considerable problems. During the period of OPEC dominance, from 1973 until 1983, it is clear that political issues affected its deliberations on price; and many of those political issues grew out of the complex events in the Middle East. If 1973 represented a turning point for the oil industry, did the two oil crises of the 1970s also represent a turning point for the Middle East?

Notes

1. Burton I. Kaufman, *The Oil Cartel Case: A Documentary Study of Antitrust Activity in the Cold War Era*. Greenview Press, Westport, Connecticut, 1978.
2. In common with many of the oil companies mentioned in this book, the company now known as British Petroleum had previously gone under other names, first the Anglo-Persian Oil Company and from 1933 to 1954 the Anglo-Iranian Oil Company.
3. David Howard Davis, *Energy Politics* (3rd edn). St Martin's Press, New York, 1982, pp. 86–7.
4. Colin Robinson, 'The Changing Energy Market: What Can We Learn from the Last Ten Years?' In David Hawdon (ed.), *The Energy Crisis Ten Years After*. Croom Helm, London, 1984, pp. 7–36, esp. p. 10.
5. British Petroleum, *Our Industry Petroleum*. British Petroleum, London, 1977, Table 2, p. 564.
6. Adnam A. Al-Janabi, 'Production and Depletion Policies in OPEC', *OPEC* Review 3 (1979), pp. 65–75, esp. pp. 66–8.
7. Seymour, *OPEC*, pp. 29–34.
8. Resolutions of the First OPEC Conference, Baghdad, 10-14 September 1960, in Skeet, *Opec*, Appendix 5, pp. 246–7.
9. For a full list of OPEC members, see Appendix 1.
10. Dankwart A. Rustow and John F. Mugno, *OPEC: Success and Prospects*. New York University Press, New York, 1976, p. 18.
11. Seymour, *OPEC*, p. 75.
12. Frank C. Waddams, *The Libyan Oil Industry*. Croom Helm, London, 1980, pp. 253–60.
13. Skeet, *Opec*, pp. 71–80.
14. Bamberg, *British Petroleum 1954–75*, pp. 468–72.
15. Gustavo Coronel, *The Nationalization of the Venezuelan Oil Industry: From Technocratic Success to Political Failure*. Lexington Books, Lexington, 1983, pp. 38–41.
16. Miriam Joyce, *Kuwait 1945–1996: An Anglo-American Perspective*. Frank Cass, London, 1998, pp. 93–115.
17. Skeet, *Opec*, pp. 64–70.
18. Waddams, *The Libyan Oil Industry*, pp. 57–83.
19. John M. Blair, *The Control of Oil*. Vintage Books, New York, 1976; Harvey O'Connor, *The Empire of Oil*. Monthly Review Press, New York, 1962; and Robert Engler, *The Politics of Oil: Private Power and Democratic Directions*. University of Chicago Press, Chicago, 1961.
20. United States Congress, Senate, Committee on Foreign Relations, Hearings, *Multinational Corporations and United States Foreign Policy*. US Government Printing Office, Washington D.C., 1973–5.
21. For example, Turner, *Oil Companies* and Blair, *Control of Oil*.
22. Romano Prodi and Alberto Clo, 'Europe', in Raymond Vernon (ed.), *The Oil Crisis*. Norton, New York, 1976, pp. 91–111, esp. pp. 103–4.
23. Kuwait's national oil company built refineries in Western Europe, as well as gasoline stations operating under the brand name Q8.
24. Simon Bromley, *American Hegemony and World Oil: The Industry, the State System and the World Economy*. Polity Press, Cambridge, 1991, p. 217.
25. Turner, *Oil Companies*, pp. 126–9.

26. Sir Peter Baxendell, 'Oil Companies and the Changing Energy Market', in David Hawdon (ed.), *The Energy Crisis Ten Years After*. Croom Helm, London, 1984. pp. 48–56, esp. p. 49.

27. Turner, *Oil Companies*, p. 124.

28. United States Congress, Joint Economic Committee, Subcommittee on Energy, *Multinational Oil Companies and OPEC: Implications for U.S. Policy* US Government Printing Office, Washington, DC, 1977.

29. Skeet, *Opec*, pp. 102–3.

30. Paul Hallwood and Stuart Sinclair, *Oil, Debt and Development: OPEC in the Third World*. George Allen & Unwin, London, 1981, pp. 39–40.

31. Skeet, *Opec*, pp. 135–6.

32. Jahangir Amuzegar, *Managing the Oil Wealth: OPEC's Windfalls and Pitfalls*. I.B. Tauris, London, 1999, p. 33.

33. Bromley, *American Hegemony*, p. 155.

34. Hallwood and Sinclair, *Oil, Debt and Development*, Table 3.3, p. 49.

35. Davis, *Energy Politics*, p. 92.

36. Bamberg, *British Petroleum: 1954–1975*, p. 203.

37. Sampson, *Seven Sisters*, pp. 193–6.

38. Øystein Noreng, *The Oil Industry and Government Strategy in the North Sea*. Croom Helm, London, 1980, pp. 51–2.

39. George W. Grayson, *The Politics of Mexican Oil*. University of Pittsburgh Press, Pittsburgh, 1980, p. 239.

40. Grayson, *Politics of Mexican Oil*, pp. 143–7.

41. William D. Nordhaus (ed.), *International Studies of the Demand for Energy*. North-Holland Publishing Company, Amsterdam, 1977, p. 289.

42. Dermot Gately, 'The Prospect for OPEC five years after 1973/4', *European Economic Review* 12 (1979), pp. 369–79.

43. Alberto Quiros Corradi, 'Energy and the Exercise of Power', *Foreign Affairs* 57 (1978–9), pp. 1144–66.

44. Alfred A. Marcus, *Controversial Issues in Energy Policy*. Sage, California, 1992, p. 10.

45. Amuzegar, *Managing Oil Wealth*, pp. 33–4.

46. Skeet, *Opec*, p. 174.

47. Fred S. Singer, 'An End to OPEC? Bet on the Market', *Foreign Policy* 45 (1981–2), pp. 115–21, esp. pp. 120–1.

48. Bromley, *American Hegemony*, p. 156.

49. Amuzegar, *Managing Oil Wealth*, p. 34.

50. Stephen Stamas, 'An End to OPEC? More is needed', *Foreign Policy* 45 (1981–2), pp. 121–5.

51. Bruce R. Scott, 'OPEC, the American Scapegoat', *Harvard Business Review* 59 (1981), pp. 6–30, esp. p. 6.

52. Scott, 'American Scapegoat', p. 28.

53. Benard, 'World Oil'.

54. Amuzegar, *Managing Oil Wealth*, pp. 35, 41, 87 and 94–6.

55. Skeet, *Opec*, p. 184.

56. Coronel, *Venezuelan Oil Industry*, pp. 224–6.

57. J.T. McMullan, R. Morgan and R.B. Murray, *Energy Resources* (2nd edn). Edward Arnold, London, 1983, p. iv.

58. Hawdon (ed.), *The Energy Crisis*, p. vi.

59. Abir, *Saudi Arabia*, p. 146.

60. Abir, *Saudi Arabia*, p. 179.

61. Peter Odell, 'The Global Oil Industry: The Location of Production – Middle East Domination or Regionalization?', *Regional Studies* 31 (1997), pp. 311–22, esp. p. 315.
62. George W. Grayson, *Oil and Mexican Foreign Policy*. University of Pittsburgh Press, Pittsburgh, 1988, p. 121.
63. Amuzegar, *Managing Oil Wealth*, pp. 38–9.
64. Marcus, *Controversial Issues*, pp. 24–5.
65. Marcus, *Controversial Issues*, pp. 8, 16–17.
66. International Energy Agency, *Renewable Sources of Energy*. OECD/IEA, Paris, 1987, p. 56.
67. Philip K. Verleger Jr., 'The Determinants of Official OPEC Crude Prices', *The Review of Economics and Statistics* 64 (1982), pp. 177–83, esp. n. 2, p. 178.
68. Paul Horsnell and Robert Mabro, *Oil Markets and Prices: The Brent Market and the Formation of World Oil Prices*. Oxford University Press, Oxford, 1993.
69. Amy Myers Jaffe and Robert A. Manning, 'The Shocks of a World of Cheap Oil', *Foreign Affairs* 79 (No. 4, 2000), pp. 16–29, esp. p. 19.
70. Gause, 'Saudi Arabia', pp. 89–90.
71. David L. Greene, 'The outlook for US oil dependence', *Energy Policy* 26 (1998), pp. 55–69, esp. pp. 56–7.
72. Amuzegar, *Managing Oil Wealth*, p. 13.
73. Stephen D. Krasner, *Structural Conflict: The Third World Against Global Liberalism*. University of California Press, Berkeley, California, 1985, p. 71.

3

A TURNING POINT FOR
THE MIDDLE EAST?

Although oil production is located around the globe, it is particularly associated with the Middle East. The United States has been, and indeed still is, a major producer (but not exporter) of oil and there are also numerous areas of oil production outside the Middle East – the ex-Soviet Union, Alaska, the North Sea, Latin America and Northern Africa – all of which play an important part in this history of the oil crises of the 1970s. Nonetheless, even when the Middle East is not the predominant source of production at any particular time, it is still at the heart of the oil industry. The Arabian Peninsula in particular can increase production rapidly if required, it has the largest volume of domestic production available for the world market, and the region possesses the largest known oil reserves in the world.

Unfortunately, these massive oil reserves are located in a region with a number of severe problems. The position in the Middle East throughout the period since the end of the Second World War has been very complex, with a series of interlocking problems reinforcing one another. Each country within the Middle East has its own internal uncertainties and instabilities, encompassing a wide range of types of regime and government. All have faced the challenge of development – some with more success than others. In areas where oil was discovered only comparatively recently, such as Dubai and Abu Dhabi, traditional economic, social and cultural patterns remained virtually unchallenged until the 1960s. There have been a number of inter-state conflicts within the region, many of them with wide-reaching repercussions. The best known is of course the general Arab–Israeli conflict, which resulted in major wars in 1948, 1967 and 1973, with further clashes such as the war of attrition between Egypt and Israel in 1970 and civil war in Lebanon leading to an Israeli occupation and fighting between Syrian and Israeli troops in 1982. However, there have also been major disagreements and tensions in the past fifty years between Iraq and Kuwait, Iran and Iraq, Bahrain and Iran, Saudi Arabia and the two Yemens, and Syria and the Lebanon. Questions of boundaries and communications, including pipeline transportation across state borders or through crucial waterways such as the Suez Canal and the Straits of Hormuz, have implications for all the regional powers (Map 2).

However, above all it has been the long-running dispute between the Arabs and the state of Israel which has destabilized the region. This not only caused continual tension, but also pitted one superpower against another as each encouraged and armed its respective clients. The proximity of the Soviet Union to the region has been a major factor in its history, particularly with regard to Iran, which has a long land border with the USSR and served as one of the major supply routes for Allied aid to the Soviet Union during the Second World War. One of the first crises of the Cold War came when Soviet troops failed to pull out from northern Iran in 1946, and demanded (unsuccessfully) oil concessions in the region as the price for their departure. Finally, the region itself has international significance: whether for religious reasons (it contains the holy places of three of the world's greatest religions), geopolitical reasons (the Middle East lies at the juncture of three continents and includes important routes of communication) or economic reasons (oil). Thus, defending the region from internal dissension, intra-regional conflict or external threat has been a major preoccupation of international relations certainly since 1945. While these factors make it difficult to assess the extent to which changes in the Middle East are as a direct consequence of the two major oil crises, or whether they represent longer term trends, both major oil crises of the 1970s were accompanied by, and indeed to a varied extent were caused by, independent developments within the Middle East, notably the Arab–Israeli War of 1973 and the Iranian Revolution of 1979.

In order to understand the problems besetting the region in the years after 1945, it is necessary to know something of the genesis of the modern Middle East. The boundaries and political structure of the region changed radically in the first half of the twentieth century. The demise of the Ottoman Empire in the aftermath of the First World War led to the creation of a number of states which had hitherto been provinces under the jurisdiction of the Turkish Sultan, such as Syria, Iraq and the Lebanon, together with the recognition of the autonomy of a number of small sheikhdoms along the Persian Gulf, including Kuwait, Bahrain and Qatar. However, the new states were not left to their own devices; by a new system of mandates, supervised by the League of Nations, each state was placed under the tutelage of another, more developed power, whose task was to guide it towards eventual self-government. France assumed responsibility for Syria and the Lebanon, and the United Kingdom for Iraq.[1] The fate of the province of Palestine was more controversial, however. During the First World War considerable support had been expressed, particularly in the United States and the United Kingdom, for the creation of a national home for the Jewish people within Palestine. The most concrete expression of this support came in the form of the Balfour declaration, a letter from British Foreign Secretary Arthur Balfour to Lord Rothschild, which committed the British Government to supporting the creation of such a home.[2] This, however, promised to cause major difficulties for the mandatory power, as the majority of the population of Palestine were Arabs. The British Government was awarded the mandate for Palestine, and created two separate governments, one for Transjordan under the leadership of King Abdullah, and the other, under much firmer British control, in Palestine. The British Government also formalized its hitherto informal protectorates over the sheikhdoms of the Persian Gulf, in which political agents responsible to the Government of India offered advice to the rulers, if necessary reinforced by the presence of British gunboats in the Gulf. The rulers signed a number of agreements with the British Government, which in effect surrendered the conduct of foreign affairs to the protecting power. In the interior of the Arabian Peninsula, a number of tribal rulers contended for influence over the various Bedouin tribes.[3]

During the interwar period, a number of developments both changed the political structure prevailing in the area, and also made the entire region of much greater importance to the rest of the world. The consolidation of much of the Arabian Peninsula under the rule of one man, Abdul Aziz ibn Saud, and the creation in 1932 of the new Kingdom of Saudi Arabia, with control over the Holy Cities of Mecca and Medina, altered the politics of the Peninsula and the Persian Gulf. Meanwhile, deposits of petroleum were found in many countries of the Middle East. Oil had been produced in Persia/Iran since before the First World War, but during the interwar years concessions were signed for Iraq, Saudi Arabia, Kuwait and Bahrain. In 1927 the British-guided Iraqi Government granted a concession to the Iraq Petroleum Company, a multinational consortium which included some of the largest oil companies in the world, including Shell, British Petroleum, the French company, CFP, and a consortium of American majors, including Exxon and Mobil. This company was later to acquire other concessions within the Persian Gulf states. At that time, little real attention was paid to the Arabian Peninsula, but during the course of the

1930s, concessions were awarded for Bahrain (to Chevron), Saudi Arabia (again, to American interests, as Texaco and Chevron formed a new joint company, the Arabian American Oil Company or ARAMCO) and Kuwait (where the American Gulf Oil and British Petroleum shared the concession through a jointly-owned company, the Kuwait Oil Company). Thus, the pattern was set; the oil concessions in the Middle East were mainly held by a network of major oil companies, in different collaborative ventures. Although there were later changes in the ownership of the main concessions, notably the admission of Exxon and Mobil to ARAMCO and, in 1954, the replacement of British Petroleum's monopoly over Iranian oil by another international consortium, the process by which the leading oil majors dominated the Middle East had been created by the late 1930s.

Although, apart from Iran and Iraq, real commercial exploitation of the oilfields did not occur until after the Second World War, it was apparent by the end of the 1930s that the Middle East as a whole promised to become a prolific producer and exporter of oil. Very small populations and an absence of other industries meant that there was virtually no domestic demand for the petroleum. By the late 1940s it was clear that for both the British and the American governments Middle Eastern oil was seen as a national security interest. For the British, seemingly without any substantial deposits of domestic petroleum, Middle Eastern oil had always been viewed as significant. For the United States, the reason was more indirect, as it was a major producer in its own right. However, periodic concern at the potential exhaustion of American oil, coupled with the financial importance of the Middle East to the profits of the large oil companies, meant that the United States Government did all that it could to protect and maintain its control over the American concessions. Middle Eastern oil was defined as crucial to national security and the companies that exploited it were also seen as more than just economic agents. Experts and financial aid were sent to Saudi Arabia to assist the government with development programmes. Elsewhere, the United States bitterly opposed attempts by the Soviets to obtain an oil concession in northern Iran, demonstrated its concern with the wider region by the Truman Doctrine, which pledged help to Turkey and Greece, and eventually, under the Eisenhower Doctrine of 1957, sent troops into Lebanon to secure peace there.

The United States had had little involvement in the Middle East prior to the interwar period; this was the direct opposite of the United Kingdom, for which the Middle East had been of strategic importance ever since the acquisition of India. During the Second World War British troops in Iran, Iraq and the massive bases in Aden and Suez helped to protect the region from German advances; the British also intervened in the politics of Iran, where the pro-German Shah was forced to abdicate in favour of his son, and Iraq, where factions in the Army were favourable to the Germans. Moreover, in both the British and American governments, postwar planning assumed that the region would continue to play a significant role, and require considerable attention, in defence plans and strategy.

The interwar period also saw the acceleration of a tendentious problem that was to be further exacerbated by the Second World War. The Balfour declaration had been carefully worded, speaking of the creation of 'a' national home 'in' Palestine. The definition of what precisely it had promised soon became the cause of bitter dispute. The British administration of the mandate for Palestine had the unenviable task of steering a path between the general duty of the mandatory power to work towards self-government in the interests of the local population (largely Arab: in 1922 there were only 83,790 Jews in Palestine out of a total population of 752,048 although this had risen to 156,481 in a population of 992,559 by 1929)[4] in the first place, but also to foster the formation of a National Home for the Jewish people. Disputes over the levels of permitted immigration plagued the interwar period. The distinction between a Jewish National Home within Palestine and a Jewish state of Palestine was one which the British administration continued to emphasize, but it was clear that no solution could be found that would be acceptable to both Arabs and Jews. There was an unbridgeable gulf between the Jewish desire for a Jewish state, incorporating, if at all possible, the biblical land of Greater Israel, and the occupation and ownership of that territory by Palestinian Arabs for centuries. Pressure for increased immigration mounted after Adolf Hitler came to power in Germany and, with the ending of the Second World War, following German persecution and the Holocaust, many of the surviving European Jews wished to emigrate to a new, Jewish state. The issue was hotly debated in the United Nations, effectively the successor to the League of Nations (which had been responsible for the mandate system).

On 29 November 1947 the General Assembly of the UN voted to set up both a Jewish and an Arab state in the mandatory area of Palestine. The proposal included suggested borders between the two states, with Jerusalem assigned a special status as an International Zone.[5] The proposals would mean a Jewish state that would have, at the time of the debate, 498,000 Jews and an Arab population of between 400,000 and 500,000. However, there was no agreement on these proposals within Palestine itself, and the consequence was an escalation in violence. In the face of mounting tension and Jewish terrorism (aimed against the British administration in Palestine), the British decided to hold fire on the implementation of partition, and in effect to do nothing before their withdrawal from the mandate on 14 May 1948. On the same date, Jewish leaders in Palestine declared a new state of Israel; the following day six Arab states – Egypt, Syria, Transjordan, the Lebanon, Saudi Arabia and Iraq – invaded Israel (although most of the fighting was done by Egypt and Transjordan). However, the new state was able to resist the Arab incursion and indeed made substantial advances. During 1948, around 725,000 Arabs fled from the new state of Israel, many to the regions originally designated for the Arab state, including the Gaza Strip, which was occupied by Egypt in 1948, and the West Bank, which was occupied by Transjordan in 1948 and then finally annexed in 1950, the year in which the name Jordan was adopted. By the armistices signed between the various belligerents in 1948, Israel acquired an additional 2,400 square miles of territory, increasing its size by about 40 per cent. These various moves effectively wiped Arab Palestine from the map.[6]

Aided by both private and state funding, especially from the United States, Israel established a democracy – an unusual phenomenon within the region. However, the Arab states refused to acknowledge its existence and a state of armed tension prevailed thereafter. As refugees fled to other Arab states in the region, in 1950 the Israeli parliament (the Knesset) passed the Law of Return which gave every Jew in the world the right to migrate to Israel. Given the need for land to support its rapidly growing Jewish population, Israel refused any attempts to agree a repatriation policy for the estimated 750,000 Palestinian refugees, many of them living in temporary camps in Jordan and the West Bank, Gaza, Lebanon and Syria.[7] Slowly groups emerged to speak for the displaced Palestinians, including al-Fatah in 1959; a federation of several groups formed the Palestine Liberation Organization in 1964 together with a Palestine Liberation Army which launched guerrilla raids on Israel. In 1956, following the Suez campaign, Israel also hoped to hold on to the land it had conquered in the Sinai Peninsula, but the United Nations and the United States pressured it into withdrawing, although a United Nations Expeditionary Force was stationed there.

This was the most immediate problem faced in the region after the Second World War. Initially there seemed little reason to worry about the Arabian Peninsula, well away from the pressing problem of Israel. Its security was guaranteed by the massive British bases in Aden and the Suez Canal area and its rulers were solidly conservative and pro-Western. Provided that the demands of the rulers for extra revenues could be met – and they were, if not always in the amounts required – the British and American governments hoped that economic prosperity would promote political stability and a continued pro-Western orientation. Insofar as these sparsely populated states faced any kind of danger, it was an external menace from within the region, as the Iranians laid claim to Bahrain and the Iraqis to Kuwait. While Britain was still the protecting power, however, even this was not a major challenge.

Elsewhere, on the other hand, the position was not so positive. In Iran, there were two main threats. One was the presence of the Soviet Union, and the other was nationalism, which was spreading rapidly. The young Shah had not yet established his power and was seen as the tool of the Western powers, which had placed him on the throne in preference to his father. In Iraq, there were strong indications of growing anti-British sentiment, a nationalist movement in the armed forces, and growing disapproval of the royal family, regarded as the tools of the British. In Egypt too, opposition to the British presence, typified by the immense Suez base, was growing. This posed the problem that was faced by imperial powers in a host of countries after 1945: should such opposition be resisted, if necessary by force, or should a compromise be sought? Individual states in the region asserted their independence of Western influence, typified by the coup in Syria in 1949, the overthrow of the pro-Western King in Iraq in 1958 and the military coup in Egypt in 1952. The resultant regimes tended to be authoritarian, anxious to pursue rapid economic and social development, and generally hostile to Western intervention.

Thus, comparatively soon after the end of the Second World War, the various elements which together comprised an explosive cocktail of problems were in place. First, the Cold War: initially the main threat from the Soviet Union was perceived as lying in Iran and Turkey. However, as the Soviets formed closer links with radical Arab nationalism, this greatly concerned the United States. In particular, the Soviet Union provided military equipment, arms and advisers to two key states, Egypt and Syria, both immediate neighbours of, and hostile to, Israel. For these states, Soviet support was invaluable, enabling them to build up military strength against Israel, and also to follow policies of state economic activity. Iraq, a major oil producer in the region, also developed stronger links with the Soviet Union. Thus, the Soviet threat was strongly linked to the second problem for the West, the growth of radical Arab nationalism, which not only transformed the Soviet threat, but also led to more support for pan-Arabism, the notion of a single Arab nation, crossing the boundaries of the existing states. Third, there was one issue which united both the radical Arab nationalists and the conservative monarchies of the Arabian Peninsula, and that was their shared dislike of, and opposition to, Israel. The Arab League, formed in 1945, had members covering a wide spectrum of political ideologies, and increasingly acted as a focus for anti-Israeli comment. The presence of Israel was a powerful complicating factor in the region's politics. It threatened to unite countries with otherwise very diverse political views and regimes. It led to massive armament programmes and a series of wars, and those wars were to have added significance as they came to pit the protégés of one superpower against those of the other. The United States remained solidly loyal to Israel and, as we shall see in more detail below, supplied it with military and financial aid, including up-to-date weaponry. Although the Soviet Union had been prompt to recognize the state of Israel in 1948, it was essentially identified with the Arab states of the region.

After the Second World War the United States and the United Kingdom tried to secure peace and stability in the Middle East in a number of ways. Clear support was given to those states which were definitely pro-Western, such as Lebanon, Jordan, Saudi Arabia, Kuwait and the other Persian Gulf states. On the assumption that economic prosperity would encourage political stability, the oil companies were aided, through complex tax regimes, to increase the revenue accruing to the host governments. If all else failed, the British were poised to take decisive military action, with a network of permanent squadrons and military bases. However, during the late 1950s and 1960s those forces for stability were steadily eroded. The pro-Western regimes were angered by the growth of American support for Israel. Meanwhile, the pattern of oil concessions, and in particular the composition of the companies operating them, was challenged. Although the main concessions remained in the hands of the leading majors, it soon became apparent that there was scope for other companies to enter the Middle East, in areas which had been excluded from the original concessions, such as the Neutral Zones set up as buffers between rival states, and the offshore oilfields. These various concessions went, in many cases, to American independents such as Getty's Pacific Western Company, and the Italian and Japanese state companies. Not only did these companies tend to offer much better terms, but they also loosened the hold of the powerful international cartel.

Meanwhile, the ultimate sanction against upheaval, the use of force, was also eroded. Until 1956 the British defence presence in the region remained very strong, but in that year they completed their withdrawal from the Suez base, and in 1967 Aden gained independence, and rapidly established the People's Democratic Republic of South Yemen, governed by the Marxist National Liberation Front. In 1958 the pro-British regime in Iraq was overturned, and in 1961 the British also ended their protectorate over Kuwait. Finally, in 1968 the British Government decided to withdraw east of Suez with effect from 1971. In that year, the Trucial States also were freed from British rule, and formed the federation of the United Arab Emirates. Thereafter, the British presence in the region had to be exercised from Cyprus. Thus, by the late 1960s, the Middle East was a region of tension and over-riding all its politics was the superpower conflict, conducted by proxy through the two superpowers' client states.

1967–1973

Through the humiliating defeat of the Arabs in 1948, the Israelis had clearly demonstrated their superiority to the Arab states, and forced the abandonment of the idea of a separate Arab Palestine. This superiority was reinforced, in part by the war of attrition between the Israelis and the Arab states, in part by the different paths and pace of development of the various states, but also by further Israeli demonstrations of their superior military capabilities, first in the Suez Crisis, and then again in 1967. In that year, a major, decisive, if short war radically changed the situation in the Middle East. Tension between Israel and its Arab neighbours had increased following the Suez crisis, and the coming to power of more radical governments in Iraq and Syria. From 1964 onwards, Palestinian guerrilla groups such as al-Fatah launched attacks on Israel from the West Bank (then part of Jordan) and the Golan Heights in Syria. In April 1967 Israeli and Syrian planes engaged in a dogfight over the Golan Heights.[8] Two months later, in June 1967, an Arab–Israeli War erupted. Although it lasted only six days, it had serious repercussions which are still unresolved today.

The war began when Israel launched a devastating pre-emptive strike against its main Arab enemies. In so doing, it was responding to signs that the main front-line Arab states were concentrating troops on their borders and might be planning an attack. On 16 May 1967 Nasser ordered the United Nations Expeditionary Force to withdraw from the Egyptian frontier with Israel, after over ten years in place. Six days later, the Egyptian Government closed the Strait of Tiran to all Israeli shipping, or indeed any ships carrying strategic goods to Israel, thus effectively shutting off the Israeli port of Eilat.[9] Three days after that, the front-line states moved troops closer to their borders with Israel. Apparently concerned that this was in preparation for an attack, on 5 June Israeli planes attacked air bases throughout Egypt, and in the course of six days, the Israelis destroyed much of the Egyptian and Syrian air forces on the ground. Their forces secured the Golan Heights from Syria, the rest of Jerusalem and the West Bank from Jordan, and the Gaza Strip, together with the whole of the Sinai Peninsula up to the Suez Canal, from Egypt. Thus, Israel was in effective control of not only mandatory Palestine, but also extensive Egyptian and Syrian territory (see Map 1). During the war, in marked contrast to 1956 when the United States had exercised pressure on Israel, France and Great Britain to cease military action, neither of the superpowers intervened to influence events. President Lyndon Johnson and Soviet leader Alexei Kosygin remained in close contact with each other, using the hotline on a number of occasions; they also both supported the call for a ceasefire. However, while the United States employed more subtle pressure, the Soviet Union broke off diplomatic relations with Israel, and threatened sanctions as Israel ignored calls for a ceasefire.[10] Eventually a ceasefire was indeed put in place. Having demonstrated its military superiority, Israel secured American support for its policy of retaining the Occupied Territories until there could be a peace settlement that would include recognition by the Arab states of Israel's existence.

The sheer speed and scale of the Israeli victory took the world by surprise and, on the face of it, appeared to consolidate the Jewish state's security and power. Israel had humiliated its traditional enemies and had struck at their capacity to consider a possible retaliatory attack. Moreover, it had improved its security through its occupation of additional territory. Much of this was regarded as part of historic Israel, including east Jerusalem; and within a comparatively short period Jewish settlers began to move into the regions. The Palestinians were even more in disarray as they were forced to flee into surrounding states, including Jordan. Shortly after the defeat, in October 1970,

President Nasser died of a heart attack, and in Syria the President was also later replaced.

During the brief war, attempts by some Arab oil producers to support the Arab war effort by declaring an oil boycott of the United States failed dismally. Europe had sizeable stocks, Iran and Venezuela increased exports and, significantly, the United States increased domestic production. The closure of the Suez Canal also affected the deliveries of oil from the Persian Gulf to Europe, but there was plenty of surplus tanker capacity, and as a result Middle Eastern petroleum could be taken round the long route, via the Cape of Good Hope. Moreover, the United States still derived most of its imports from the Western hemisphere and Europe already relied strongly on the new North African suppliers. The main consequence of the boycott was that the boycotters lost revenue: Sheikh Yamani calculated that Saudi Arabia lost 21 million dollars in the period 5–29 June alone.[11] In August the boycott was dropped. However, in the aftermath steps were taken to set up a specific Arab petroleum organization and on 9 January 1968 the Organization of Arab Petroleum Exporting Countries (OAPEC) was created, initially by Kuwait, Saudi Arabia and Libya, at that time all conservative monarchies. In 1970 a number of other states joined the organization, including more radical governments (of which Libya was now one) and a number whose oil production was too low to qualify for membership of OPEC, such as Bahrain and Egypt. It also included the transit states, across whose territory ran the massive pipelines carrying Arabian and Iraqi oil to the Mediterranean. As well as coordinating any future oil action, the organization had clear objectives to encourage mutual economic development and technological advances.[12] This new organization notwithstanding, however, the apparent lesson from 1967 was that the use of the oil weapon in support of the Arab side in the Arab–Israeli conflict was unlikely to be effective.

Nonetheless, although ostensibly the war had been a striking victory for Israel,[13] there were some negative consequences for the Jewish state. The war created for the Israeli Army, and hence the Israeli state, a military reputation which encouraged them to ignore compromise, and at the same time encouraged the United States to arm Israel, in order that it might become a regional power capable of controlling possible Soviet influence. The most potent symbol of its military prowess, the Occupied Territories, nonetheless caused a number of problems. By this vast extension of territory, with its large Arab population, Israel greatly increased its defence responsibilities, while it also caused further instability through the displacement of refugees into other states in the region. In the Golan Heights alone, 35,000 left during the fighting, never to be allowed to return, and another 95,000 either fled or were forced to leave over the following six months.[14] Moreover, while the international community was impressed by the extent of the Israeli victory, the sheer size of occupied territory was less favourably regarded, particularly as it became apparent that the Israeli Government intended to incorporate at least part of it into the Israeli state. East Jerusalem, captured from Jordan, included the biblical Western wall, so there were strong historical reasons in the Israeli view for their retention of the whole of Jerusalem; while the West Bank was part of Greater Israel (Judea and Samaria) and both it and the Gaza Strip had been used as bases to launch attacks on Israel. On 28 June 1967 the Knesset declared that it had the right to apply the jurisdiction of the state to any part of Eretz Israel (land of Israel–Palestine), and in the following month declared that Jerusalem was one city, indivisible, and henceforth the capital of Israel.[15]

However, on 22 November 1967 the United Nations passed Resolution 242, calling for the withdrawal of Israeli troops from the Occupied Territories. The resolution was the result of American and Soviet consultation, and was carefully worded, at British instigation, referring to 'withdrawal of Israeli armed forces from territories occupied in the recent conflict'. The use of the term 'occupied territories', rather than 'the occupied territories', left the way open for Israel ultimately to retain at least some of the territory, presumably that most crucial to her security. However, it also called for 'acknowledgement of the sovereignty, territorial integrity and political independence of every state in the area and their right to live in peace within secured and recognized boundaries'.[16] While the Resolution lent international support to the Arab demands for the return of the territory, Israel continued to consolidate its position by creating a belt of Jewish settlements along the Jordan valley, with a religious settlement outside Hebron. Moreover, the Egyptian oilfields in the Sinai, occupied by the Israelis, made a substantial contribution to Israel's oil needs, supplying 70 per cent of its total needs in 1973.[17]

As a consequence of the war, the fate of the Palestinians was again brought dramatically to the attention of the world; not only was the scale of the refugee problem increased, but also the Occupied Territories controlled by Israel contained more than one million Palestinians. Moreover, within that community, there was growing support for guerrilla movements, particularly for the PLO which was reorganized in 1968. Yasser Arafat became its chairman, and stepped up guerrilla operations, many of them launched from Jordan. The war radicalized Arab opinion; at the Khartoum Arab summit in 1967 the 'three noes' policy was adopted: no peace, no recognition, no negotiations. The Arab states were now more determined than ever to build a powerful opposition to Israel. In the face of their humiliating military defeat, they recognized the need for economic pressure to support any future military action. As Arab oil became more significant in the international oil trade, Egypt in particular, under the leadership of President Anwar Sadat from 1970, was determined to work in liaison with the major oil producers.

During the next six years the superpower dimension to the Arab–Israeli conflict was intensified. In 1970 there was a war of attrition along the Suez Canal; during that 'war' the Israeli air force conducted deep air raids into Egypt which threatened to destabilize Nasser's Government, already undermined by the 1967 defeat. The Soviet Union considerably strengthened its relationship with Egypt by building up Soviet arms and personnel in Egypt, thus increasing the possibility that Israeli and Soviet military personnel might directly engage each other. The conflict became in many ways 'bigger than itself', heightening the possibility of a direct superpower confrontation. As a consequence, there was a fear in some circles that an Israeli victory would carry too high a cost in terms of increased superpower tension. Yet at the same time American support for Israel was more freely given, once its Arab enemies were perceived as Soviet clients. To some extent, it allowed the two superpowers to judge, by proxy, the comparative performance of their most advanced weaponry systems. Because in any prolonged war, replacement supplies of spare parts and destroyed armaments would be critical, both superpowers could directly influence the course of the war. In its most threatening dimension, there remained a possibility that one or the other superpower might actively intervene in order to prevent the defeat of its own client. However, having said that, the Arab–Israeli conflict took place against a background of *détente*, in which both superpowers were aware of the dangers of allowing regional conflict to affect their global relationship. In April 1972 the Nixon–Brezhnev communiqué called for a relaxation of the military tension in the Middle East.[18] As the account of the October 1973 crisis demonstrates, however, this patently did not occur.

To understand the Cold War elements of the October 1973 war, it is important to look at the way in which the two sides came to be identified with the respective superpowers in the preceding six years. The so-called 'special relationship' between Israel and the United States has no formal basis, as the United States has not entered into a military alliance or a defence pact with Israel; the relationship also seems very one-sided, as the United States has provided economic and military assistance and advanced weaponry (from 1948 until 1996 Israel received more than 65 billion dollars in economic and military aid from the American Government, thus making it the largest single recipient of US aid). Yet in 1962, in a much-quoted comment, President Kennedy apparently told Israeli Foreign Minister Golda Meir, privately, that 'the United States has a special relationship with Israel in the Middle East, really comparable only to that which it has with Britain over a wide range of world affairs'.[19] President Carter used the phrase publicly in 1977.

However, although the United States had been one of the first countries to recognize the new government of Israel, and the domestic Jewish lobby exercised strong influence on its behalf, successive administrations also tried to build strong relationships with Arab states, and Israel looked to other countries, notably France, for many of its arms supplies prior to 1967. It took time to construct the special relationship, which certainly did not exist when, in February 1957, President Eisenhower declared that the United States would support United Nations sanctions unless Israel withdrew from Egyptian territory seized during the 1956 Suez Crisis.[20] By 1958, however, President Eisenhower and Secretary of State John Foster Dulles saw radical Arab nationalism as the main threat to regional stability, particularly as that radical nationalism built links with the Soviets. Kennedy's move towards a more supportive policy for Israel not only reflected a changing perception of the potential role of Israel within the Middle East,[21] but also sought to divert Israel from the creation of a nuclear capability by the provision of modern military hardware and promises of support.[22] Even before 1967 the United States had begun a policy of arming Israel, in response to Soviet arms deals with its main Arab adversaries, Egypt and Syria. Kennedy lifted the American embargo on the sale of arms to all the countries involved in the Arab–Israeli conflict which had been in place since 1950 and in August 1962 he agreed to sell Hawk missiles to Israel, although he stressed that these were intended for defence purposes only.[23] Kennedy's successor, Lyndon Johnson, began to build up Israel as a counter to radical, Soviet-supported Arab regimes, and six months after the 1967 war, in January 1968, his administration agreed to provide Israel with 50 Phantom warplanes; these were offensive rather than defensive weapons, and thus marked the beginning of a very different arms relationship between

Israel and the United States, which by 1968 had replaced France as the former's main arms supplier.[24]

After 1968 President Nixon and his administration continued to provide support – both financial and military – for Israel. National Security Adviser Henry Kissinger saw the Arab–Israel conflict in Cold War terms, and perceived the main threats as lying in Arab radicalism and Soviet intervention (which meant that it was important that Israel should prevail). President Nixon increasingly defined Israel as a strategic asset to the United States, one which could serve American security interests in the region. Links between the two countries were strengthened when, in September 1970, civil war broke out in Jordan between King Hussein and Syrian-backed Palestinian organizations, which had been constructing a virtual 'state within a state'. The United States Government encouraged Israel to intervene, promising to deter any Soviet or Egyptian response. Israeli military manoeuvres played a significant part in enabling Hussein to prevail, forcing the Syrians to withdraw. One consequence of this was that the Palestinians, expelled from Jordan, moved their headquarters to Lebanon instead, a development that was to have serious consequences a decade later. In December 1971 the United States signed a long-term military supply agreement with Israel, and American aid to Israel increased from 269.6 million dollars in 1968–70 to 1.5 billion in 1971–3, with military aid accounting for over 1 billion of that sum.[25] More and more, the aid package was presented, not in terms of economic development (which imposed limits on use, required economic justification and careful monitoring) but on the basis of security.[26]

President Nixon and Henry Kissinger (by then Secretary of State) both viewed the international scene essentially as a global, bilateral struggle for power between the United States and the Soviet Union, and this was reflected in their reactions to the 1973 Arab–Israeli War. It was important that states supported by the Soviet Union should not win a clear victory, as this would heighten the likelihood of other radical states in the region building closer links with Moscow. However, there were other concerns. Egypt's President Sadat had made some overtures to the United States, and the administration was eager to build on those. The steadfast support for the Arab cause by such conservative monarchies as that of Saudi Arabia caused added difficulty for the United States, which was anxious not to alienate moderate Arab opinion. These included the major oil producers who declared the oil boycott in support of the Arab belligerents. For many reasons, including domestic politics, the United States Government could not afford to renounce its support for Israel; yet at the same time there were other policy objectives which made a total Israeli victory undesirable. The decision by the administration, to avow publicly its continued support to Israel through the provision of arms supplies, while at the same time working to avoid total Arab defeat, addressed these contradictory policy objectives. By calling for a ceasefire jointly with the Soviet Union, the Cold War dimension of the crisis was publicly downplayed (at least until the red alert provoked in the closing stages of the war); Israel was not defeated, but neither were the Arab forces utterly humiliated.

The construction of the American special relationship with Israel was in part a response to Soviet policies in the region, and in particular the USSR's support for radical Arab regimes. This had begun prior to 1967. As radical nationalism changed the face of Middle Eastern politics from the 1950s onwards, the Soviets began to seek bases and then alliances in the region. The intensive development of the Soviet Mediterranean Squadron as part of a general expansion of the Soviet fleet in the 1960s required support in the form of port facilities and air support as the Soviet fleet was slow to acquire aircraft carriers, with only one in operation as late as 1973. Egypt and, after the expulsion of Soviet advisers from there in 1972, Syria proved invaluable in that respect. From 1969 until 1972 the Soviets had extensive rights in six or seven Egyptian air bases and at least two ports.[27] By 1973 the Soviets were strongly identified with the Arab side in the conflict with Israel, although Sadat had already begun to signal his intentions to reorient Egyptian foreign policy away from a close tie with the Soviet Union and ultimately he was to seek a more positive relationship with the United States.

The Soviet Union had begun to supply arms to radical Arab states well before the United States changed its policy on arms sales. In 1957 Syria was the first Arab state to be offered credits by the Soviet Union (equivalent to 98 million dollars) and in 1958 Egypt was given a 175 million dollar loan, the largest granted to a Third World state by that time.[28] After the Iraqi Revolution of 1958, the Soviets also began to develop closer relations with this traditional rival of Egypt for regional influence, providing financial and technical assistance for the state development of Iraqi oilfields. The first Soviet arms deal with Iraq came in November 1958 and by the end of 1967 there were 1,300 military advisers in the country; moreover, Iraq was one of only five Third World countries to receive a Soviet nuclear reactor. The Soviet Union also signed a number of formal treaties of friendship and cooperation with states in the region, the first with Egypt in May 1971 and thereafter with Iraq in 1972, South Yemen in 1979, Syria in 1980 and North Yemen in 1982.

The 1967 war had a number of implications for the Soviet position in the region. In the short term it had the effect of increasing Soviet influence in Egypt: to restore its own prestige, which had been undermined by the poor performance of Soviet-trained personnel and weaponry during the war, the USSR stressed instead the poor performance of the Arab forces, and began to play a much greater role in restructuring and training the Egyptian army and police. In January 1970 the Soviet Union assumed responsibility for the air defence of Egypt, sending 15,000–20,000 'advisers', including trained personnel to operate the SAM-3 air defence system, which had never before been installed outside the Soviet Union. However, as Soviet pilots were actually flying the planes, there was a distinct possibility of an escalation into direct Soviet involvement.[29] In return, the Soviets gained important rights in air bases and ports within Egypt. However, the Soviet Union was in fact playing an ambivalent role; on the one hand proposing a peace plan in which it was willing to acknowledge Israel's borders as those in place before June 1967 (as opposed to those set out in the 1947 partition plan, which had been its earlier position) and at the same time sending large numbers of military advisers to Egypt and signing in May 1971 a Soviet–Egyptian Treaty of Friendship and Cooperation. Even this was in many respects an attempt to 'salvage something from a faltering relationship',[30] as the Soviet denials of advanced offensive weaponry to the Egyptians had angered Sadat.

Although the United States had responded to the 1973 war in ways that implied that this was a superpower war fought by proxy – which, to some extent, it was – in fact the Soviet influence in the region had begun to decline even before the war. Prior to the outbreak of war, the Soviet Union had attempted to curb President Sadat's threats of war with Israel by withholding Soviet arms; in response, in July 1972 Sadat ordered that the Soviet advisers, sent to Egypt at Nasser's request in 1970, should be withdrawn. However, naval facilities in Egypt remained crucial to the Soviets, and there was a *rapprochement* in the winter of 1972–3. In late 1972 the Soviets returned the SAM missiles to Egypt, along with a few hundred advisers, while Sadat also renewed Soviet naval rights in Egyptian ports for another five years. But Egypt still did not receive the MIG-23s they had requested and although the Soviets did deliver SCUD missiles, that was not until early 1973. In the period around the 1973 war, faced with a decline in its position in Egypt, the Soviet Union increased its existing links with Syria, which after 1973 surpassed those with Egypt. In July 1972 Syria was given a 700 million dollar arms deal, some of which, including MIG-21s and SAM equipment, arrived in September 1972.[31] After 1973 Syria was supplied with the offensive weaponry that had been either denied or only reluctantly given to Egypt, although the most advanced Soviet weaponry was denied to it until the Israeli invasion of the Lebanon in 1982. In 1976 Iraq also received a large arms deal from the Soviets. However, Egypt's move towards a much closer relationship with the United States was nonetheless a blow to the Soviet position in the region.

Given the critical role of the Soviet regional protégés in launching the 1973 war, the question arises: Was this in fact a Soviet-inspired move controlled by Moscow and intended to serve its own interests? Certainly in providing advanced weaponry the Soviet Union had given the Arab front-line states the means to launch such an attack, and it supplied both Syria and Egypt with additional supplies during the war itself. However, its influence in Egypt had clearly been shaken when Sadat expelled the Soviet advisers in July 1972. The provision of SCUD surface-to-surface missiles and a few hundred Soviet advisers in particular might have been read by Sadat as evidence that the Soviets had now accepted his arguments for a military solution, at least to the point where they would not actively oppose it. There are few signs that the Soviets actually encouraged their clients to pursue war, and during the 1973 crisis they in effect tried to follow two different policies: on the one hand, avoiding possible confrontation with the United States which might lead to an escalation in tension; on the other, retaining their prestige and influence in the region by providing aid and support. Galia Golan concludes that while the Soviets were indirectly aware of Arab plans, they did not collaborate with the Arab states nor were they party to the planning of the war.[32] Even Kissinger, whose perception of the 1973 war was clearly coloured by his determination to curtail Soviet influence in the region, rejected thoughts that the Soviets had actually encouraged the war, although he concluded that they had made no effort to halt it.[33] However, the Soviets could not afford to see another decisive defeat for the Arab armies, which might require the kind of intervention that would threaten its broader, Cold War objectives. This issue became particularly acute as the Israelis ignored cease-fire agreements and continued to encircle the Egyptian Third Army, which ultimately led to Brezhnev's letter to Nixon, resulting in the DEFCON 3 alert.

Thus, in the six years between 1967 and 1973 a number of developments had converged to create the preconditions for crisis. The world was heavily dependent upon the prolific, and cheap, Middle Eastern oil. By then, however, the West's options for controlling events in the region had been considerably reduced. The oil companies still had a lot of power, but the host governments were learning the advantages of diversification. The British were no longer able to enforce peace in the region, while the United States was also in no position to replace them. Its main centres of influence in the region were Iran, Saudi Arabia and, of course, Israel. Although the Shah of Iran had embarked on a massive programme of defence spending, he was still unable to maintain stability in the region as a whole. As an increasingly vociferous opponent of Israel, Saudi Arabia was an uncertain ally. Israel was the cause of instability, rather than its cure. Moreover, the region was dominated by a series of interlinked tensions: Arab nationalism, the Soviet threat and Cold War tensions threatening superpower conflict, and the Arab–Israeli conflict. Hence, in a potentially crucial region, economic policy and imperatives had become inextricably linked with political tensions including the potentially explosive superpower confrontation. As we have seen, those elements coincided at the time of the 1973 oil crisis.

After 1973

After October 1973, events moved quickly in the Middle East, with many consequences that would not have been foreseen in the period leading up to the oil crisis. Although the region remained the source of considerable tension and conflict, the focus in the Arab–Israeli conflict moved away from interstate conflict between Israel and the united front-line states to prolonged negotiations over the fate of the Occupied Territories and the future of the Palestinians. Meanwhile, Iran – the regime that appeared to be one of the strongest in the Middle East, and obtained much United States support as a consequence – underwent a major revolution. Moreover, as a consequence of the Shah's overthrow and the nature of the succeeding regime, a wave of Islamic fundamentalism threatened the internal stability of the apparently secure conservative monarchies of the Arabian Peninsula. In part, these changes grew out of the consequences of 1973.

Once the initial ceasefire was in place, a new stage began in Arab–Israeli relations and in the role of the United States in the region.

While clearly one of the goals of the front-line Arab states was to recapture at least some of the land occupied by Israel in 1967, they believed their objectives were more likely to be won by international pressure than military victory, as evidenced by their liaison with the major oil producers on the use of the oil weapon. This proved to be a successful strategy. At an early stage, it became clear that the Nixon Administration, and more particularly Secretary of State Kissinger, was willing to intervene directly to broker a peace, rather than simply support their protégé, Israel. The United States began to play an active role in the peacemaking process, one which it has continued to the present, acting as mediator and facilitator. There are a number of reasons for this. The Arab states had demonstrated a far greater military capacity in 1973 than in 1967; although Israel had managed to launch a successful counter-offensive, the two sides were more evenly matched than in previous wars, making the negotiation of a compromise settlement a more realistic option. There were indications that President Sadat of Egypt would welcome American intervention, which would serve Kissinger's goal of limiting Soviet influence in that country. Moreover, the use of the oil weapon emphasized Western dependence upon Middle Eastern oil, demonstrated the level of support for the Arab cause among the leading oil producers in the region and, in the short term, provided cogent domestic political reasons for the Nixon Administration to seek an end to the oil boycott.

Initially the question of peace was referred to an international conference, to be held in Geneva, opened in December 1973 under the joint chairmanship of the United States and the Soviet Union. However, as it soon became apparent that a multilateral, public conference was unlikely to reach a conclusive and comprehensive peace, Henry Kissinger embarked upon what has become known as his 'shuttle diplomacy'. In its first stages, Kissinger won support for the initial ceasefires on the Egyptian and Syrian fronts, and for the six-point plan in November 1973 which addressed the most immediate difficulties in the Sinai. However, with these ceasefires 'in place', the rival armies were left facing each other, and more permanent disengagement agreements were required to avoid a resumption of the war. Travelling from capital to capital in the Middle East, Kissinger slowly negotiated bilateral agreements between Syria and Israel and Egypt and Israel. Addressing the problems piece-by-piece, or step-by-step, trying to find common ground on some issues while postponing more controversial and intractable problems, if necessary indefinitely, the Secretary of State began to make progress. It was slow, and painstaking, and left many key issues, not least the fate of the Palestinian people, unresolved, but eventually interim agreements were reached. On 18 January 1974 Egypt and Israel signed a disengagement agreement, by which Israel was to withdraw from all the territory that it held on the Western side of the Suez Canal; on the Eastern side, an area 30 kilometres wide was divided into three zones, of which Egypt was to have control over the zone closest to the canal, subject to a ceiling on the number of troops that could be kept there; Israel was to have the Eastern zone, subject to the same conditions; and the United Nations would control the buffer zone.

The Sinai was an easier issue to settle, however, as Israel could surrender a lot of territory and still retain control over areas which it regarded as central to its national security. The Golan Heights were more sensitive, and it took Kissinger 34 days and 41 flights between Israel, Syria and other countries before an agreement was reached.[34] Its provisions were similar to the Egyptian front, with each state in control of a specified zone, and a United Nations presence in the middle. However, the situation in the Sinai was still volatile and in need of a more permanent solution. It was not until March 1975 that Kissinger was able to return to his shuttle diplomacy, by which time the Israeli position had hardened; it was only when the Secretary of State announced a reassessment of American Middle Eastern policy and suspended negotiations on an Israeli request for 2.5 billion dollars in aid, including the purchase of F-15 fighter planes, that progress was made. However, the United States combined the carrot with the stick, signing memoranda of understanding which provided assurances and guarantees to the Israelis on the issue of oil supplies, as well as promising not to recognize or negotiate with the PLO until the latter agreed to recognize Israel and accept UN Resolution 242. The United States pledged aid, some of it military, to Israel at a level of roughly 4 billion dollars annually for the next three years – a very considerable increase in existing aid levels.[35]

The second Sinai agreement was signed on 4 September 1975, on terms very similar to the first, but including an Israeli agreement to withdraw from the Abu Rodeis oilfield and the Sinai passes, which would become part of the UN-controlled demilitarized buffer zone. The various disengagement agreements removed possible points of friction between the various sides that might have led to a resumption of war, but did not address the issue of much of the Occupied Territories, on which both international and Israeli domestic opinion was divided. Thus, there were no negotiations with Jordan, as any agreement with that country would inevitably have to address the issue of the Palestinians. The new Israeli Prime Minister, Yitzhak Rabin, was willing to accept these agreements, in part to play for time at a period when Arab power was strong and superpower rivalry threatened to engulf the conflict. Rabin believed that after a few years (in biblical terms, he anticipated seven lean years being replaced by seven fat ones) Arab oil power would decline, and in the meantime it was critical to avoid any situation that might lead to Israel being forced to return to the pre-1967 borders, as the Soviet Union, for example, had demanded.[36] Meanwhile, through sponsoring such a gradualist approach, Kissinger was able to achieve one of his key aims – the reduction of Soviet influence in the region. The Geneva Conference remained adjourned, and Egypt moved more and more towards the United States, a swing away from the Soviets that was symbolized when, in March 1976, Egypt unilaterally abrogated its 1971 Friendship and Cooperation Treaty with the Soviet Union. The initiative in seeking peace in the region appeared to be solidly in American hands.

However, although Presidents Nixon and Ford both supported Kissinger's approach, the victory of Jimmy Carter in the 1976 election resulted in a change in Middle Eastern policy. President Carter's foreign policy placed a strong emphasis on moral imperatives and also reflected a concern with problems of development and North–South relations. Rather than viewing the Arab–Israeli conflict entirely through a Cold War prism, the Carter White House preferred to see it also as a Third World issue, and one that could be addressed by a new joint initiative with the Soviet Union. Abandoning Kissinger's piece-by-piece approach, Carter and his Secretary of State Cyrus Vance called for a resumption of the Geneva Conference, in the hope that the two superpowers could find a comprehensive regional settlement. They believed that what was needed was the negotiation of a full peace between Israel and its Arab neighbours, to include an Israeli withdrawal to the pre-1967 borders and the creation of a homestead for the Palestinian people.

This opened up the possibility of Soviet involvement in the peace process. The Soviet Union had its own peace plan which proposed that Israel should withdraw from all territory occupied in 1967; that a Palestinian state should be established in the West Bank and the Gaza Strip; and that the right of all states in the region, including Israel, to exist should be recognized. Robert Freedman is very critical of this basic plan, which he argues was intended to keep Arab–Israeli hostility alive, preserve the Soviet role as the main arms supplier to the Arabs, and create a Palestinian state which, it assumed, would be pro-Soviet.[37] However, while it departed from the letter of Resolution 242 in its call for Israeli withdrawal from all of the Occupied Territories, it recognized the importance of addressing the future of the Palestinian people. Under President Carter, American government opinion was closer to the Soviet view, and in October 1977 the two governments issued a joint communiqué, which called for a resumption of the Geneva Peace Conference and referred to 'the legitimate rights of the Palestinian people'.[38] However, this approach soon ran into problems, not least because, since the initial convening of the Conference, the PLO had assumed a new importance, increasingly recognized as the main, if not the sole, representative of the Palestinian people. The Arabs now demanded that the PLO should be present at Geneva to represent the interests and views of the Palestinians, but the Israelis refused to sit at the negotiating table with the PLO. This hard line in part reflected the views of the new right-wing Likud Government elected in 1977 under Prime Minister Menachem Begin, which brought an end to the Labour Party's domination of Israeli governments since the state's creation. Begin regarded the West Bank as the 'Liberated Territories' of Judea and Samaria, part of Greater Israel. Few of the participants welcomed Carter's initiative: the Israelis were furious at the higher profile granted to the Palestinians, while Sadat was furious that the proposal was for a unified Arab delegation when Egypt had been putting itself at arm's length from other Arab states.

Thus, President Carter's attempts to broker a comprehensive settlement appeared to have stalled the entire peacemaking process until, in a dramatic gesture, Sadat made his historic visit to Jerusalem in November 1977, where he addressed the Knesset and called for peace. This paved the way for bilateral Egyptian–Israeli talks and in September 1978 Prime Minister Begin and President Sadat met at the American President's summer retreat at Camp David. After nearly two weeks of hard bargaining, on 18 September 1978 the two men signed a comprehensive agreement, including a timetable for the withdrawal of Israeli forces from Sinai and the guarantee of free passage for Israeli ships through the Suez Canal. In a separate 'Framework' the two governments also agreed in principle that Resolution 242 should be the basis of settlement for the broader peace; the proposed solution to the Occupied Territories was to set up an elected self-governing authority in the West Bank and the Gaza Strip, with a withdrawal or redeployment of Israeli troops.[39] However, not only were the other parties to the problem, notably Jordan and the Palestinians themselves, not consulted or involved in the negotiations, the terms were sufficiently vague, lacking any practical time-scale, that it is hardly surprising that this second agreement was not implemented, although the withdrawal from Sinai was completed. It was much easier for an Israeli Government to agree to withdrawal from the Sinai, despite the presence of oil and the strategic significance in terms of defence, than from lands which, to many in Israel, constituted part of 'Greater Israel'. This was a classic 'land for peace' deal by which, in return for land which had no historic importance for Israel, the Jewish state achieved peace with its leading Arab adversary. On 26 March 1979, again with the aid of President Carter's mediation, a peace treaty was signed between Egypt and Israel, dealing with issues specific to the two countries rather than the wider problems of the Palestinians and the other Occupied Territories. This was, however, a highly significant step, for without Egypt it was highly unlikely that Israel would ever face a concerted onslaught from the combined Arab states. By 25 April 1982 the Sinai occupation was over. Meanwhile Egyptian links with the United States were strengthened: in September 1981 Anwar Sadat expelled the Soviet ambassador, and the United States provided military and economic assistance.

While much attention focused on the bilateral talks between Egypt and Israel, other states were also concerned about the issue, and a significant development came in 1974 when, at a meeting of Arab heads of state in Rabat, the PLO was recognized as the sole legitimate representative of the Palestinian people, signalling that the issue was not simply regarded as a refugee problem. In effect, the PLO was accorded, at least by the Arab states, the role of a government in exile. On 22 November 1974 the UN General Assembly also voted to accept the PLO as an observer at all UN meetings as the representative of the Arab Palestinians. In the summer of 1975 there was a campaign to expel Israel from the UN, which only just failed, and in November 1975 the General Assembly passed a resolution in which Zionism was associated with racism.[40] This meant, *inter alia*, that in any future attempt to reach a comprehensive settlement of the Arab–Israeli conflict, the PLO would need to be involved. Israel, however, was determined not to negotiate with what it regarded as a terrorist organization. Moreover, Egypt's unilateral decision to pursue a policy of negotiation with Israel met with little support within other Arab states. One consequence of this was that the balance of power within the Arab world began to shift away from Egypt, particularly after peace talks began in 1977, towards Saudi Arabia. Arab anger increased when the Israeli Knesset declared in

August 1980 that an undivided Jerusalem was the capital of Israel and in 1981 extended Israeli jurisdiction over the Golan Heights.

In the ten years after the 1973 crisis, the United States played a prominent role as peace mediator under successive Presidents and, as will be discussed later in the chapter, that role continued even after the Egyptian–Israeli peace treaty. American policy in the region, although still strongly tied to the support and security of Israel, became more even handed, as both political and military support was provided for Egypt and Saudi Arabia. Although still perturbed by the support given to radical Arab regimes by the Soviets, and while it still provided aid, particularly military aid, to the Israeli state, the United States Government also sought to encourage moderate elements within Arab states. Thus, the 1973 oil crisis led to a more decisive American intervention in the region to promote peace.

However, despite the apparent lessening of tension between Israel and at least one of its immediate neighbours, problems elsewhere ensured that the region would continue to exercise international policy makers. After 1979 attention swung to the Persian Gulf area: a combination of the Soviet invasion of Afghanistan and the Iranian Revolution threw into sharp focus the real problems of protecting the massive oil-producing states of the Arabian Peninsula, many of them with small populations and limited defence capabilities.

Iran and the Persian Gulf

Chapter 1 set out the immediate background to the second oil price shock in 1979. However, to understand the nature of its political impact, it is necessary to explore in a little detail how the Persian Gulf, for a full decade after 1979, surpassed the Arab–Israeli conflict as a source of instability in the troubled region. The 1973 crisis demonstrated how potent was the mixture of oil and politics in the Arab–Israeli conflict. The Persian Gulf was to prove no less potent a cocktail of economic and political issues during the 1980s. As discussed earlier in the chapter, the six years prior to 1973 were critical in the evolution of the factors which produced the crisis in October of that year. In the Persian Gulf, the years from 1971 until 1979 fulfilled a similar function.

Until 1971 the United Kingdom had maintained a permanent presence in the Persian Gulf, as part of a chain of naval, military and air facilities stretching from the Suez Canal through the Indian Ocean to Hong Kong, and could be relied upon to protect the massive oilfields of the region. In 1968, however, the Labour Government under Prime Minister Harold Wilson announced that it had decided, in the face of continuing economic and financial crises, to withdraw nearly all British forces from the Middle East and Asia by the end of 1971. In a worrying indication of possible problems to come, within a few months of Wilson's 1969 announcement, a Soviet naval flotilla had paid its first visit to the Gulf.[41] Following Britain's departure, for most of the 1970s, the West essentially relied upon two regional policemen, Saudi Arabia and, in particular, Iran, to protect the region's oil supplies and political stability. This was in line with the Nixon Doctrine, which aimed at providing economic assistance for regional allies, rather than American troops, to maintain peace or fight to secure the region.

Saudi Arabia was significantly placed with regard to the Suez Canal and Red Sea, was in close proximity to the two radical Yemeni states and was also of worldwide importance as the centre of the two main Holy Places of Islam (see Map 2). In 1974 King Feisal of Saudi Arabia visited the United States and agreed a wide-ranging programme of economic, technical and military cooperation. A large proportion of the vastly increased Saudi Government's budget was spent on defence, over 20 per cent of the total cost of the second Five Year development plan of 1975–80, which was estimated at 142 billion dollars.[42] In September 1978, Saudi Arabia asked the United States to sell it F-15 aircraft, and it was sufficiently confident of its position in American foreign policy to present the sale as a test of the Saudi–American relationship. The Carter Administration linked the proposed sale to others proposed for Israel and Egypt, and presented them to Congress as a single package to be accepted or rejected as a whole: it was accepted. The relationship was two-way, however: in 1979 Saudi Arabia opposed proposals from other Arab states to impose an oil embargo on Egypt and the United States in protest at the Camp David Agreement. After the Iranian Revolution, when Saudi Arabia's role as regional protector was immensely enhanced, the Saudi Government quietly provided money to the Reagan Administration for use in Nicaragua and Angola in return for the Administration's full support in trying to persuade Congress to sell the Airborne Warning and Control System (AWACS) aircraft to Saudi Arabia for its own defence.[43] This was finally agreed by Congress, albeit by a very narrow margin (52 votes to 48 in the Senate).

However, arming Saudi Arabia was fraught with political difficulties, because of its standing as a resolute opponent of Israel. This limited the extent to which the American Congress was prepared to provide the Saudis with advanced offensive weaponry. By far the preferred American partner in the region was Iran, whose long border with the Soviet Union had already rendered it vulnerable to Soviet pressure. The combination of the massive increase in Iranian oil revenues after 1973, and the determination of the United States to build up Iran as a strong regional policeman in the wake of the British withdrawal east of Suez, led to American arms sales totalling around 20 billion dollars in the period between 1972 and the downfall of the Shah in 1979, sales that included such advanced weaponry as the F-14 aircraft, attack helicopters and various missiles.[44] Unlike Saudi Arabia, Iran was not hostile to Israel, indeed it supplied that country with much of its oil. Iran had a larger population and a more advanced military, thus making it a greater buffer against the Soviet Union and, in addition, it directly overlooked the strategically crucial Straits of Hormuz – a vulnerable gateway through which, at the time, over half of the world oil trade passed.[45]

In 1979 the security of the Persian Gulf was radically threatened by a number of events. The escalation of Cold War tensions in 1979 had an immediate impact upon the Middle East. Soviet incursions into Afghanistan increased the pressure upon Iran, while their involvement in the Horn of Africa also threatened the route through the Red Sea and the Suez Canal. The West, and especially the United States, was perturbed by these developments, but more unexpected and dramatic were domestic developments in Iran. Events in that country demonstrated that the flood of extra oil revenues into the economies of the oil producers in the Middle East would not necessarily produce only positive consequences. Iran saw its oil revenues, and hence its GDP, increase significantly from over 11 billion dollars in 1970 to 52.6 billion in 1975,[46] yet, despite that vast influx of revenues, the Shah's reign, for reasons discussed in Chapter 1, came to an abrupt end in January 1979. The Iranian Revolution had a number of implications for oil diplomacy and the stability of the Middle East. At a time when the successful negotiation of a peace treaty between Egypt and Israel suggested a lessening of tension in the Arab–Israeli conflict, the revolution concentrated international attention on the Persian Gulf. It cast the security of the region into turmoil, and suggested for the first time that a ruthless policy of modernization and economic development might have costs as well as benefits.

This lesson was emphasized in November 1979 when the Grand Mosque at Mecca was seized by a group of men led by a Saudi dissident, Juhayman bin Muhammad bin Sayf al-Utaybi, protesting against what he saw as religious laxity within the kingdom. There was also unrest in the oil-rich province of Hasa, a region with a predominantly Shia population. In many respects the Mecca Rebellion was a failure: no spontaneous mass uprising accompanied the seizure of the Ka'ba, while the religious establishment of Saudi Arabia supported the royal family and authorized the storming of the Grand Mosque. However, in response to this, Crown Prince Fahd strengthened the position of religious leaders in education, gave more authority to the Morality Police, and partially reduced the trend towards centralized government by shifting more influence to the provinces.[47] As was pointed out at the time, the Saudis had experienced at least some of the same forces of instability as in Iran, including 'suddenly acquired riches, overambitious development plans, an enlarged military establishment armed with all kinds of new weapons, a great influx of foreigners, and the growth of new groups seeking political expression'.[48] Certainly, the Mecca Rebellion, taken with earlier signs of concern within the kingdom at the pace of modernization, encouraged the Saudi Government to stress traditional values and increase the authority of the religious establishment, the Iranian equivalent of whom had proved so potent a source of opposition. The growth of Islamic fundamentalism challenged the common assumption that, as a developing country became more modern, it would become more secular.

Moreover, with the Iranian Revolution, the American strategy for maintaining the security of the crucial Gulf region was immediately undermined. The Soviet invasion of Afghanistan reinforced the need for an alternative to the now defunct regional policeman. The United States acted swiftly to emphasize that it would tolerate no threats to Western oil supplies. In January 1980, a month after the Soviet invasion, President Carter used his State of the Union Address to set out what became known as the Carter Doctrine: 'An attempt by any outside force to gain control of the Persian Gulf region will be regarded as an assault on the vital interests of the United States of America. And such an assault will be repelled by any means necessary, including military force.'[49] This, taken together with the formation of a Rapid Deployment Force prepared to intervene in case of any future threat, demonstrated that the United States was prepared to intervene actively in Persian Gulf affairs. The Soviets protested at this assumption of power, pointing out that they also had long-standing interests in the region. In December 1980 Brezhnev suggested a plan for the neutralization of the Persian Gulf region, but the United States refused. However, on the whole the two superpowers managed the situation well, despite the prevailing Cold War atmosphere: in effect they agreed, after the disastrous attempt to rescue the American hostages, that Iran was a mutual no-go area as far as intervention in domestic affairs was concerned.[50] The United States was forced to re-evaluate its policy towards Saudi Arabia in particular. Its plans for a Rapid Deployment Force had to take into account the lack of American access to bases in the region, other than on a limited scale in Oman, Kenya and Somalia. It was in this context that in 1981 the Reagan Administration pushed a plan through Congress for the sale of an airborne warning and control system (AWACS) to Saudi Arabia: this provided significant support for possible American action, but also contributed to the new regional defence alliance formed in 1981, the Gulf Cooperation Council. From 1983 American aircraft also had access to Pakistani air bases.[51]

As well as the need to defend the region from external threat following the collapse of the Shah's regime, however, another problem remained: the internal security of the states in the Persian Gulf region. Islam has two main strands, Sunni and Shia. While the majority of Muslims are Sunni, Iran has always been strongly Shiite. Many of the states in the Gulf region, including Kuwait and Bahrain, had Shia minorities, and also substantial groups of foreign workers, some of them Shia. Saudi Arabia acted as host to large numbers of Shia pilgrims at the annual pilgrimage. These groups were quickly perceived as Iran's potential fifth column, and indeed in late 1981 there was an abortive coup attempt in Bahrain which was linked with the Iranian regime. Shortly afterwards, the government of Bahrain signed a bilateral mutual security pact with Saudi Arabia, a precedent followed by all the Gulf states with the exception of Kuwait.[52] Added to the fear of potential internal unrest following the Iranian Revolution, the states had also to consider whether the powerfully armed fundamentalist government in Iran might threaten the stability of the region. This fear became particularly acute when war broke out between Iran and Iraq in September 1980. There was a real possibility that the Iranian regime would use its strategic position at the Straits of Hormuz to threaten the passage of tankers carrying Iraqi oil to market, although later on Iraq opened up new pipelines through Saudi Arabia and Turkey. Moreover, Iraq looked to its fellow Arab states in the region for support, thus presenting them with an awkward dilemma: Iraq was a powerful regional actor, with an existing territorial claim on Kuwait, but Iran also posed an immediate threat, particularly as it sought to win support by calling for a generalized Islamic revolution. For the small and under-populated states of the Gulf, lacking strong defence capabilities, this posed a considerable problem and they turned to their large neighbour, Saudi Arabia. In February 1981 representatives of the five Gulf states (Kuwait, Bahrain, Qatar, Oman and the UAE) and Saudi Arabia met to discuss the problem, and in May 1981 they formed a Gulf Cooperation Council.

The problem of Gulf security continued throughout the eight years of the Iran–Iraq War, and increasingly the Gulf states threw their support behind Iraq, giving that country large sums in aid, even at a time when, after 1983, oil revenue was declining sharply. The West, too, deeply suspicious of the Islamic state in Iran, and aware of the importance of Persian Gulf oil, chose to back the Iraqi leader, Saddam Hussein. This tension developed in a particularly volatile region: in the period from the early 1970s through the 1980s, the share of military expenditure in GNP in the Middle East was three times the world average.[53] This contributed to growing budgetary problems in these countries, which again contributed to the failures to agree oil production quotas in OPEC. The impact of the conflict reached new heights in 1986–7, when Iranian forces attacked oil tankers, particularly Kuwaiti ones, sailing through the Gulf and the Straits of Hormuz. This led the Kuwaiti Government to appeal to the five permanent members of the United Nations Security Council for practical assistance in allowing Kuwaiti tankers to re-register under their flags. Both the Soviet Union and the United States responded positively to this request. After an Iraqi Exocet missile accidentally hit the USS *Stark* on 17 May 1987, the United States Government expanded its naval presence in the region, and in July it took a further step, providing a naval escort for Kuwaiti tankers that had re-flagged. As tension mounted, on 31 July 1987 riots broke out in Mecca at the time of the pilgrimage, resulting in the deaths of several hundred people, and in August the Saudi and Kuwaiti embassies in Teheran were attacked and occupied. In early November 1987 the seriousness of the problem in the Gulf region was acknowledged by the Arab League, when for the first time the problem of the Gulf states took centre stage, and the League strongly supported Saudi Arabia and Kuwait. In this atmosphere, Egypt was once more seen as an important Arab state, and in May 1989 Egypt took part in the all-Arab summit in Casablanca, while in December of the same year Syria restored full diplomatic relations with Egypt. However, in 1988 the war finally ended with a compromise peace.

After 1990, while events in the Persian Gulf continued to demand international attention, the Arab–Israeli conflict, this time centred much more on the question of the fate of the Palestinians, again returned to centre stage. Before moving on to the Gulf War and its consequences, it is time to return to the Mediterranean littoral, to consider events there since 1979.

The Arab–Israeli conflict after 1979

Although the Iranian Revolution and subsequent events in the Gulf shifted some of the attention away from the Arab–Israeli conflict – now increasingly a struggle for the Occupied Territories between the Palestinians and the state of Israel – it nonetheless continued to have considerable implications for regional politics, and also continued to involve the United States in particular. The problem of the Palestinians also spilled over into the Lebanon, previously regarded as an ocean of stability in the Middle East, but torn between Muslims and Christians – a position complicated by the presence of Palestinian refugees, whose numbers increased after 1967 and who threatened to set up a state within a state, from which to attack Israel. Palestinian links with the Lebanese Muslim community prompted Israel to pursue a policy of assisting the Christian community, which had once been dominant in the country. Instability in the Lebanon also threatened Syria, which in 1976 intervened, sending troops into the north of the country but carefully avoiding any areas that might be seen as important to Israel's security.

However, in June 1982 Israel invaded Lebanon in an attempt to destroy the PLO bases in south Lebanon and Beirut. What initially appeared to be a short-term, punitive raid soon turned into a full-scale incursion, with direct clashes between the Syrian forces in Lebanon and the Israelis. Following Israel's invasion, in which its troops went well beyond their declared objectives, there seemed a real possibility of another major war, in which Israel, armed with the latest American weaponry, would be directly set against a Soviet-armed Syria. On 9 June 1982 Syrian and Israeli forces engaged in major clashes in the Beka'a Valley. The then Minister of Defence, Ariel Sharon, played a full role in planning for this full-scale incursion, which led to a setback in his career; after a commission of enquiry found that Israel was indirectly responsible for the massacres of hundreds of men, women and children at the Sabia and Shatila refugee camps (by Christian Phalangist militia forces who were allowed to enter by Israeli troops). As Israel launched a major assault on Beirut, repeated attempts to negotiate a ceasefire failed, until American President, Ronald Reagan, made his displeasure clear. Even so, Israel appeared to have gained one of its objectives when PLO guerrillas were forced to leave the Lebanon, supervised by a multinational force. Its headquarters were moved to Tunis. Although in some ways Israel succeeded in achieving its objectives, it did so at the cost of a loss in international sympathy, particularly after the Shatila and Sabia massacres. Moreover, Israel had begun an intervention in the Lebanon that was to last nearly twenty years.

The Israeli invasion of Lebanon took place during the Presidency of Ronald Reagan, who greeted with pleasure the expulsion of the PLO from Beirut. Like Presidents Nixon and Ford before him, Reagan defined the situation in the region in terms of superpower conflict, and provided Israel with substantial economic and military aid. During the eight years of the Reagan presidency Israel received nearly 23 billion dollars, much of it as grants rather than loans.[54] On 30 November 1981 the United States signed a Memorandum of Understanding on Strategic Cooperation with Israel, providing for strategic cooperation and closer liaison on military and intelligence matters, a clear reflection of the extent to which Israel was seen as an important anti-Soviet power in the 'second Cold War'. However, the following month the Israeli Government announced that it intended to annex the Golan Heights, a move which alarmed the United States and, indeed, some groups within the Israeli population. This violated international law and Resolution 242, as well as the disengagement arrangements put in place in 1974, and succeeded in annoying even the American Government. The Reagan Administration suspended the Memorandum of Understanding and also voted in support of a UN Security Council Resolution condemning the move. However, the memorandum was reinstated two years later, and on the whole the usual close relationship prevailed. Nonetheless, Reagan was prepared to signal his displeasure on occasion, for example when Israel mobilized its supporters in Congress to protest against the proposed sale of AWACS and F-15 aircraft,[55] and in some instances – for example, the Israeli attacks on an Iraqi nuclear reactor and the PLO headquarters in Beirut – this led to a suspension of arms deliveries.

The position was complex for, as Reagan had found out in the issue of the Golan Heights, the problem was not simply one of a Cold War struggle but an essential conflict between Israel and the Palestinians. This did not completely eliminate the superpower dimension: the Soviets continued to support the idea of an international peace conference, under its co-chairmanship, to bring about a lasting settlement based on its long-standing peace plan. However, it was in many respects the question of the Occupied Territories, still unsolved since the 1967 war, which caused the most difficulty. Although many in Israel believed firmly that most, if not all, of the Occupied Territories on the West Bank and the Gaza Strip should be retained and settled by Jews, opinion was mixed, with some Israelis questioning the policy of their government.[56] At the same time, the view was being expressed by some Palestinians at least that it was time to accept a negotiated settlement with Israel, incorporating the two-state approach.[57]

At this point, Reagan decided to follow in the footsteps of a number of his predecessors in attempting to broker peace. On the same day as the PLO left Beirut, 1 September 1982, President Reagan chose to outline the American plan for peace. Rejecting the idea of a separate independent Palestinian state, he nonetheless recognized the importance of addressing the aspirations of the Palestinians: he suggested self-government by the Palestinians in the West Bank and the Gaza Strip in association with Jordan. Although the President made clear that he did not expect Israel to return to the original pre-1967 boundaries, which had placed the bulk of the population living within artillery range of potential Arab enemies, he also stressed that the homelessness of the Palestinian people had to be addressed.[58] He also expressed his opposition to any further settlements in the Occupied Territories, although he called for a freeze rather than a withdrawal from existing settlements. In effect, most of the Occupied Territories would be surrendered by the Israelis in return for recognition and secure boundaries. This proposal was immediately rejected, however, by both the Israeli Government and the Arab states.

Events in the Occupied Territories continued to pose a threat to the stability of the region, particularly after the Palestinians in the Gaza Strip and the West Bank launched the spontaneous protests and demonstrations, known as the *Intifada*, in 1987. This was to last until the Oslo Accords in 1993. Jewish settlements in the West Bank and the Gaza Strip, despite President Reagan's calls for restraint, had continued to grow, until by 1991 there were over 90,000 Israeli settlers in the West Bank and 3,800 in the Gaza Strip.[59] Until that point, as Avi

Shlaim points out, 'Israel had won wide acceptance, not only in the United States, for its version of the Arab–Israeli dispute: the violence of its opponents was "terror"; its own was "legitimate self-defence".'[60] However, the brutality with which Israeli troops curbed the *Intifada* undermined that acceptance. Protest by the Palestinians was spontaneous, widespread and unpremeditated, but it rapidly gathered momentum as a political struggle, with the goals of self-determination and the establishment of a Palestinian state. Although the PLO had not orchestrated the *Intifada*, the strength of political feeling it demonstrated contributed to a reappraisal by the United States of the Palestinian issue. This included the recognition of the PLO as a legitimate party in the negotiations, and the direct involvement of George Schulz, the Secretary of State, who tried (unsuccessfully) to persuade both sides to accept a deal based on territory for peace.

The *Intifada* had other consequences. In 1987 Egypt attended the Arab summit and in effect was welcomed back into the fold. On 31 July 1988 King Hussein of Jordan announced that his country was severing its administrative and legal responsibilities for the West Bank, thus not only meaning that Jordan could no longer be used as the negotiating agent for the Palestinians, but also that one solution much favoured in Israel, of in effect persuading the Palestinians to accept the East Bank – i.e. Jordan – as 'Palestine' was no longer an option. It also closed off the American hope for a self-governing Palestinian authority linked with the state of Jordan, rather than having a separate national and state identity. In addition, the *Intifada* also led to the formation of Hamas as a radical resistance movement.[61] However, there was one positive step, when in mid-November 1988 the PLO agreed to accept UN Resolution 242, and the existence of Israel as a legitimate state, although within a few months it also issued a declaration of independence for a Palestinian state in the West Bank and Gaza, with East Jerusalem as its capital.

1990 to the present

At the opening of a new decade, in 1990, tension appeared endemic in the region. In the Persian Gulf, the Iran–Iraq War had ended with a compromise peace, but the threat of Islamic fundamentalism and, it was soon to emerge, intra-regional disputes still remained. In the Occupied Territories the Palestinians were in revolt, the problems of their future aspirations seemed as far off a solution as ever, while the United States had been unable even to elicit discussion of the Reagan peace plan in 1982. The region was also to be powerfully affected by two significant developments at the beginning of the 1990s. The first was the changing position of the Soviet Union in the Middle East and indeed in global politics as a whole. The Cold War had continued to be a significant backdrop to the region's politics, particularly after the outbreak of the Second Cold War in 1979. However, the position began to change in the mid-1980s, as a result of Soviet leader Mikhail Gorbachev's emphasis on the need for international stability and improved relations with the West to allow concentration upon domestic issues, including cuts in defence spending. In the Middle East this policy took the form of promoting a regional peace, ideally reached through a multilateral settlement involving the Soviets. Gorbachev was still reluctant to restore the diplomatic link with Israel, severed in June 1967, but he did follow a more relaxed policy towards the Soviet Jews wishing to emigrate to Israel. However, the task of assimilating this massive influx of newcomers encouraged the Israelis to continue their policy of creating further settlements in the Occupied Territories. The Soviets also made conciliatory gestures towards Egypt, with the resumption of consular and economic relations in 1987. The Cold War ceased to be a major factor in the politics of the region, as compared to the position of the Occupied Territories, the fate of the Palestinians, the outcome of the Iran–Iraq War and the threat posed by Islamic fundamentalism. With the effective end of the Cold War in the late 1980s and the ultimate collapse of the Soviet Union, the Cold War ceased to be, for the first time in fifty years, an important factor in Middle Eastern politics.

The move to a world now dominated by one superpower made possible the second major development: the Iraqi invasion of Kuwait in 1990 and its subsequent liberation by an international coalition led by the United States. In August 1990 Saddam Hussein of Iraq invaded Kuwait, resurrecting an old territorial claim over that country. The dispute had a number of different causes, including Iraq's desperate need for funds to restore its economy after eight punishing years of war against Iran (it was a net debtor to the sum of around 70 billion dollars).[62] Moreover, Iraq was anxious to secure the cancellation of its debt to Kuwait and indeed demanded that Kuwait pay compensation for Iraq's losses in defending Arab interests against Iran, but Kuwait refused.[63] The Iraqi Government wanted to divert domestic and international attention from various internal problems, including the Kurdish issue. However, as so often in the region, oil also played a significant part. The boundary between Iraq and Kuwait, originally drawn by British administrators in the pre-oil days, divided the Rumeileh oilfield, which Iraq wished to control in its entirety. In addition, Iraq's general strategy towards oil production and pricing was at odds with that followed by Kuwait. Saddam Hussein's Government was keen to increase its oil revenue, and this could be done in two ways: first, by increasing its own production, while other producers maintained their allocated levels; and also by pushing up the price per barrel. However, this was going to be difficult to achieve, given that there was an oil glut in the world market, and that the proportion of the free world's oil produced by OPEC members had fallen. Kuwait, on the other hand, often exceeded its quota. As a country with very substantial reserves, it had less interest in taking action which, if it did succeed in increasing prices, might encourage a return to conservation and large-scale exploration for new reserves elsewhere.

The crucial importance of the Gulf reserves for the long-term supply of petroleum was clearly recognized by the West in their response to the invasion. Contemporary suggestions that Saddam Hussein might also attack Saudi Arabia raised the spectre of his securing control over, at the very least, the oilfields in the north-east of that country, thus placing under his direct control a very substantial proportion of the world's known oil reserves and, perhaps even more critically, reserves which could be exploited relatively cheaply. This is not to imply that the war was solely about oil; complex issues relating to the post-Cold War world order were clearly also significant. The United Nations was swift to take action. UN Security Council Resolution 660 was passed on the same day as the invasion, and over the next three months a series of nine more resolutions condemned the invasion, demanded withdrawal of Iraqi forces and imposed a series of sanctions against Iraq, including the use of a naval blockade to enforce them.[64] Gradually the UN built up a substantial force which culminated in Operation Desert Storm to liberate Kuwait. A multinational force, comprising ground, air and naval forces, together with non-combat support units, and financed by a number of states including not only Kuwait and Saudi Arabia, but also with very large contributions from Germany and Japan, launched an intensive air bombardment on Iraq and then a short but decisive ground war which forced Iraqi troops out of Kuwait in less than a week. It is salutary to compare the willingness of the UN members to enforce Resolution 660 as compared to the years of debate concerning Resolution 242.

The speed of international, and in particular American, response to the Iraqi invasion was made possible by the end of the Cold War. This was a significant departure. Efraim Karsh rightly points out that the major Middle Eastern conflicts did not originate from Cold War tensions[65]; neither the Soviet Union nor the United States prompted the decisions of their respective client states to take military action (as in, for example, 1967, 1973, 1980 and 1990). The Soviet Union remained committed throughout to the concept of a regional, comprehensive settlement arrived at through a peace conference on the Geneva model, predicated upon a mutual recognition of the right of all states in the region to exist – including Israel. However, a significant factor in the 1973 crisis was the rapid development of superpower tension as events unfolded – a tension only eased when both the United States and the Soviet Union joined together to call for a ceasefire. Superpower rivalry remained a potent factor shaping the development, as opposed to the origins, of the major Middle Eastern conflicts. From 1973 onwards one of the preoccupations of the United States had been to hold the Soviet Union as aloof from the region, and the peacemaking process, as possible, and to a large extent they had succeeded. However, in the case of Kuwait, the United States and the Soviet Union issued a joint statement condemning the invasion the day after it took place, and the UN was able to assemble a large multinational force in the region without any repercussions on the part of the Soviet Union.

Both of these events – the Gulf War and the end of the Cold War – also had an impact upon the Arab–Israeli conflict. During the Gulf War, Iraq launched direct attacks on Israeli territory, seeking to win wider Arab support for an anti-Israeli jihad; even before the war broke out in January 1991, in August 1990, Saddam Hussein had specifically linked Israel and Kuwait by offering to withdraw from Kuwait, if Israel withdrew from all occupied territories and Syria withdrew from the Lebanon. The PLO, in what can only be called an error of judgement, supported Saddam Hussein. Israel responded to American requests not to retaliate militarily, but was forced to take a passive role, as the Bush Administration did not wish to propose its inclusion in the international coalition, which had a number of Arab contingents, and was reliant upon one of Israel's traditional enemies, Saudi Arabia, for bases.[66] This was significant, as it demonstrated an emerging new American Middle Eastern strategy, based on cooperation with Arab states. With the mounting disintegration of the Soviet Union, Israel's importance as a staunchly pro-Western state, with advanced military and intelligence capacity significant to the defence of the region, declined. Meanwhile, the brutal measures used by Israeli forces to quell the Palestinian *Intifada* caused consternation in the United States and elsewhere in the outside world,[67] as did the attacks on Israeli civilian targets by groups such as Hamas.

After the Gulf War, particularly with the end of the Cold War, the Arab–Israeli conflict underwent another transformation. President George Bush Sr used the opportunity to launch another attempt to find a comprehensive peace settlement for the region, and those peace efforts were continued by his successor, Bill Clinton. Both of the strategies originally considered in 1973 – a multilateral peace conference and direct personal mediation – were employed. In 1988 George Schulz had visited the region to discuss peace, and after the end of the Gulf War, in the changing climate caused by the end of the Cold War, the United States once again returned to the goal of a comprehensive peace settlement for the region, including a political system acceptable to the Palestinians in the West Bank and the Gaza Strip. James Baker visited the region ten times before announcing on 16 October 1991 that peace talks would be opened later in the month in Madrid. Shlaim described this initiative as 'the most serious attempt ever on the part of the United States to promote a comprehensive settlement of the Arab–Israeli conflict'.[68] The Soviet and American governments acted jointly in inviting the intended participants, Israel, Syria, Lebanon and Jordan (with the Palestinians forming part of the Jordanian delegation), along with the United States, the Soviet Union, the European Community and Egypt acting as participants, and the Gulf Cooperation Council and the United Nations invited to send observers. In a marked departure from previous practice, President Assad of Syria agreed to participate in direct talks with the Israelis, rather than continuing to insist upon a full UN conference and multilateral, rather than bilateral, discussions.

The goal was to negotiate a lasting peace on the basis of United Nations Resolutions 242 and 338, incorporating a comprehensive settlement of all the remaining issues, including a political system acceptable to the Palestinians in the West Bank and the Gaza Strip, with the transition of authority to a self-governing authority. The United States made it plain that while it did not support the creation of an independent Palestinian state, neither did it countenance the continuation of the Israeli rule or annexation of the Occupied Territories.[69] It also opposed the continued building of new settlements in the

Territories, which had been justified in part by the need to accommodate the large numbers of Jewish immigrants from the Soviet Union (370,000 after 1989). However, this massive wave of new migrants provided leverage to the Bush Administration, which threatened to withhold a 10 billion dollar loan guarantee, needed to ease the absorption of such a rapid growth in population, as a way of driving Israel to the negotiating table.[70] Nonetheless, the number of settlers increasingly posed a serious obstacle to agreement: by 1992, in addition to 97,000 in the West Bank, and a further 3,600 in Gaza, 14,000 had settled in the Golan Heights and 129,000 in East Jerusalem.[71] The presence of these settlements in the Occupied Territories restricted the options open to the Israeli Government.

At Madrid, both the PLO (whose standing had been undermined by its support for Saddam Hussein) and the new Israeli Prime Minister, Yitzhak Rabin (who had to take account of domestic opinion), were more inclined to compromise. The Israeli election had focused on the peace issue, and the result was a landslide victory for the Labour Party, which was willing to trade territory for peace. Many Israelis were becoming increasingly concerned about the impact upon their politics of the permanent retention of the whole Occupied Territories, which would bring into Israel a substantial Arab minority hostile to the state. With an Arab population already accounting for some 20 per cent of the population, the total annexation of the West Bank and Gaza would have increased the Arab minority to 40 per cent of the population.[72] Indeed, Rabin was prepared to take the historic step of recognizing the PLO as the legitimate representative of the Palestinian people. The PLO had already, in 1988, acknowledged the right of Israel to exist, thus implicitly dropping its insistence upon reclaiming all of mandatory Palestine for the Palestinian people, and in effect adopting the two-state solution, with Israel on the one hand and a Palestinian state in the West Bank and Gaza on the other.

However, it soon became apparent that the two sides had totally different conceptions of the interim self-governing authority and the transitional transfer of power. The Palestinians assumed that the ultimate goal was complete independence in the West Bank and Gaza, accomplished through the transfer of growing authority, including power over law and order and security, to the Palestinians. The Israelis, on the other hand, proposed a slow transfer of only limited power, in which they would maintain responsibility for defence and security, as well as the areas of settlements and the network of roads between them; the new authority would only have no legal jurisdiction over Israeli settlers.

Moreover, it was emphasized that Jerusalem was the capital of Israel, and should not be regarded as part of the Occupied Territories.[73]

The peace process stalled in May 1992, reviving again in August. In January 1993 President Clinton's Secretary of State, Warren Christopher, resumed shuttle diplomacy in an attempt to revive the peace process. Although the formal talks were still locked in stalemate, informal discussions were consecutively taking place in Norway, directly between Israel and the PLO, and the result, although signed in Washington DC, is generally called the Oslo Accords. On 13 September 1993, Israel and the PLO agreed on a Declaration of Principles on Interim Self-Government Arrangements. These arrangements were transitional, for a period not exceeding five years, leading to a permanent settlement based on UN Resolutions 242 and 338. The agreement provided for the creation of a Palestinian Interim Self-Government Authority, and also an elected Council for the Palestinian people in the West Bank and the Gaza Strip. A process of gradual transfer of authority still had to be agreed, but responsibility for external defence and the security of Israeli settlers remained with Israel, although the Palestinian Authority was intended to have a strong police force. Israel would first organize a staged withdrawal of its troops from the Gaza Strip and Jericho, with a redeployment of troops elsewhere, if possible away from populated areas.[74] This agreement, however, isolated Syria, and indeed once the agreement was in place Israel showed less interest in negotiating with Syria, particularly once a peace agreement was signed between Israel and Jordan in July 1994.

Initially, it appeared as though progress was being made towards the self-governing Palestinian authority in keeping with the planned timetable, which envisaged agreement on a permanent arrangement within five years. In May 1994 a token force of thirty Palestinian policemen arrived in the Gaza Strip, followed in July 1994 by Yasser Arafat. On 28 September 1995 the Israeli–Palestinian Interim Agreement on the West Bank and the Gaza Strip (often known as Oslo II) was signed in Washington, DC, by Yitzhak Rabin and Yasser Arafat, providing for elections to a Palestinian Council and transfer of legislative authority to this council, accompanied by the withdrawal of Israeli forces from Palestinian centres of population. However, the agreement gave the Palestine Authority exclusive control over only 4 per cent of the West Bank, with shared control over a further 25 per cent. The remainder, nearly three-quarters of the whole, remained in Israeli control, as did around a third of the Gaza Strip. Yet the Jewish settler population in the Gaza Strip numbered under 5,000, as against one million Palestinians.[75]

This reflects a major problem with the historic agreement on the future of the Occupied Territories. On the Israeli side, even a partial withdrawal from the Occupied Territories raised severe problems with some groups and political parties to whom the West Bank was part of Greater Israel, the biblical lands of Judea and Samaria. There was continual pressure on the Israeli Government to allow further settlement, including the construction of a network of roads, thus enlarging the area under the exclusive control of the Israelis. The growth of right wing protest was reflected in the assassination, on 4 November 1995, of Prime Minister Rabin. Negotiations on the final status of the Occupied Territories were scheduled to begin on 4 May 1996, but Rabin's successor, Shimon Peres, suspended talks with the Palestinian Authority, and instead resorted to what was to become a frequent tactic, the closure of Israeli borders to workers from the West Bank and the Gaza Strip, and demands for strong action against Hamas leaders. Matters worsened after the election as Prime Minister on 29 May 1996 of Binyamin Netanyahu, a fervent believer in Greater Israel, and an opponent of any kind of Palestinian state. He encouraged the further building of settlements in the Occupied Territories, and the construction of more roads – subject to Israeli control – between them. Rather than trade land for peace, he demanded that the Palestinian Authority should curb extremists and used every excuse to delay progress on the Oslo Accords. Jewish settlements in East Jerusalem were also vigorously encouraged. His eventual proposals for a final settlement of the Occupied Territories meant that Israel would retain 60 per cent of the West Bank, with the 40 per cent controlled by the Palestinian Authority in two separate areas with no link between them.

By the fiftieth anniversary of Israel's foundation, on 14 May 1998, negotiations had not even started on a permanent arrangement, yet they were scheduled for completion by 4 May 1999. Not even the intervention of President Clinton, and a visit to the area by his Secretary of State Madeleine Albright, was able to achieve progress. For the Palestinians, while the creation of the Palestinian Authority represented a symbolic first step, the slow pace of transfer was a source of concern. Meanwhile, Israel responded to any security threat by closing the crossings from the West Bank and Gaza into Israel, and imposing further restrictions on movement. The standard of living for Palestinians actually dropped, and as it became clear that Israel was reluctant to surrender meaningful power, or give the Palestinian Authority control over even a substantial minority of the land, protest grew among the civilian population. Throughout, militant groups opposed to any agreement with Israel, such as Hamas and Islamic Jihad, carried out a campaign of terrorist attacks on Israel, including a new form of terror, the suicide bomber.

Moreover, not even partially addressed in the process until then, were two questions critical to the Palestinians; the first was the status of East Jerusalem. Israel had already declared that Jerusalem was indivisible, and that it was the capital of Israel, although most countries still retained their embassies in Tel Aviv. However, to the Palestinians, not only was East Jerusalem part of the Occupied Territories and hence not under Israel's jurisdiction, but the old Walled City was particularly significant, containing as it did the Dome of the Rock or Haram al Sharif, the third holiest place in Islam. Problems arose, however, because the Dome was built on the Western Wall, a site of great religious significance to Jews. For Yasser Arafat to surrender the claim to East Jerusalem was impossible if he were to retain his political authority, especially as that was eroded by Israeli refusal to abide by the timetable for withdrawal and the movement to full autonomy; yet it was also inconceivable that any Israeli Prime Minister could surrender East Jerusalem to the Palestinian Authority. The other problem related to the status and property of the Palestinians who had fled from the new state of Israel in 1948. The Israelis refused to accept that these refugees, who had now swollen to nearly four million, had any right of return and maintained that they no longer had any rights to their abandoned property, which had been effectively confiscated by the Israeli state. Nor is it easy to envisage that Israel would willingly accept the return within its borders of so large a group hostile to the Jewish state.

It was these two issues which were eventually to bring about an end even to the faltering peace process, despite the concerted efforts by President Clinton, lasting to within a matter of hours before he left the Presidency, to broker a final agreement. In July 2000 the two sides had come closer to an agreement at Camp David, when Prime Minister Ehud Barak offered the Palestinian Authority limited municipal control over areas of East Jerusalem with a predominantly Arab population. However, Yasser Arafat felt unable to accept this, and the talks broke down. Chances of progress were undermined yet further when in September 2000 Likud Party leader Ariel Sharon visited Haram al Sharif, in defiance of security advice to the contrary, thus reinforcing the Israeli claim to jurisdiction over the region. The response was an outburst of Palestinian protest, which soon became known as the second *Intifada*; like the first, it met with a violent response and a policy of repression by Israel. The election of Ariel Sharon as Prime Minister of Israel in February 2001 exacerbated conflict between the two sides. As the political position of Yasser Arafat was eroded yet further, militant groups such as Hamas escalated their response in the form, particularly, of suicide bombers, to be met by further Israeli repression. The position at the point of writing (January 2002) offered little grounds for optimism.

Let us therefore move to an assessment of the importance of the two oil crises of the 1970s to Middle Eastern politics. The Middle East has remained, in the nearly thirty years since the 1973 war, one of the most troubled regions in the world. While we can point to other important dates – the capture of the Occupied Territories in 1967, the British withdrawal from east of Suez in 1971 – the years 1973 and 1979 were both important turning points for the history of the region. The 1973 crisis both increased Arab self-confidence, without which it was unlikely that Anwar Sadat would have taken the dramatic initiative which ultimately led to the Camp David Accords, and it also raised awareness in the international community, and particularly the United States, of the complexity of the problem. Moreover, the United States had to abandon a number of its assumptions: that Israel was so superior militarily that it could be solely responsible for maintaining stability in the region; that the Arab–Israeli conflict was in effect a microcosm of the Cold War; and that the predominant reason for instability in the region was Soviet intervention.[76] On the other hand, the domestic changes in Egypt, and the collapse of the United Arab Republic in 1961, had already begun a process by which radical pan-Arabism was undermined. The 1973 war reinforced that process, by the close alliance between the front-line states and the conservative regimes in the Arabian Peninsula; by the awareness that a military solution could only achieve limited objectives and that American pressure on Israel was an important component of any settlement of the Arab–Israeli conflict; and by the stimulus it gave to Egypt's move away from the Soviet Union towards the United States. The vexed question of the Occupied Territories and their Arab inhabitants, which first arose as a result of another major war in 1967, continued to pose a major threat to the stability of the region. Successive Israeli governments found it impossible to reconcile the many different demands upon them, from within Israel itself for security, control and new land for settlements, from the Occupied Territories for autonomy, liberty and economic opportunity, and from the rest of the world for compromise and peace. However, although the Arab–Israeli conflict still remains one of the most pressing international issues, it has taken a rather different form since 1973. In particular, it has now become overwhelmingly a problem between Israel and the Palestinians, with no general war in the region (as opposed to individual flashpoints such as the Lebanese Civil War and Israeli occupation) since 1973. However, it is difficult to foresee a permanent settlement in the immediate future to the problem of one land claimed by two peoples.

The Iranian Revolution of 1979 was in part stimulated by internal developments within that country caused by the vast expansion of oil revenues, but was also a response to unequivocal Western support for the Shah's autocratic regime which now bore the main responsibility for the defence of the Persian Gulf and its massive oil deposits, after the final British withdrawal from the region. The removal of Iran as a regional policeman, the disputes between states on oil policy, and the considerable increase in spending on arms by governments, taken together with the potent forces of Islamic fundamentalism and the difference between Sunni and Shia Muslims, have contributed to a period of both international and internal upheaval. The conservative monarchies of the Gulf have so far retained political power, but the events of 1978 and 1979 in Iran showed that even repressive regimes are vulnerable to upset. As the Middle East still contains the majority of the world's known oil reserves, and as issues such as the future of the Palestinians and the Occupied Territories, Islamic fundamentalism and the future development of countries as different as Iraq and Saudi Arabia continue to be unclear, its centrality to international relations is as strong now, if for different reasons, as it was in 1973.

Notes

1. Fraser, *Arab–Israeli Conflict*, pp. 9–45.
2. The Balfour Declaration, 2 November 1917, in John Norton Moore (ed.), *The Arab–Israeli Conflict: Volume III. Documents*. Princeton University Press, Princeton, New Jersey, 1974, pp. 31–2.
3. The particular status of the Gulf states is discussed in Glen Balfour-Paul, *The End of Empire in the Middle East: Britain's Relinquishment of Power in her Last Three Arab Dependencies*. Cambridge University Press, Cambridge, 1991, pp. 96–136.
4. Fraser, *Arab–Israeli Conflict*, pp. 9–10.
5. Institute for Palestine Studies, *The Palestinian–Israeli Peace Agreement: A Documentary Record*. Institute for Palestine Studies, Washington, DC, 1994, pp. 173–96.
6. Kaufman, *Arab Middle East*, p. 9.

7. Fraser, *Arab–Israeli Conflict*, pp. 52–7.
8. Douglas Little, 'The Making of a Special Relationship: The United States and Israel 1957–1968', *International Journal of Middle Eastern Studies* 25 (1993), pp. 563–85, esp. pp. 576–7.
9. Kaufman, *Arab Middle East*, p. 54.
10. Golan, *Soviet Policies*, pp. 61–4.
11. Mary Ann Tetreault, *The Organization of Arab Petroleum Exporting Countries: History, Policies and Prospects*. Greenwood Press, Westport, Connecticut, 1981, p. 43.
12. Tetreault, *OAPEC*, pp. 58–87.
13. Aaron David Miller, 'The Arab–Israeli Conflict, 1967–1987: A Retrospective', *Middle East Journal* 41 (1987), pp. 349–60.
14. Erik L. Knudsen, 'The Syrian–Israeli Political Impasse: A Study in Conflict, War and Mistrust', *Diplomacy and Statecraft* 12 (2001), pp. 211–34, esp. pp. 219–20.
15. Institute for Palestine Studies, *Documentary Record*, p. 247.
16. United Nations Security Council Resolution Number 242, Institute for Palestine Studies, *Documentary Record*, pp. 201–2.
17. Uri Bialer, *Oil and the Arab–Israeli Conflict 1948–63*. Macmillan, London, 1999, p. 245.
18. Golan, *Soviet Policies*, pp. 78–80.
19. Yaacov Bar-Siman-Tov, *Israel, the Superpowers and the War in the Middle East*. Praeger Press, New York, 1987, p. 231.
20. Little, 'Special Relationship', p. 563.
21. Abraham Ben-Zvi, *Decade of Transition: Eisenhower, Kennedy, and the Origins of the American–Israeli Alliance*. Columbia University Press, New York, 1998, pp. 1–17.
22. Little, 'Special Relationship', pp. 563–4.
23. Kaufman, *Arab Middle East*, p. 39.
24. Yaacov Bar-Siman-Tov, 'The United States and Israel since 1948: A "Special Relationship"?', *Diplomatic History* 22 (1998), pp. 231–62, esp. p. 242.
25. Bar-Siman-Tov, 'The United States and Israel', p. 246.
26. Abraham Ben-Zvi, *The United States and Israel: The Limits of the Special Relationship*. Columbia University Press, New York, 1993, p. 83.
27. Golan, *Yom Kippur*, pp. 5–7.
28. Robert O. Freedman, *Moscow and the Middle East: Soviet Policy since the Invasion of Afghanistan*. Cambridge University Press, Cambridge, 1991, p. 7.
29. Golan, *Soviet Policies*, pp. 73–5.
30. Golan, *Soviet Policies*, p. 78.
31. Golan, *Yom Kippur*, p. 29.
32. Golan, *Yom Kippur*, pp. 21–42.
33. Kissinger, *Years of Upheaval*, pp. 469–70.
34. Kaufman, *Arab Middle East*, pp. 90–1.
35. Avi Shlaim, *The Iron Wall: Israel and the Arab World*. Allen Lane: The Penguin Press, London, 2000, pp. 337–8.
36. Shlaim, *The Iron Wall*, pp. 327–8.
37. Freedman, Robert O., 'The Soviet Union and a Middle East Peace Settlement', in Janice Gross Stein and Paul Marantz (eds), *Peacemaking in the Middle East: Problems and Prospects*. Croom Helm, London, 1985, pp. 156–98.
38. Kaufman, *Arab Middle East*, p. 106.
39. Text of both Camp David agreements, 18 September 1978, may be found in Institute for Palestine Studies, *Documentary Record*, pp. 235–47.
40. Fraser, *Arab–Israeli Conflict*, p. 114.
41. Shadram Chubin, 'The superpowers and the Gulf', in Roy Allison and Phil Williams

(eds), *Superpower Competition and Crisis Prevention in the Third World*. Cambridge University Press, Cambridge, 1990, pp. 144–64, esp. pp. 147–8.

42. Abir, *Saudi Arabia*, pp. 128–140.
43. Rosemarie Said Zahlan, *The Making of the Modern Gulf States: Kuwait, Bahrain, Qatar, the United Arab Emirates and Oman*. Unwin Hyman, London, 1989, p. 132.
44. Karsh, Efraim, 'Cold War, post-Cold War: does it make a difference for the Middle East?' *Review of International Studies* 23 (1997), pp. 271–91, esp. p. 278.
45. R.K. Ramazani, 'Security in the Persian Gulf', *Foreign Affairs* 57 (1978–9), pp. 821–35, esp. p. 821.
46. Scott, 'American Scapegoat', p. 20.
47. Abir, *Saudi Arabia*, pp. 167–74.
48. John C. Campbell, 'The Middle East: The Burdens of Empire', *Foreign Affairs* 57 (1978-9), pp. 613–32, esp. pp. 628–9.
49. Jimmy Carter, State of the Union Address, 23 January 1980, *Public Papers of the Presidents of the United States: Jimmy Carter, 1980–81* (3 vols), Vol. I. US Government Printing Office, Washington, DC, 1981, p. 197.
50. Roy Allison and Phil Williams, 'Introduction', in Allison and Williams (eds), *Superpower Competition*, pp. 12–21.
51. Bromley, *American Hegemony*, pp. 224–8.
52. Zahlan, *Modern Gulf States*, pp. 62–3, 90.
53. Simon Bromley, *Rethinking Middle East Politics: State Formation and Development*. Polity Press, Cambridge, 1994, p. 114.
54. Bar-Siman-Tov, 'The United States and Israel', p. 253.
55. Kaufman, *Arab Middle East*, pp. 123–4.
56. Amnon Cohen, 'The Future of the West Bank: The Diversity of Israeli Opinion', pp. 49–57 and Abraham Diskin, 'Israel's Parties and the Arab–Israeli Conflict', pp. 58–79, both in Stein and Marantz (eds), *Peacemaking in the Middle East*.
57. Nafez Nazzal, 'The Palestinian Perspective on the Future of the West Bank and the Gaza Strip', in Stein and Marantz (eds), *Peacemaking in the Middle East*, pp. 80–95.
58. President Reagan, Address to the Nation on United States Policy for Peace in the Middle East, 1 September 1982, *Public Papers of the Presidents of the United States: Ronald Reagan, 1982* (2 vols), Vol II. US Government Printing Office, Washington, DC, 1983, pp. 1093–97.
59. Calvin Goldscheider, *Cultures in Conflict: The Arab–Israeli Conflict*. Greenwood Press, Westport, Connecticut, 2002, pp. 98–9.
60. Shlaim, *The Iron Wall*, p. 441.
61. Shlaim, *The Iron Wall*, pp. 455–60.
62. Fred Halliday, 'The Gulf War and its aftermath: first reflections.' *International Affairs* 67 (1991), pp. 223–34, esp. p. 226.
63. Miriam Joyce, *Kuwait 1945–1996: An Anglo-American Perspective*. Frank Cass, London, 1998, pp. 165–6.
64. The resolutions are reproduced in Dilip Hiro, *Desert Shield to Desert Storm: the Second Gulf War*. Paladin, London, 1992, pp. 526–31.
65. Karsh, 'Cold War, Post-Cold War'.
66. Shlaim, *The Iron Wall*, pp. 472–9.
67. Ben-Zvi, *Limits*, pp. 137, 152–89.
68. Shlaim, *The Iron Wall*, p. 485.
69. For documents on the peace talks, including opening and concluding remarks by the Palestinian and Egyptian delegations, see Institute for Palestine Studies, *Documentary Record*, pp. 3–37.

70. Shlaim, *The Iron Wall*, pp. 487–91.
71. Fraser, *Arab–Israeli Conflict*, pp. 141–2.
72. Fraser, *Arab–Israeli Conflict*, pp. 153–4.
73. The text of the various proposals and counter-proposals may be found in Institute for Palestine Studies, *Documentary Record*, pp. 39–116.
74. Declaration of Principles, 13 September 1993, Institute for Palestine Studies, *Documentary Record*, pp. 117–28.
75. Shlaim, *The Iron Wall*, pp. 527–30.
76. Kaufman, *Arab Middle East*, p. 87.

4

A TURNING POINT FOR
THE CONSUMERS?

In looking at the evolution of the 1973 oil crisis, it is clear that OPEC was only able to fix a much higher price unilaterally, first in October 1973 and then in January 1974, because of the situation prevailing within the market for crude oil, in which the balance between demand and supply was precarious, and was increasingly dependent upon the OPEC oil. In 1979 the upward pressure on market prices, which ultimately persuaded OPEC to increase its own official price, was again partly the result of competition between oil companies and consuming countries for the available supplies. In other words, the consumers' demand for petroleum played into the oil producers' hands. This was in marked contrast to the position prevailing for most of the postwar period, when supplies of cheap oil had been plentiful, and companies had been able to accommodate the massive expansion in demand for petroleum to fuel the West's phenomenal economic growth; by the beginning of the 1970s, instead of a buyers' market, it had turned very clearly in favour of sellers.

Consumption and cooperation before 1973

Changes in the domestic American oil industry played a major role in this transformation of the world oil market. For much of the preceding three-quarters of the century, the United States had been the world's largest oil producer. However, it was also the world's largest oil consumer, to the extent that from 1948 onwards it relied upon oil imports to meet some of its energy requirements. Initially foreign oil provided only a comparatively small proportion of overall consumption, and until the early 1970s, even though the United States was importing oil, it was not producing to its full capacity: individual oil-producing states set their own limits on production to prevent undue competition. However, by 1971 the two leading states operating this system, Texas and Louisiana, were permitting production at 100 per cent capacity. By the time of the oil crisis, the United States was importing over a third of its oil requirements (see Table 4.1).

Other industrialized nations were also heavily dependent upon imported oil, in some cases, notably Japan, for virtually all of their petroleum needs. Moreover, the role of petroleum within the overall pattern of energy generation expanded, as did transportation fuelled by petroleum. West Europe's dependence on imports for energy grew from 33 per cent in 1960 to 65 per cent in 1972[1]; as far as individual economies were concerned, France relied upon crude oil imports for three-quarters of its total energy needs while the two major coal producers in Europe – the United Kingdom and West Germany – were reliant on imports for 10 per cent and 42 per cent respectively. In 1955 coal had accounted for three-quarters of West Europe's energy usage, and as a consequence 78 per cent of its energy was produced within West Europe: by 1972 less than a quarter of its energy came from coal.[2] The growth in road and air transport also increased demand for petroleum products. Moreover, European dependence on imported oil was heavily tied to the Arab oil producers. In 1972 the European Community relied on Saudi Arabia for 23 per cent of its oil imports, Kuwait and Libya both contributed 14 per cent, while Iran supplied 11 per cent.[3] This increased reliance upon an imported commodity – one, moreover, which for Europe and Japan in particular came from a politically troubled region – had given some cause for concern even before 1973. However, given how critical petroleum was to the smooth running of the industrialized economies, more forward planning might

Table 4.1   United States production and imports, 1973–1982 (mbd)

Year	1973	1974	1975	1976	1977	1978	1979	1980	1981	1982
Production Crude oil	9.2	8.8	8.4	8.1	8.2	8.7	8.6	8.6	8.6	8.6
imports	3.2	3.5	4.1	5.3	6.6	6.3	6.5	5.3	4.4	3.5
Total imports	6.3	6.1	6.0	7.3	8.3	8.4	8.5	6.9	6.0	5.1

Source: Adapted from US Bureau of the Census, *Statistical Abstract of the United States: 1995* (115th edn). Bernan Press, Washington, DC, 1995, Table 995, p. 598.

have been expected. In part the lack of such planning reflected an assumption that any problems, if they were to occur, lay some time in the future: in part, it was as a consequence of the difficulties inherent in reaching a consensus, both within and between nations, on an appropriate policy to adopt.

In many respects, the United States should have been well placed for energy: in addition to a substantial domestic petroleum production, it also had substantial reserves of coal and natural gas. As early as 1958 the American Government had taken steps to limit the amount of imported foreign oil, although this was partially a response to fears that cheaper foreign oil would undercut domestically produced petroleum, to the detriment of the many independent producers.[4] The Eisenhower Administration imposed a mandatory system of oil import quotas, intended to keep the proportion of imported oil roughly stable. This encouraged the use of American oil, rather than the (cheaper) foreign supplies, but by the early 1970s the consequences of this policy were clearly apparent. As consumption soared, new crude oil discoveries within the United States failed to keep pace with the level of demand. Whereas just before the Second World War the US produced 62 per cent of the world's oil, by 1972 that figure was down to 21 per cent. Moreover, other sources of potential energy – particularly coal and nuclear power – were, for various reasons, subject to considerable restrictions.[5] As a consequence the demand for oil imports grew, leading to concern within the American Government that the growing reliance on foreign petroleum was a potential threat to national security. It was this which prompted the creation in March 1969 of President Nixon's Cabinet Task Force on Oil Import Control.[6] The task force reported in February 1970 and suggested that the quota should be replaced with a tariff, which would keep imported oil prices high but still allow additional imports. However the quota system protected the domestic oil companies against a potentially damaging flood of cheap foreign oil, and was still too politically sensitive to be easily overturned. The task force's proposals were rejected, predominantly on domestic grounds, apparently on the political advice of the Secretaries of Commerce and the Interior and the chairman of the Federal Power Commission.[7]

Yet, with hindsight it became apparent that the task force had taken too optimistic a view of the situation. Whereas it had worked on the premise that by 1980 the United States would be importing no more than 5 mbd, largely from the Western Hemisphere, an amount that was under 30 per cent of total requirements, in fact by 1973 the

United States was already importing well over 6 mbd, with over 10 per cent of American oil consumption coming from the Eastern Hemisphere. The task force also assumed that the price of foreign crude would, if anything, decline; that domestic US production would reach 3.94 billion barrels in 1975 (it was actually 3.05 billion) and that Venezuela would double its output in the 1970s (production in that country actually declined by a third during the decade).[8] In April 1973, in the face of rising demand, the Nixon Administration finally abolished oil import quotas and replaced them with a tariff. However, the federal government's control of energy prices, introduced as part of the general price freeze in August 1971, continued until 1981, unlike all other prices which were decontrolled by 1974. Thus, the American consumer was partially isolated from the impact of rising world prices after 1973.

Energy policy was not simply a matter of economics, however. The American State Department's concern over this worsening position was clearly reflected in an article published in the prestigious journal, *Foreign Affairs*, even before the oil price crisis, by James Akins, the Department's oil expert.[9] In this article, he set out the new predictions which the State Department was then using in planning foreign oil policy. It assumed that American consumption would reach 24 mbd by 1980, of which 50 per cent would be imports, the majority of which would come from the Eastern Hemisphere. Akins also predicted that the price of crude oil in the Persian Gulf would have increased to a startling 4.50 dollars per barrel. These prognostications were mainly economic in scope, and reflected established patterns of supply and demand. However, the political dimension was also highlighted. As the United States built an ever-closer relationship with Israel, and the Arab oil producers – now combined in OAPEC – became more significant in the world's oil export market, the traditional American policies by which the United States combined both its support for Israel and its awareness of the national security dimension of Middle Eastern oil came into question. Akins explicitly addressed the possibility of an oil boycott, and concluded that it could have very severe consequences for the United States. The Americans initiated discussion within the OECD on the possibility of collective consumer activity, but this met with little support. In part, this was because it was assumed that the political use of oil as a weapon in the Arab–Israeli conflict was unlikely following the unsuccessful boycott in 1967; the potential supply problem was therefore seen as a gradual and medium-term one, rather than an immediate and abrupt one. Even when the Saudis made a number of statements in the course of 1972 and 1973, first in 1972 suggesting a bilateral deal by which the United States would have a guaranteed supply of Saudi oil in return for exemption for that oil from tariffs and quotas and, second, explicitly linking the issues of oil and American support for Israel, the United States failed to accept the first or heed the second.[10] Moreover, the European nations presumed that any political oil boycott would be aimed predominantly at the United States. Thus, the United States assumed that they faced no real threat from the political use of the oil weapon, and the Europeans assumed that any such threat did not really apply to them. Both assumptions, of course, were proved false in October and November 1973.

Nonetheless, despite the prevailing level of apathy, there had been some initiatives addressed at the problems of conservation and the development of alternative – preferably renewable – sources of energy prior to 1973. One possible forum which industrialized oil consumers could use to pursue collective energy policies was the Organization of Economic Cooperation and Development (OECD), a large group comprising the main industrialized economies in the non-Communist world. In May 1972 American Under Secretary of State Irwin addressed an OECD meeting, calling for the creation of an international organization to coordinate the policies of major consumers in the case of any restrictions on supplies from producing countries, and to encourage increased availability of alternative sources of energy. However, he suggested that the projected energy shortage would emerge at the end of the decade, rather than before, and at this stage his main proposal was for a study to examine the likely long-term energy shortages, which was agreed.[11] Moreover, the United States suggested that the pooling should be of water-borne imports (thus excluding domestic production and any oil brought from Canada by land); Western Europe, and particularly Japan, obtained far more of their supplies by sea.

The European Community also had the remit to discuss energy, although responsibility for energy policy was split between the European Coal and Steel Community (coal), the European Atomic Energy Community (nuclear energy) and the Community itself, which under the Treaty of Rome had responsibility for oil, natural gas and electricity. The member states agreed a number of strategies, including the diversification of sources of energy, the creation of individual stockpiles of petroleum products equivalent to 60 or 90 days' usage, and the promotion of conservation. In 1968 a directive obliged member states to keep oil stocks equivalent to 65 days' consumption,[12] and in October 1972 the heads of state agreed to raise the stockpile required to 90 days' usage.[13] A year later, at the time of the October crisis, although not yet at the 90-day level, Europe generally had built up reserves equivalent to 70 days of usage. However, there was certainly no united energy policy in terms of allocation or distribution, and member states were wary about too strong a direction coming from the Commission. Above all, no government was prepared to surrender control over its energy policy or petroleum and coal supplies to the European Community. In May 1973 the energy ministers of the European Community met to discuss a collective policy, but decided that any negotiations, for example with the United States or the OECD, should be conducted by individual governments, not the Community.[14] Moreover, the differences in interests that were to emerge more strongly at the time of the crisis were already in place: the United Kingdom was at that time a major oil importer, but it was poised to become a producer in its own right as a consequence of the North Sea discoveries, and it was also the parent government for British Petroleum (in which the Government held a majority shareholding) and the 40 per cent British share of the Royal Dutch Shell Group. Both France and Italy had state-owned companies involved in foreign production and seeking further overseas production capabilities – in France the CFP and also Elf-ERAP and in Italy Ente Nazionale Idrocaburi. The Netherlands contained one of the world's largest spot markets for petroleum in Rotterdam. It was most unlikely that a common position on energy policy would emerge, particularly in the face of what appeared to be a medium-term problem.

Indeed, when President Nixon sent an energy proposal to Congress in April 1973, it contained one immediate change – the abolition of the oil import quota – otherwise it too looked to the medium term, proposing measures to limit dependence on imported oil through a combination of conservation and expansion of production. Although President Nixon had asked John Erlichman, George Schultz and Henry Kissinger to study the potential links between energy policy and foreign affairs, again this was not seen as a pressing priority.[15] Despite the few cautionary voices raised before 1973, even those who foresaw the possibility of a potential oil shortage for consuming nations assumed that, if politically motivated, it would be directed predominantly against the United States, which took comparatively little of its oil needs from the Middle East, and of limited impact. The economic position was seen as more challenging, but in the medium rather than the short term. October 1973 demonstrated the fallacy of that position, and forced consumer governments, both individually and collectively, to give pressing attention to future energy policy.

In many ways, the consumers were well placed to make an effective response to the dramatic changes in the oil market. High patterns of energy usage predicated upon cheap supplies of energy, and oil in particular, left a lot of scope for initiatives in the fields of conservation; the higher price of oil made the exploitation of alternative sources of petroleum in less accessible areas such as Alaska, the North Sea and other offshore oilfields, as well as the development of alternative, renewable sources of energy, more financially viable; and not only were there a number of international organizations, such as the OECD and the European Community, in which energy could be discussed, but the issue had already been raised, albeit in an inconclusive manner. Prompt, effective action through the individual and collective action of the main industrialized nations might therefore be expected.

However, the combination of economic and political factors in October 1973 came as a shock for consuming governments, whose future planning had tended to separate out the two trends. In the space of a few weeks, they were simultaneously faced with a number of different problems: first, they were made critically aware of the potentially disruptive impact of abrupt interruptions to supplies, for whatever reason; second, it became apparent that, at least in the short to medium term, the demand for oil products was relatively price inelastic, meaning that if prices suddenly increased, there were only limited options in the short run to adjust demand accordingly; and finally the realization of the first two factors emphasized their dependence upon petroleum and its various products. Although the consequences for all oil-importing nations had much in common – notably an adverse effect on the balance of payments and escalating oil import costs, coupled with an indirect effect on the costs of energy, transportation and all other goods – less developed countries fared particularly badly in the longer term, not least because they used less petroleum in electricity generation, and were thus unable to employ substitutes. Thus, in developing countries, oil consumption continued to grow in the 1970s and early 1980s at a level roughly equivalent to income growth.[16] Their problems are discussed in Chapter 6: in this chapter, the main focus is on whether the industrialized consuming countries, which in effect means the states that were members of the OECD, were able effectively to counter the power so graphically illustrated by the oil-rich developing countries of OPEC, and also the degree to which they were able to implement policies to deal with the second oil price shock in 1979 and for any potential changes in the oil market thereafter.

Responses to the 1973 crisis

Should the oil consumers choose to respond actively to the oil crisis, rather than simply accept the economic consequences of increased prices, that response could be at the level of the individual state or through collective action (although the two were not of course mutually exclusive). Indeed, although they were often seen as alternatives, Lieber points out[17] that it was critical to follow both routes if an effective strategy was to result. As discussed above, individual countries already had energy policies in place, and there had been some previous attempts to act collectively. Petroleum, however, in many ways was not just another commodity. As discussed in the introduction, oil was critical for energy generation and transportation (including trade and defence). This, therefore, meant that adequate supplies of petroleum and its products went beyond just economics; as Robert Keohane has pointed out, energy is a matter of high politics, directly affecting issues of both economic growth and national security. Hence, it is an issue on which individual nation states could not afford to compromise their key interests.[18] This, of course, militated against collective action, in that governments are generally slow to transfer responsibility and control over the most sensitive areas of national politics to others. Moreover, the complex situation in 1973 meant that consuming nations had to act on two different fronts at once: the economic dimension of the crisis required action in energy policy to reduce consumption; meanwhile, the political oil boycott demanded a political response to the Arab–Israeli conflict. While it is impossible to look at all the major oil consumers, it is important to consider the key figures.

The United Kingdom had to take into account a number of different factors in shaping its response to the oil price and Middle Eastern crises. On the Middle East, the Heath Government had attempted in the previous three years to encourage multilateral discussions between the United States, the Soviet Union, the French and the British, looking for a settlement on the lines of Resolution 242. However, this did not accord with Kissinger's desire to exclude the Soviets from the politics of the region and isolate the radical Arab states. With no physical presence in the region following its withdrawal east of Suez, the British Government could do little more than withhold cooperation from the American operation to resupply Israel, and lend its support to European calls for a settlement on the basis of the various UN resolutions.

As regards the economic dimension of the crisis, the British faced a particularly acute short-term problem. Although their position as a parent government and a potential producer suggested that in the medium term their position was comparatively positive, the Heath Government had been engaged in a lengthy series of disputes with the National Union of Miners, which had led to widespread strike action in January to February 1972, during which time British industry was put on to a three-day week. In November 1973 further problems in the coal industry, coupled with the possible impact of the oil embargo, led to the introduction of a State of Emergency and severe restrictions on the use of power. Once the British had been awarded preferred (later most favoured) status in the boycott – meaning that it should receive whatever petroleum it required – the government attempted to put pressure on the oil companies to ensure that its status was honoured. In view of the turmoil in the coal-mining industry, this was particularly significant. However, this ran counter to the companies' own strategy, which was to share the burden of production cuts among all their customers. Faced with company intransigence, Prime Minister Edward Heath summoned the chairmen of British Petroleum and Shell to Chequers, to demand that they provide the United Kingdom with the oil it needed. In his autobiography Heath suggested that the oil companies, in not giving the United Kingdom as much oil as it needed, were motivated by the fact that they could make higher profits else-where. In his account, when he met the chairmen of Shell and BP at Chequers, they completely refused to cooperate. 'I was deeply shamed by the obstinate and unyielding reluctance of these magnates to take any action whatsoever to help our own country in its time of danger.'[19] As discussed in the last chapter, BP company historian James Bamberg has suggested that the situation was less clear-cut, but no public mention was made at the time of whatever assistance was given.

In looking to the longer term, the United Kingdom was very conscious of its position as an oil producer, whose supplies of natural gas and petroleum in the North Sea became more economically viable with a high price for oil. The British Government was determined not to agree to a Community policy based upon the pooling of supplies, let alone one which might threaten its absolute control over North Sea oil. At the time of the Conference on International Economic Cooperation, the United Kingdom insisted that it would not accept the idea of a single European representative, but would need to be separately represented as an oil producer in its own right. Supplies of natural gas and oil from the North Sea transformed the British energy position during the 1970s and thereafter, making it essentially self-sufficient in energy as well as an oil exporter.

Like the United Kingdom, France had a long history of involvement in the Middle East, most recently as the mandatory power for both Syria and the Lebanon during the interwar years; moreover, it had intervened in Lebanon in May 1978 on behalf of the United Nations. The French Government already took a strong pro-Arab position.[20] Not only had France called on Israel to withdraw from the Occupied Territories long before the 1973 crisis, but since 1969 it had implemented a total arms embargo to Israel, while continuing to supply Arab states with arms. Thus, France's belief that the major obstacle to a Middle Eastern settlement was Israeli intransigence was not merely a response to the threatened boycott. However, economically it needed its status as a preferred nation. With little indigenous energy production, by 1971 France was dependent upon member states of OAPEC for nearly 75 per cent of its oil, and 50 per cent of total energy consumption.[21] Like the United Kingdom, it tried to persuade state-owned or controlled companies to supply it with full oil requirements.

Looking to the future, France, on the one hand, opposed any attempts by the United States to organize a confrontational consumers' organization; and, on the other, it adopted a multi-pronged energy policy aimed at reducing its vulnerability to any future action. One important element of the French energy policy was already in place: the use of state-owned or controlled companies to exploit foreign oil resources. This policy had been introduced in the interwar period when France secured a share in the multinational Iraq Petroleum Company through the CFP, and extended after the Second World War as two of the three largest French oil companies were state owned or controlled. The government owned Elf-ERAP completely, as well as 35 per cent of CFP.[22] In addition, the government wished to reduce the need for oil imports by energy conservation and the development of a domestic nuclear energy programme. It succeeded in doing this, reducing the share of petroleum in energy consumption from 66 per cent in 1973 to 46.7 per cent in 1982.[23] By the mid-1990s France obtained over a third of its primary energy consumption, and nearly three-quarters of its electricity, from nuclear sources.[24] The government also sought to develop bilateral arrangements and relationships with the major oil producers, which included a contract with Iraq in 1975 to construct an enriched uranium reactor in that country. Moreover, increased arms sales to major oil producers (including Saudi Arabia, Kuwait, Libya and Nigeria as well as Iraq) helped to offset the steep increase in the energy import deficit from 18 billion francs in 1973 to 60 billion in 1976.[25]

While France tried to lessen its dependence upon oil imports, and to build political links with the oil exporters, West Germany on the other hand defined the key strategy in dealing with the impact of higher oil prices as increasing its own exports, especially to the Middle East, to offset higher oil import bills. It also sought to increase its energy efficiency; and, of course, unlike France it had substantial indigenous coal deposits which supplied around half of its energy requirements. Its response was predominantly economic although, in a number of ways, the West German Government sought to distance itself from Israel, through its eventual request to the Americans not to use their bases in Germany for resupplying Israel during the war, and through support for the various Community-wide pro-Arab statements and initiatives.

Although individual West European countries necessarily devised their own individual domestic responses to the oil crisis, the European Economic Community had the potential for collective action and, indeed, had already set in place some precautionary measures on oil stocks, as well as encouraging the development of alternative sources of energy. However, opinion differed within the Community as to whether it should be in effect a coalition of the individual member states, in which case national energy policies would be paramount, or a supranational union, in which the collective entity of 'Europe', represented by the European Commission, would steadily gain more influence and power. Energy policy was central to these two conflicting ideas, as a Community-wide policy would plan for its combined energy resources – including coal and oil, nuclear power, and any alternative sources of energy. Alternatively, each country could control its own energy policy, utilizing its own resources as it saw fit, and cooperating with other Community members only if it was deemed to be in its interests. Although the Commission reviewed the overall energy position in the Community as a whole, on energy policy the individual member remained supreme, pursuing the domestic and foreign policies that it deemed most likely to meet its individual national energy needs. During the boycott, the Dutch requests for an intra-Community allocation system that would share available oil equally fell on deaf ears.[26]

However, despite the wide diversity of views on the Arab–Israeli conflict within Europe – France, Britain and Italy were by tradition pro-Arab, the Netherlands and Denmark were definitely pro-Israel, while West Germany, which for historical reasons had tended to be supportive of the Jewish state, was attempting to move towards a more neutral stance – there were some important initiatives on a Community level. On 13 October (before the boycott was announced) the European Council of Ministers was able to agree to a joint statement calling for a ceasefire and negotiations on the basis of UN Security Council Resolution 242, followed by a firmer statement on 6 November calling on Israel to withdraw from the Occupied Territories and recognize the legitimate rights of the Palestinians.[27] However, while this might appear as little more than a knee jerk reaction to the oil boycott – in line with Kissinger's interpretation of European policy as driven solely by immediate considerations that were mainly oil-based – the original six members of the European Economic Community had in fact agreed as early as May 1971 on a united position on the Arab–Israeli conflict, based on a call for withdrawal from the Occupied Territories and the right for every state in the region to enjoy secure and recognized boundaries. Thus, the declaration on 6 November was a reassertion, not a reappraisal of policy.[28] On 31 October President Georges Pompidou called a summit meeting to discuss the European policy towards the energy crisis, and in December 1973 the heads of state met at Copenhagen. Five Arab foreign ministers attended the summit for talks with their European counterparts. The British and French governments reluctantly agreed to authorize the Commission to prepare proposals for ensuring the orderly functioning of the energy market in future, but little was done on this once the boycott of European countries was loosened by the end of the year. What is significant, however, is that the European Community, still unsure of the extent to which it would adopt anything resembling a common foreign policy, nonetheless was able to agree on the pursuit of an Arab–European dialogue, even though it was at pains to distance this dialogue from the Arab-Israeli conflict itself. In July 1974, twenty-one members of the Arab League met the nine members of the European Community, as a result of which cooperation was agreed in areas of development, albeit ultimately with very limited results.[29]

Outside Europe, the main industrialized oil consumers were the United States and Japan. Since 1945 Japan had traditionally followed the American lead in foreign policy; however, its booming economy relied very heavily on the import of raw materials, including virtually all of its energy. In 1973 Japan imported around 99 per cent of its crude oil requirements, and about 40 per cent of it came from producers that were members of OAPEC.[30] Moreover, in 1973 oil provided nearly 78 per cent of Japan's total energy requirements. The country had tried where possible to import crude oil for refining within Japan, thus opening the way for direct deals with producers or for Japanese companies to take on overseas production contracts. However, the impact of the oil price increases was rapidly apparent in the balance of payments: whereas in the latter half of the 1960s oil imports had accounted for around 16 per cent of the total import bill, in 1974 and 1975 it was over a third of the total.[31] Japan was therefore severely threatened when, in the initial stages of the oil embargo, it was defined as neutral. The Japanese Government had already given its support to Resolution 242 but on 22 November 1973 it specifically reinforced this point and at the same time stressed its support for the Palestinians' right of self-determination and total Israeli withdrawal from the Occupied Territories. Over the winter of 1973–4 Japan sent a series of special envoys to the oil-rich states of the Persian Gulf – Syria, Egypt, the Sudan, Algeria, Morocco and Jordan – offering economic and technical assistance. The government promised economic and technical assistance to the oil producers and encouraged Japanese firms to build up exports to OPEC countries, while also seeking joint ventures with the producers on, for example, the development of refining and petrochemical capacity. Moreover, in December 1973 Vice Premier Miki visited the Middle East, and generally Japan assumed a more independent attitude, for example by calling in 1976 for a direct dialogue between the PLO and Israel.[32] The pro-Arab line fitted in with Japan's traditional emphasis on economic rather than political goals in foreign policy. By 1976 Japan had signed economic agreements with Iraq, Saudi Arabia, Iran and Qatar, and by 1980 direct deals with producers accounted for 45 per cent of its oil imports.[33] These political changes reflected the seriousness of the economic impact on Japan. In 1974 Japan had a negative growth rate for the first time since 1945, accompanied by inflation, rising unemployment, recession, and a balance of payments deficit, while in the second oil price shock, Japan's budgetary surplus of nearly 12 billion dollars in fiscal year 1978 turned into an 11 billion dollar deficit in 1979, largely due to the oil price hike.[34]

The United States was directly affected both economically and politically: in addition to the oil price increase, it was designated an unfriendly nation during the oil boycott and faced a complete suspension of imports from the Arab Middle East. The Nixon Administration (and more specifically its Secretary of State Henry Kissinger) dismissed suggestions that the boycott had in any way shaped its Middle Eastern policy, and certainly in the immediate aftermath it continued to give substantial support, including military supplies, to Israel. However, as a country with a large domestic production (even if it was well below required consumption levels), a limited dependence on Middle Eastern oil, and another major oil producer, Venezuela, within close proximity – not to mention its role as parent government for five of the Seven Sisters – it should have been in a strong position to withstand even the boycott. However, despite the best efforts of the oil companies, President Nixon's announcements that supplies might be expected to fall by anything up to 17 per cent produced panic, culminating in massive queues at petrol-filling stations. Meanwhile, the concurrent developments in the Watergate affair made public support critical to the beleaguered President Nixon. According to a Gallup poll conducted in December 1973, nearly a quarter of the population felt that the federal government was responsible for the energy crisis, and 19 per cent specifically blamed the Nixon Administration, while only 7 per cent blamed the Arab nations (a quarter thought that the oil companies were primarily to blame).[35] Nixon had great hopes of being able to announce a successful American initiative to broker peace, or at the very least a lifting of the oil boycott, as a result of American mediation. Henry Kissinger however, while claiming that 'Europe seemed to have no specific aim except to seek the goodwill of the oil producers', consistently maintained that, unlike the panic-stricken Europeans, his policies were based upon political, and particularly Cold War, considerations, not on short-term energy opportunism.[36] However, the administration did adopt a more even-handed approach to Middle Eastern issues, in a deliberate attempt to reduce Soviet influence in the region and build a closer relationship with Egypt.

The oil boycott concentrated American attention on the longer term implications of its dependence on imports. As the world's largest consumer, the United States was in a position to make a considerable impact on the overall level of oil consumption, and over the following years a number of initiatives were taken by successive administrations in order to reduce both consumption and imports. Unfortunately the ambitious plans remained just those: plans. It proved exceptionally difficult to persuade American consumers to make effective changes in their energy usage. Meanwhile, the American Government continued to take a firm stand towards the oil-producing states, at times threatening the use of force if necessary. In January 1974 United States Defence Secretary Schlesinger publicly warned that the American Government would not rule out the option of reprisals against oil producers. At several points in the winter of 1974–5 prominent American officials, including President Gerald Ford, Secretary of State Kissinger and Pentagon officials, warned that the United States would be prepared to resort to the use of force to counteract possible substantial cutbacks in production.[37] President Ford also explicitly linked food with oil, pointing out that the United States was the world's largest food exporter.[38] However, such belligerent threats could only really apply to the use of oil as a political weapon: the economic side of the equation, the need to address the greatly increased cost of oil imports, called for more long-term policies of conservation and the development of alternative energy sources.

Whereas Nixon's call for a medium-term energy policy had fallen on deaf ears in April 1973, the oil boycott had demonstrated to the American public, and indeed to Congress (which had dragged its feet on the initial proposals), that there was a problem to be faced in reconciling the growing demand for oil at cheap prices with increased conservation concerns, and policies intended to push up prices in the producing countries. The first major programme to address American dependence on imported oil came a month after the October crisis began, when on 7 November 1973 President Nixon introduced what he called 'Project Independence' aimed at encouraging conservation and the use of alternative sources of energy, to make the United States self-sufficient in energy by the end of the decade.[39] His proposals included a number of obligatory measures to cut production, such as speed restrictions on roads, cut backs in air flights, and the encouragement of voluntary conservation (he suggested that Americans might lower their thermostats to 66–68 degrees Fahrenheit, rather than the prevailing norm of 75–78 degrees). He also stressed the need for initiatives to increase production, including the relaxation of environmental regulations. On 16 November 1973 the controversial Alaskan Pipeline bill became law, and later in the month Nixon elaborated on his initial proposals. However, the American Government still used price controls and regulations to keep domestic prices lower than OPEC prices, but all attempts to decontrol prices failed to get through Congress until April 1979, after the second oil price shock. The energy crisis generated a lot of domestic interest, much of it looking for a possible scapegoat for the problems, such as OPEC itself, or the multinational oil companies which were suspected of cooperating with the oil producers to the detriment of the American consumer. In the 94th Congress alone, by October 1975 about a thousand bills on energy had been introduced, although only a handful were passed.[40] However, presidents seeking support for their successive energy proposals had problems getting support from Congress, in the face of pressure from a number of conflicting interest groups: the pro-Israeli Jewish lobby, the environmentalists, the domestic 'independent' oil producers, the coal industry – and, of course, the large multinational oil companies.

Gerald Ford, Nixon's successor, also made energy one of his main priorities when he entered office. In January 1975, explicitly linking the energy crisis with recession and inflation, he called for a number of other measures with the goal of reducing foreign oil imports by 2 mbd by the end of 1977; where Nixon had called for self-sufficiency by the end of the decade, Ford now set the target date at 1985. He proposed the creation of a strategic petroleum reserve, the decontrol of natural gas, delayed implementation of the Clean Air Act, and also the decontrol of oil prices to stimulate the domestic oil supply.[41] However, while the Energy Policy and Conservation Act, subsequently passed by Congress, included many of Ford's proposals, it did not include price decontrol. Instead of seeing a move towards self-sufficiency, the period from 1973 to 1976 saw American dependence on foreign oil increase from 36 to 46 per cent.[42] In 1977 President Jimmy Carter also made energy policies one of his first priorities on coming to office. In April 1977 he stated that 'with the exception of preventing war, [the energy problem] is the greatest challenge that our country will face during our lifetime', and referred to it as the 'moral equivalent of war'[43] Like Ford, he tried to increase prices; but, as before, Congress refused. None of these efforts succeeded in changing the long-term dependence of the American public on imported oil. By 1975 the United States was the world's largest importer of crude oil and petroleum products.[44]

However, in trying to reach individual strategies for dealing with the oil crisis, consuming nations found themselves in a difficult position, reluctant to impose policies – for example on energy conservation – which might increase the burden on the manufacturing sector. The measures introduced tended to be comparatively minor in terms of the overall energy picture, and were often directly aimed at the individual consumer, who had to contend with the burden of speed limits, reductions in Sunday driving, and the curtailment of energy-intensive leisure pursuits. In fact, over the winter of 1973–4, which was unusually mild, there were no real shortages of oil products: reserves of oil products in the European Community member states never fell below the equivalent of 80 days of consumption, suggesting that any reductions in consumption were a response to changes in demand, rather than supply.[45] However, even if the immediate impact was perhaps less than had been anticipated, the long-term problem of dependence and the likely impact of a severalfold increase in prices could not be ignored. Each individual country's successes in reducing petroleum consumption would have little impact upon prices and OPEC power unless they were mirrored in other major consuming economies. This, however, raised the relationship of economic and political priorities and policies, and whether collective action should embrace only the economic, or also the political dimensions of the problem. Conflicting priorities and interests were to make difficult what should have been comparatively simple: the evolution of a common and collective consumer policy among nations which, unlike the producers, already had much in common in terms of political systems and ideologies.

There were, however, problems with the existing institutions through which collective action could be discussed. The OECD in some respects might have appeared the most obvious forum for the consumers; however, the sheer diversity of its members, both in terms of their political stance towards the Arab–Israeli conflict and their situation *vis-à-vis* energy, crude oil production and consumption, militated against an effective policy. The European Community, which had already discussed energy, could not speak for the United States and Japan. The Group of Seven – comprising the heads of state of the seven most industrialized states in the West, thus including the United States and Japan as well as the leading European economies – did not exist until 1975. Moreover, initiatives on energy cooperation, whether before or after the various oil crises, intersected with a number of other important issues, including the identity, structure and leadership of the European Community, the role of the United States in the defence and stability of Europe, economic rivalry between the European Community and the United States, and the claims and demands of the United States in its perceived role as leader of the free world.[46]

Outside the European Community, leadership in seeking a collective response to the oil crisis rested with the United States, partly for economic but also for political reasons, as the American Government sought to avoid a wedge being driven between itself and its European allies and Japan by calling for concerted consumer action. This needs to be considered in the wider context of the changing position of the United States in the world, and more particularly American foreign policy during the Nixon Administration. In the period after 1945, the United States had been the dominant Western power, one of the two superpowers straddling the globe. Its power was based not only on military capacity (particularly nuclear weaponry) but also on economic power. Until the end of the 1960s, it was the undisputed economic leader of the Western world and it also provided the leadership and direction for Western policy. In filling this decisive role, it faced no real rival.

Possible alternatives, such as the United Kingdom, France, West Germany and Japan, were all, for various reasons, unable or unwilling to challenge American hegemony.

By the early 1970s the situation had changed: the American economy ran into difficulties by the end of the 1960s, and other nations were challenging its economic predominance, notably West Germany and Japan. However, while economically strong, neither of these two powers had exercised major military power outside their own boundaries since 1945. Combined, on the other hand, the European nations could bring together considerable defence capability, political influence, international understanding and economic power. It is in this context that we need to consider the policies adopted by the Nixon Administration. President Nixon and Henry Kissinger both emphasized the Cold War context of their policies, and regarded the United States as having the primary leadership role in the West's resistance to the Soviets. At the same time, growing economic difficulties, reflected in calls at home for a reduction in defence costs, led to the Nixon Doctrine, which stressed the importance of regional states taking prime responsibility for their own defence, albeit with American financial and military aid; the United States would only consider direct intervention in exceptional circumstances. It was clearly time for a reappraisal of the trans-Atlantic relationship, and in April 1973 Henry Kissinger, then National Security Adviser, called for a new Atlantic Charter to define relationships between the United States and Europe. While stressing that, given the close military balance between East and West, Europe must be prepared to take more responsibility for its own defence, Kissinger also argued that Europe should follow the American lead on foreign policy matters because American interests were global, while Europe's main preoccupations were regional. Aware of Europe's growing economic strength, he also stressed the linkage between American military protection on the one hand, and Europe's economic policies on the other.[47] The speech, however, which called for a 'Year of Europe', was not sympathetically received, reinforcing France's traditional independence in foreign affairs. British Prime Minister Edward Heath, who – unlike many British Prime Ministers – regarded relationships with Europe as more important than the so-called 'special relationship' with the United States, clearly expressed his annoyance at the idea of a 'Year of Europe' in his later memoirs.[48] The United States had no reason to assume, after October 1973, that Europe would automatically follow its lead.

Indeed, in terms of Middle Eastern policy, there was very little trans-Atlantic harmony. Kissinger made clear in his memoirs that he regarded

European policy as pusillanimous, and driven by short-term considerations, i.e. the oil boycott. This simply reinforced the American opinion that, while their own Middle Eastern policy took into account
Western interests in a Cold War context, its allies were too prone to
look at their own specific and particular interests. The United States
was unswerving in its opposition to the boycott, and tended towards
belligerency in its public statements. The European countries and
Japan, however, were more inclined to be conciliatory. Japan's change
in policy was clearly linked to the energy issue, but some individual
European nations had already adopted a pro-Arab stance, while the
European Community had made its first statement on the crisis several
days before the boycott was put in place. Moreover, from an economic
standpoint, West Europe relied on the Middle East for around 60 per
cent of its total oil supplies while the United States obtained under 15
per cent of its needs from the region.[49] However when, in early March
1974, the European Community decided to encourage a European–
Arab dialogue on a number of different issues, the United States was
furious, and saw this as Europe wanting it both ways: to have American
involvement in the defence of Europe on the one hand, yet pursue
their own economic interests on the other. Having already taken a
united stand – at odds with American policy – on the Arab–Israeli conflict, the European Community continued to do so. In March 1980
the European Community voted to support a UN General Assembly
resolution condemning Israeli settlements in the Occupied Territories;
and in June 1980, while stressing the right of all states in the region,
including Israel, to exist, the EC also called for Palestinian self-determination and the participation of the PLO in negotiations.

Although, in his memoirs, Kissinger did not hide his annoyance and
frustration at what he interpreted as narrow-minded European policies
motivated by considerations of oil, he was also determined to create a
united front of consumers against the producers' organization. Bromley
suggests that the United States saw in the oil crisis a means of regaining
its position as leader of the West.[50] Although the OECD might seem
appropriate for this purpose, as it did have both an oil committee and
an energy committee, it had not proved particularly successful during
the 1973 crisis.[51] On 12 December 1973 the Secretary of State used the
prestigious Pilgrims Dinner speech to call for cooperation on energy
policy across the Atlantic.[52] Shortly afterwards, he invited the leading
consuming nations to an energy conference in Washington, DC. There
was some resistance to the very idea of such a conference, but in
February 1974 the meeting of the industrial consumers took place.

France in particular, which preferred its chosen policy of bilateral deals with the main producers, called for a multilateral United Nations Conference to include the producers as well as the consumers, and only attended the Washington Conference to prevent an unacceptable commitment on the part of the European Community in its absence. The conference forced the Community to decide whether to adopt a common attitude towards the American initiatives, or respond on an individual basis. While the French called for a common Community policy of caution and resistance, with an emphasis instead upon fostering a collective Community approach to the oil producers, the United Kingdom and West Germany were more favourably inclined towards the United States' initiative.

The participants were able to agree on certain important strategies, if not necessarily the means of achieving them. First, there was a need to shift from a reliance on the Middle East towards less politically sensitive sources of oil where possible; second, where feasible there should be a move away from oil as a source of energy towards alternatives; and finally there should be a reduction in consumption. Moreover, while cautious of American motives, the majority of European Community members were also prepared to cooperate in the creation of a new organization to represent the interests of the consumers, the International Energy Agency (IEA). France, however, chose to remain outside it (although it finally joined in 1992).[53] In November 1974 the IEA was formed as an adjunct of the OECD. It had a varied brief, but at the heart of its agenda was the task of creating and implementing schemes for emergency oil sharing if overall supplies were cut by 7 per cent or more, with provision for pool arrangements.

It was intended that these allocation arrangements should be automatic, and a bureaucratic structure was created to implement them. If the IEA – and not, it should be noted, the individual member governments – decided that there had been a sufficient reduction in supplies, then member states were bound to take certain steps and accept IEA allocations of oil, which on the face of it amounted to a significant delegation of state authority to an international organization.[54] However, with no coercive powers, the IEA would still be dependent upon the individual governments agreeing to take action in an emergency. An added difficulty was whether the oil companies, whose cooperation would be required, would put consumer plans above producer demands. As yet, this has never been put to the test. The IEA, however, also had a range of other tasks, including the collection of statistical and other information and the encouragement of consumer cooperation on energy issues.

In March 1975 a further step was taken, this time to protect Western economies from volatile downward prices, which might undermine attempts to explore for alternative sources of oil and develop alternative sources of energy. It was agreed that there should be a minimum safeguard price (MSP) below which each member government would prevent oil from being sold in its domestic economy. The assumption underpinning the proposal, which originated from the Americans, was that otherwise OPEC might engineer a collapse in prices to undercut the development of viable alternative energy sources.[55] However, there were problems in agreeing either the principle of the MSP or its initial level. As eventually set, the MSP was very low; its advantages therefore probably did not outweigh the negative impact of the disputes between the oil producers in the organization (notably the United States and the United Kingdom) who wanted a minimum price and consumers, such as West Germany, who did not.

While the emergency pooling of supplies was at the heart of the IEA, central also to its brief was the assumption that steps should be taken to reduce consumer dependency upon OPEC oil in the future. There were a number of possible strategies that could be adopted by the consumers, either individually or acting in concert. The first was to reduce reliance upon imported oil, and particularly OPEC oil, by a variety of domestic strategies including conservation, the encouragement of energy efficiency, exploration for domestic sources of petroleum, and the development of alternative (preferably renewable) sources of energy. The second was to assume that the increase in oil prices would achieve a reduction in oil usage without active government intervention, as individual consumers adjusted to higher costs; this in turn would reduce demand, and might then provoke a crisis within OPEC, as the organization faced the task, for the first time, of achieving agreement on the reduction of production. This, however, implied a reliance on market forces. The third was a more confrontational approach towards the oil producers, either at the level of economics (by encouraging a reduction in demand for OPEC oil) or, possibly, at the military level. The latter was contemplated on occasion, but never implemented, by the United States: the other consumers preferred more peaceful means of achieving their goals.

In claiming leadership of the West in the crisis, the United States could point to a number of supporting factors: it was comparatively less dependent on oil imports, especially from the Middle East than West

Germany and Japan: it was a significant, if inadequate producer in its own right; and it had the political and economic power, in particular the privileged role of the dollar, to sustain it. However, to justify leadership it needed to lead from the front. In terms of strong rhetoric, the American Administration did just that, but in terms of the goals agreed at the Washington Energy Conference, of conservation, reduction of oil import dependence, and the development of alternative sources of supply and energy, it was far less convincing. With domestically controlled prices for much of the 1970s, US petrol prices as late as March 1981 were roughly half the prevailing price in Western Europe. Congressional hearings frequently reflected the desire to locate a scapegoat, for example OPEC or the oil companies, to blame for the energy crisis rather than address the underlying domestic sources of the crisis. In hearings held by the joint economic committee in 1976, for example, the view was expressed that American oil companies were more concerned with the need to secure long-term access to oil supplies – implying therefore a cooperative attitude towards OPEC and its member states – than with achieving lower prices for consumers.[56] Oilmen were quizzed on the extent to which they had worked with OPEC to control the oil market, including the reduction of production in order to keep up prices. However, not only did the American Government have few sanctions that it could realistically use against the companies, but as the representatives of the oil industry themselves stressed, with the growth in the participation percentage of the producing governments, their control over supplies of crude oil had diminished substantially.

The combination of lower prices, a tendency to treat the energy crisis as an artificial problem manufactured by external agencies (the oil producers, the oil companies) for their own profit, and Congressional unwillingness to introduce unpalatable policies that would directly affect their constituents, meant that the United States signally failed to cut consumption significantly. As a consequence, therefore, American imports went up, not down (see Table 4.2). Congress did agree to set up a Strategic Petroleum Reserve, but it was not until the end of 1977 that a start was even made on its creation, and by December 1978 it held only 67 million barrels – the equivalent of less than nine days of oil imports. When President Ford attempted in 1975 to increase import duties on petroleum and at the same time decontrol all domestic oil prices, Congress proved obstructive. President Carter tried to put in place a crude oil equalization tax, but that was defeated in Senate.[57] It was not until July 1978, following the Bonn Summit, that President

Table 4.2 Petroleum consumption by selected areas, 1971–1978 (mbd)

Year	1971	1972	1973	1974	1975	1976	1977	1978
USA	14.85	15.99	16.87	16.15	15.88	16.98	17.93	18.26
W. Europe	13.28	14.16	15.16	14.17	13.51	14.47	14.23	14.62
Japan	4.44	4.74	5.46	5.27	5.02	5.19	5.35	5.42

Source: Adapted from *BP Statistical Review of World Energy 2001*. BP Plc.

Carter was finally able to deregulate oil prices and this was not complete until January 1981. The pressure from fellow industrialized countries to act on imports continued, and in July 1979, at the Tokyo summit, objectives were set on the oil imports to be met by 1985. Europe was particularly furious when, in 1979, the United States tried to divert Caribbean oil intended for Europe to the United States. The sharp recession in 1980, however, had the additional effect of reducing oil consumption in the United States as elsewhere.

Thus, at a time when the oil-producing states were still solidly united through OPEC, the oil consumers were less well organized. Even within Europe very little was achieved in the way of a common policy. There were still doubts about the shape and direction of the Community in future. The United Kingdom, under the new Labour Government, was demanding a renegotiation of the terms of entry. There was an undoubted tension between the economic strength of West Germany, compared to that of the other members. There was not even a consensus upon the crucial question of whether the Community would develop as a supranational community largely led by European institutions such as the Commission, or as an intergovernmental federalist organization in which national governments would retain the main authority, and decisions would be taken at meetings of Heads of Government, the Council of Ministers and so forth. Energy policy, of course, directly addressed this profound difference of opinion.

So, although in terms of consumption levels, the European Community did rather better than the United States[58] this was more a sum of national policies than an example of Community action. There were too many divergent interests within the Community, with one significant oil producer (the United Kingdom), two members with extensive, if expensive, coal supplies (the United Kingdom and West Germany) and also differences on nuclear policy. Moreover, the key Community members all favoured different energy strategies. West

Germany, which had its own coal reserves already, was contemplating the use of natural gas from the East. France traditionally emphasized a mixture of nuclear energy with support to state-sponsored companies and bilateral relationships with oil producers (particularly Iraq). The United Kingdom had become a major oil producer in its own right. Debates within the European Community on the formation of a common energy policy also continued, but ran into the expected differences of national interest, as well as raising questions about the role of the Community as a whole, whether as a supranational organization or a federation of individual states. The Community encouraged conservation, reduced dependence on imports and research and development, but these were all policies likely to be promoted also by individual states. What was in the interests of the Community as a whole – for example, for the United Kingdom to maximize its North Sea oil production – would not necessarily suit the individual national interest. Moreover, while the Group of Seven 1979 summit in Tokyo agreed to control oil imports, there were substantial disagreements on how to set and calculate the goals. There was also the question of whether there should be a target for the whole European Community (in which case British oil production would have a significant effect) or for individual countries (which would allow the United Kingdom to claim its due credit for reducing its imports by over 60 per cent between 1973 and 1978). Individual targets prevailed.

By the time of the second oil shock, the consumers had not succeeded in reaching the goals set at the Washington Energy Conference. There had, admittedly, been some diversification of oil supplies away from the Middle East, but that region remained sufficiently significant that a threat to its supplies generated panic. It also became apparent that dependence upon oil – or, to put it another way, the potential to substitute other products for petroleum derivatives – varied according to commodity. While the use of residual fuel oil, predominantly used in the generation of electricity, could and did decline after 1978 as alternative sources of electricity generation were developed,[59] it was much harder to develop alternatives to gasoline and aviation fuel. Not only had individual consuming nations found it difficult to implement fully the goals set out in 1974, there was little evidence of a coherent consensus among them as to how best to implement those goals. Lieber rightly points to a number of causes for conflict among consumers: the need to secure adequate national supplies; the competition for export markets as a number of countries sought to increase exports to help offset higher oil import bills; the differences in policy between producers and consumers; the lack of awareness among some publics, especially that of the United States, of the extent and seriousness of the energy crisis; and the problems of persuading all countries to follow voluntary policies of restraint, for example on consumption and the use of spot markets, when the rewards for the 'free rider' breaking the common front were likely to be not dissimilar from those actually cooperating.[60]

1979 and after

As Table 4.2 demonstrates, at the time of the second oil price increase, in 1979–80, overall consumption remained high, due largely to American reluctance to embrace the cause of conservation. It soon also became apparent that the plans and structures put in place after the 1973 crisis were inadequate to meet this new crisis. The International Energy Agency (IEA) had predicated its emergency schemes on the assumption that any future crisis would be caused by shortage of supplies, whether by political action or market forces. In order to prevent politically inspired action being directed towards selected members of the IEA, as had happened in 1973, it had set up an automatic pooling system, designed to share out scarcity equitably. However, this was not a crisis of supply but of confidence. Without the discipline created by a pre-agreed plan, countries were free to follow their own interests. Despite six years of planning, the oil-consuming nations were still less effective and coherent than the producers of OPEC.

Nor did the second massive increase in oil prices encourage greater coordination among the industrialized states. The question of Soviet energy contributed to the strains within the trans-Atlantic alliance, as the United States bitterly opposed plans for increased natural gas to Europe through a new pipeline. In 1983 the American Government and the Europeans agreed, through the mechanism of the IEA, that the former would drop its demand that Western Europe should limit Russian imports to no more than 30 per cent of total gas supplies, but at the same time all members pledged to take heed of the security issues this raised, and consider alternatives to increased imports from the USSR where possible. However, this was only part of a general determination on the part of Western Europe, and particularly West

Germany, to engage in increased East–West trade as part of Ostpolitik, i.e. a policy aimed at political reconciliation and increased trade with the East.[61]

However, in the period after 1980 there was a drop in global demand for petroleum. There are a number of reasons for this. The sharp recession undoubtedly reduced demand, but this changed as the economy recovered. In 1984 world consumption of oil grew by nearly 4 per cent, although the rate of growth dropped slightly to 2.5 per cent in 1985.[62] In addition, alternative sources of energy and energy conservation measures could not be implemented overnight, and undoubtedly some of the measures introduced after 1973 did not become effective until after 1979. However, the fall in oil prices after 1983 eliminated the main reason for energy conservation. Alternative sources of energy were often very expensive to develop, and the world economy continued to function on the basis of cheap transportation. Although crises in the Middle East did trigger short-term increases in prices, as in 1990 at the time of the Iraqi invasion of Kuwait, the remaining oil producers, both within and outside OPEC, were able to increase supply and hence exert downward pressure on price. In the past twenty years, the price of oil has generally remained below 30 dollars a barrel, and on occasion has fallen below 10 dollars. This enabled consumers to move energy conservation lower down both domestic and international agendas. With the changes in the Arab–Israeli conflict, the likelihood of a politically motivated oil boycott lessened, as did its potential potency in the face of increases in non-Arab oil production. Energy policy still remained in the sphere of high politics, in view of its importance to the economy, but the agenda widened beyond oil. However, the dream of a nuclear future was soon tarnished. In 1986 more than ten times as much nuclear electricity was produced as in 1971,[63] but in the same year there was the second of two major accidents that raised public concern about the nuclear industry. In 1979 there had been an accident at Three Mile Island nuclear power station in the United States, and in 1986 came the Chernobyl disaster in the Soviet Union when contamination from the nuclear plant spread over much of Europe, including the United Kingdom. The following year, following a referendum, Italy introduced a moratorium on all nuclear energy – a symbol of declining faith in this alternative source of energy.[64]

After 1981, and more so after 1983, there was a shift in national oil policies, reflecting the changes in economic policy towards privatization, deregulation and a reliance on market forces. The removal of oil price controls in the United States meant higher prices, which triggered a drop in demand. On the other hand, the Reagan Administration was less willing to take an interventionist approach to oil policy. While it continued to support the Strategic Petroleum Reserve, it also reduced its cooperation with both domestic (Department of Energy) and international (IEA) efforts to expand emergency provision, and gave only limited support to energy conservation measures, including a proposed increase in gasoline taxes. The United States continued to consume energy at roughly twice the rate of other major industrial countries in Western Europe. In 1981, with a daily consumption of 15.6 million barrels, the United States consumed almost as much oil as Western Europe (12.8 mbd) and Japan (4.7 mbd) combined (Table 4.3). The United Kingdom changed from being a net importer of energy to being effectively self-sufficient in energy. Under the influence of the Thatcher Government, the energy sector was largely privatized and the government's main concern was to ensure a free market insofar as possible. It continued to oppose any attempts by the European Community to develop an energy policy of its own that might supersede the British right to control its own energy.

During the decade from 1985 to 1995 the introduction of the internal market and deregulation were the main factors driving European Community energy policy, along with building links with Eastern and Central Europe, particularly in terms of natural gas. It had, of course, to deal with very different national approaches to energy issues, with the British Government in favour of a *laissez faire* approach, unlike France which retained its commitment to state intervention. Attempts by the Commission to strengthen its position – for example, its 1990 proposals that it should control an emergency 60-day oil reserve and take sole responsibility for determining its use, and that it should apply for membership of the IEA with the right to vote in place of the member states on specific issues – were rejected by the members.[65] Despite the demise of both oil crises, energy policy still remained central to national interest.

Table 4.3 Oil consumption by selected areas, 1979–1982 (mbd)

Year	1979	1980	1981	1982
USA	17.91	16.46	15.55	14.77
West Europe	14.68	13.63	12.78	12.21
Japan	5.49	4.94	4.70	4.40

Source: Adapted from *BP Statistical Review of World Energy 2001*. BP Plc.

Table 4.4   World petroleum consumption, 1983–1993 (selected years – mbd)

Year	1983	1985	1986	1988	1990	1991	1992	1993
World, total	58.4	60.10	61.76	64.83	66.16	66.71	66.57	66.72
U.S.	15.23	15.73	16.28	17.28	16.99	16.71	17.03	17.24
West Europe	12.38	12.39	12.79	13.08	13.25	13.86	13.81	13.80
Japan	4.40	4.38	4.44	4.75	5.14	5.28	5.45	5.38

Source: Adapted from US Bureau of the Census, *Statistical Abstract of the United States: 1995* (115th edn). Bernan Press, Washington, DC, 1995, Table 957, p. 599.

Left to the market, oil consumption continued to grow, if not at the levels seen prior to 1973 (see Table 4.4). The United States, in particular, became increasingly dependent upon imports, as its domestic production again turned downward (Table 4.5). The direct link between rates of growth in the economy, on the one hand, and in energy usage on the other, has been eroded. Improved technology, greater energy efficiency and a continued emphasis on conservation, at least in some consuming countries, have been successful in achieving that. However, with the lower oil prices prevailing since 1983, conservation tends to be seen as part of the environmental agenda, rather than as an economic imperative. Signs of a tighter oil market, such as appeared in September 2000, once again led to concerns about consumer vulnerability, and demands that OPEC should increase its production to stabilize prices.

Were the two oil crises a turning point for the consumers? They certainly succeeded in raising awareness of the consumers' vulnerability and dependence upon imported petroleum. Supplies were diversified

Table 4.5   United States production and imports, 1985–1994 (mbd)

Year	1985	1986	1987	1988	1989	1990	1991	1992	1993	1994
Production	9.0	8.7	8.4	8.1	7.6	7.4	7.4	7.1	6.8	6.6
Crude oil imports	3.2	4.2	4.7	5.1	5.8	5.9	5.8	6.1	6.8	7.0
Total imports	5.0	6.2	6.7	7.4	8.1	8.0	7.6	7.9	8.6	8.9

Source: Adapted from US Bureau of the Census, *Statistical Abstract of the United States: 1995* (115th edn). Bernan Press, Washington, DC, Table 955, p. 598.

away from the previous heavy reliance on the Middle East: however, the continued dominance of that region over future reserves, as opposed to current production, suggests that this position might not continue. Thus, the other goals – conservation and developing alternative sources of energy – may well be more significant in the future. The industrialized states (though not the developing countries) have managed to break the tight link between rates of economic growth and increases in energy usage, but consumption levels have continued to rise, and while the comparative importance of petroleum in electricity generation has declined, the massive transportation network at the heart of the global economy still relies upon aviation fuel, gasoline and diesel.

Notes

1. Thomas O. Enders, 'OPEC and the Industrial Countries: The Next Ten Years', *Foreign Affairs* 53 (1974–5), pp. 625–37, esp. p. 625.
2. Romano Prodi and Alberto Clo, 'Europe', in Vernon (ed.) *The Oil Crisis*, Table 1, p. 92.
3. Bromley, *American Hegemony*, p. 166.
4. Reasons for the import quotas are discussed in Richard H.K. Vietor, *Energy Policy in America since 1945: A Study of Business–Government Relations*. Cambridge University Press, Cambridge, 1984, pp. 91–100.
5. James W. McKie, 'The United States', in Vernon (ed.) *The Oil Crisis*, pp. 73–90, esp. pp. 74–7.
6. Vietor, *Energy Policy*, pp. 140–3.
7. Henry Kissinger, *White House Years*. Weidenfeld and Nicolson, London, 1979, p. 859.
8. Rabe, *The Road to OPEC*, pp. 18–19.
9. James A. Akins, 'The Oil Crisis: This Time the Wolf is Here', *Foreign Affairs* 51 (1973), pp. 462–90.
10. Seymour, *OPEC*, pp. 110–12.
11. Statement by Under Secretary of State Irwin to the OECD meeting, 26 May 1972, *American Foreign Relations: A Documentary Record: 1972*. New York, 1976, pp. 519–21.
12. European Community, *Official Journal*, No. 4, 308/14, 23 December 1968. Luxembourg, Office for Official Publications of the European Community, 1968.
13. Louis Turner, 'The Politics of the Energy Crisis', *International Affairs* 50 (1974), pp. 404–15, esp. p. 405.
14. Turner, 'Politics', p. 406.
15. Seymour, *OPEC*, pp 112-13.
16. Dermot Gately, 'Do Oil Markets Work? Is OPEC Dead?', *Annual Review of Energy* 14 (1989), pp. 95–116, esp. p. 102.
17. Lieber, *The Oil Decade*, p. 2.
18. Robert O. Keohane, 'The International Energy Agency: State Influence and

Transgovernmental Politics', *International Organization* 32 (1978), pp. 929–51, esp. pp. 931–2.

19. Edward Heath, *The Course of My Life: My Autobiography*. Hodder & Stoughton, London, 1998, p. 503.

20. Dominique Marisi, 'Europe and the Middle East', pp. 18–32, in Steven L. Spiegel (ed.) *The Middle East and the Western Alliance*. George Allen & Unwin, London, 1982, p. 19.

21. Harrison, *Reluctant Ally*, p. 174.

22. G. John Ikenberry, 'The Irony of State Strength: Comparative Responses to the Oil Shocks in the 1970s', *International Organization* 40 (1986), pp. 105–37, esp. pp. 124–6.

23. Lieber, *The Oil Decade*, p. 82.

24. Janne Haaland Matlary, *Energy Policy in the European Union*, Macmillan, London, 1997, pp. 36-7.

25. Harrison, *Reluctant Ally*, pp. 185–201.

26. Prodi and Clo, 'Europe', in Vernon (ed.), *The Oil Crisis*, pp. 91–111, esp. p. 98.

27. Harrison, *Reluctant Ally*, pp. 175–6.

28. Stephen J. Artner, 'The Middle East: A Chance for Europe', *International Affairs* 56 (1980), pp 420–42, esp. pp. 430–1.

29. Marisi, 'Europe and the Middle East', pp. 26–7.

30. Yoshi Tsurumi, 'Japan', in Vernon (ed.), *The Oil Crisis*, pp 113–27, esp. p. 113

31. Hiroaki Fukami, 'The Japanese Economy and Oil Importation', in R.W. Ferrier and A. Fursenko (eds), *Oil in the World Economy*. Routledge, London, 1989, pp. 116–28, esp. pp. 117, 121 and 127.

32. Masahiro Sasagawa, 'Japan and the Middle East', in Spiegel (ed)., *The Middle East and the Western Alliance*, pp. 33–46, esp. p. 36.

33. Bromley, *American Hegemony*, pp. 184–5.

34. Sasagawa, 'Japan and the Middle East', p. 39.

35. McKie, 'The United States', p. 85.

36. Kissinger, *Years of Upheaval*, p. 537.

37. Peter Mangold, *Superpower Intervention in the Middle East*. Croom Helm, London, 1978, pp. 72–6.

38. Gerald Ford, Address to the 29th Session of the General Assembly of the UN, 18 September 1974, *Public Papers of the Presidents of the United States: Gerald Ford, 1974*, US Government Printing Office, Washington, DC, 1975.

39. Richard Nixon, Address to the Nation Policies to deal with the Energy Shortage, 7 November 1973, *Public Papers of the Presidents of the United States: Richard Nixon, 1973*. US Government Printing Office, Washington, DC, 1974, pp. 916–22.

40. Mason Willrich, 'Energy Independence for America', *International Affairs* 52 (1976), pp. 53–66, esp. p. 53.

41. Gerald Ford, Address to the Nation on Energy and Economic Programs, 13 January 1975, *Public Papers of the Presidents of the United States: Gerald Ford, 1975*. US Government Printing Office, Washington, DC, 1977, pp. 30–5.

42. Vietor, *Energy Policy*, p. 258.

43. Jimmy Carter, Address to the Nation on the Energy Problem, 18 April 1977, *Public Papers of the Presidents of the United States: Jimmy Carter, 1977*. US Government Printing Office, Washington, DC, 1978, pp. 656–62. Actual quotations from p. 656.

44. Willrich, 'Energy Independence', pp. 54–5.

45. Prodi and Clo, 'Europe', p. 101.

46. This is discussed in more detail in Fiona Venn, 'International Co-operation versus National Self-Interest: The United States and Europe during the 1973–4 Oil Crisis', in Kathleen Burk and Melvyn Stokes (eds), *The United States and the European Alliance since 1945*. Berg, Oxford, 1999.

47. Henry Kissinger, 'The Year of Europe' speech 23 April 1973, *American Foreign Relations 1973: A Documentary Record*. New York, 1976, pp. 181–9.
48. Heath, *Autobiography*, pp. 492–3.
49. Lieber, *The Oil Decade*, p. 59.
50. Bromley, *American Hegemony*, p. 139.
51. Ulf Lantzke, 'The OECD and Its international Energy Agency', in Vernon (ed.), *The Oil Crisis*, pp. 217–27, esp. pp. 218–20.
52. Henry Kissinger, Pilgrims Dinner speech, 12 December 1973, *American Foreign Relations 1973*, pp. 566–75.
53. Henri Simonet, 'Energy and the Future of Europe', *Foreign Affairs* 53 (1974–5), pp. 450–63.
54. Keohane, 'International Energy Agency', pp. 934–7.
55. Skeet, *Opec*, pp. 124–5.
56. United States Congress, Joint Economic Committee, Subcommittee on Energy, *Multinational Oil Companies and OPEC: Implications for U.S. Policy*. US Government Printing Office, Washington, DC, 1977, p. 2.
57. Lieber, *Oil Decade*, p. 105.
58. See figures in Lieber, *Oil Decade*, Table 2.3, p. 23.
59. Gately, 'Is OPEC Dead?', pp. 98–9.
60. Lieber, *Oil Decade*, pp. 48–58.
61. Arthur Jay Klinghoffer, *The Soviet Union and International Oil Politics*. Columbia University Press, New York, 1977, pp. 223–5.
62. British Petroleum, *Statistical Review of the World Oil Industry 1986*. British Petroleum, London, 1986, p. 1.
63. BP, *Statistical Review 1986*, p. 1.
64. Matlary, *Energy Policy*, p. 39.
65. Matlary, *Energy Policy*, pp. 58–9.

5

A TURNING POINT FOR
THE WORLD ECONOMY?

During the period from 1950 until the early 1970s the world economy, and particularly the individual economies of the industrialized nations within it, enjoyed a sustained period of growth. The real GDP of the top sixteen OECD countries rose at an average annual rate of 4.8 per cent while the rate of growth of productivity rose by a similar amount, of around 4.5 per cent on average.[1] However, in the period since 1970 there have been a number of downturns in the world economy, in 1974–5, in 1980–2, and again at the end of the 1980s and beginning of the 1990s. At least two of these downturns coincided with sudden dramatic increases in oil prices, and caused speculation as to the level of correlation between the two phenomena. The economic problems were resented the more because the period from 1950 until around 1973 was one of economic growth and affluence, at least for the main industrialized nations of the West. Their populations enjoyed increasing affluence, improved standards of living and a vastly changed lifestyle to incorporate the products of a mass production economy. Western Europe enjoyed many of the developments which had characterized the United States in the 1920s, notably the move to a mass–production/mass–consumption economy based upon the premise that the individual worker was also increasingly the consumer of the goods which he or she produced. Thus, relatively high wages enabled the mass production of popular consumer products, particularly those developed as a consequence of the rapid advances in technology and premised upon the use of cheap energy. Lifestyles altered out of all recognition, with improved education, increased opportunities for those lower down the social scale, and a greater emphasis upon the service sector of the economy. The contrast between the standard of living in most Western countries in the 1950s and 1960s with that prevailing in the interwar period was considerable.

The postwar boom

Certain characteristics were common to many Western economies. First, after the depression of the 1930s, followed by six years of total war, government management of the economy, with the goal of full employment, if necessary achieved by public spending, was very common. This took a number of different forms, however. Many governments were involved in increased government spending on welfare provision, including education and in some cases medical care. Investment in infrastructure, particularly in the period of reconstruction after 1945, both created employment and improved economic activity. In addition, as superpower conflict escalated into Cold War, many governments in First, Second and Third Worlds spent heavily on armaments.

Active government intervention did not just extend to domestic economies. Driven by the United States, the world's strongest economic and political power, there were a number of explicit agreements and institutions intended to regulate the world economy through a more interventionist policy. The series of multilateral agreements signed at the Bretton Woods conference of 1944 were intended to prevent the damaging economic nationalism which had been so prevalent during the 1930s and had effectively paralysed the world economy. The agreements included an arrangement for the free convertibility of currencies, relying not only upon gold, but also reserve currencies, of which by far the most significant was the American dollar, whose value was fixed at 35 dollars per ounce of gold. In addition, the International Monetary Fund (IMF) was created to provide assistance to countries facing temporary difficulties with their currency convertibility or balance of payments. Hence, temporary difficulties experienced by one member of the international economy would not have so devastating an impact upon the world. The International Bank for Reconstruction and Development (popularly known as the World Bank) provided assistance, including funds and advice or encouragement to assist development projects in the Third World. In addition, the General Agreement on Tariffs and Trade, signed in 1947, sought to remove barriers to free trade among the world's nations. These various measures prompted an increase in the volume of trade: between 1950 and 1973, world trade increased at roughly twice the rate of growth in output, at an average of nearly 10 per cent increase per year in trade.[2]

146

It also encouraged a shift towards global markets, with the consolidation of an integrated world trade system, enhanced by continuing improvements in worldwide transport and communications.

The Bretton Woods system did not come into effect overnight: many governments were concerned at too rapid a transition to free convertibility, and American estimates of the amounts needed to support the IMF and the World Bank proved to be too low. However, the Cold War and fears of a future downturn in the world economy with the removal of war expenditure, prompted greater American aid to the two main defeated belligerents of Japan and West Germany and also, through the Marshall Plan of 1948, to Western Europe as a whole. The task of reconstructing war-torn Europe proceeded apace, and so too did progress towards a new liberal economic world order, which was fully in place by the mid-1950s, with free convertibility of all major currencies achieved by 1959.[3]

The world economy for the thirty years after the end of the Second World War was, therefore, well managed, organized and, to a great extent, dependent upon the willingness and ability of the United States to act as the international organizer and bank manager. This was a role that it was well equipped to fill: in 1945 the United States produced something like 50 per cent of the world's goods.[4] Although to some extent this was a product of unusual war conditions, in 1950 the United States still accounted for half of the gross world product. The United States Government pursued a postwar economic foreign policy aimed at expanding trade openness and increasing monetary stability, and was prepared to use its resources to provide favourable international conditions, not only for itself but for other nations as well. It sought to win support for its international economic policies from other governments by a consensual approach, summed up by Charles Maier as 'the politics of productivity'; in other words, policies based upon an emphasis on international cooperation in pursuit of economic growth, which in turn promoted internal political stability.[5] This long period of prosperity was enhanced by the rapid pace of technological innovation and development, and in particular rapid improvements in communications and electronics.

The scale and longevity of the postwar boom is important in highlighting the contrast with economic recession in the 1970s. Much of the enhanced consumption in the developed world was due to the cheap energy prices prevailing throughout the period; that in turn was as a consequence of the switch from coal to very cheap oil, first from the Middle East and then from North Africa. The net result was a phenomenal increase in the consumption of petroleum, which doubled every decade. Cheap energy underpinned the era of mass production of commodities, hitherto regarded as luxuries, at a price that the everyday consumer could afford. This required lower production costs, to which cheap petroleum contributed, both in terms of the energy used in a more mechanized production process and the transportation of raw materials and finished products. The spreading globalization of the world economy, with regional specialization based on comparative advantage and a worldwide division of labour, was only possible because of far cheaper and more effective transportation networks. Moreover, many of the new commodities relied on cheap electricity – refrigerators, vacuum cleaners, televisions, ovens, irons, freezers, microwaves, computers. These labour-saving devices played a significant role in the development of new lifestyles, with an increase in leisure time and activities. The new forms of leisure, such as cinema and television, themselves relied upon plentiful energy. One very important element in these transformed lifestyles was the increased use of the private car, a major consumer of petroleum. However, the cost was increased reliance upon energy, and in particular on imported energy. Europe's dependence on energy imports grew from 33 per cent of total requirements in 1960 to 65 per cent in 1972.

For many countries, the postwar boom was accompanied by active management of the economy, in accordance with Keynesian principles, aimed at full employment. Internationally the world economy was encouraged to remain stable through international agreement and American management, and the dollar provided an important part of the postwar economic order. As long as the value was firmly pegged to gold, dollars were treated as though they were gold for the purposes of international monetary exchange and in central reserves built up by foreign governments. Quite literally, the dollar was 'as good as gold'. As governments or central banks sought to manage their currencies' exchange rates, they often sold their own currency for dollars, or exchanged dollars for their own currency. As the dollar was also used by many international companies and banks for their working balances, its centrality to the world economy was beyond doubt. Moreover, unlike gold, dollars held as reserves or working balances could be invested on the capital market and earn interest.[6] In addition, there was a massive Eurodollar market, particularly in the 1960s and 1970s, consisting of dollar deposits held in banks outside the United States, and this increased the availability of reserves in the international economy.

This placed the United States in a privileged position: it could pay its overseas debts with what were, in effect, dollar IOUs. As Maier points out, 'in effect, the United States taxed its allies for part of the costs of the Indochina War ... by trying to insist upon the unaltered reserve status of an eroding dollar'.[7] As a consequence, the American Government did not need to address problems with its balance of payments but could continue to pursue economic expansionary policies, including growing imports; however, this increased world reserves by more than was desirable, encouraging inflation. As the American balance of payments increasingly swung into deficit, this meant that the system rested, to a great extent, upon foreign confidence in the dollar. As the United States attempted to undertake ambitious foreign and domestic policies without asking its citizens to pay the full price in taxation, more dollars entered the international monetary system to such an extent that during the three years from the end of 1969 to the end of 1972 world monetary reserves doubled from 79 billion dollars to 159 billion.[8]

Problems within the world economy before 1973

The use of the date '1973' as signalling the beginning of the world economic downturn implies that the Western economies were enjoying affluence until the October energy crisis raised the price of crude oil severalfold and drove the world economy into recession. This is somewhat similar to the argument that the Wall Street Crash was responsible for the Great Depression of the 1930s. Although 1973 is often taken as the break point between prosperity and recession, in some ways it has close parallels with 1929, a year in which historians can point to a dramatic event which had undoubtedly negative economic consequences – a year which has been used ever since to denote the onset of 'hard times'. However, in both the United States and the world economy there were indications before 1929 of underlying structural problems as well as more immediate difficulties. The same is true of 1973. While the rapid and considerable increase in oil prices undoubtedly had an adverse effect upon the world economy, at the same time the rise in oil prices was as a result, as well as a cause of the problems in the world economy, which was already showing signs of difficulty long before the 1973 oil crisis.

Although the United States had enjoyed undoubted prosperity in the years since the Second World War, its role as leader of the world imposed strains upon it. Thus, for example, it provided financial and military aid on a vast scale throughout the world, it had a massive global military presence from the late 1940s onwards, and its currency acted as the reserve stabilizing factor in the international monetary system. As the world economy expanded, so too did the need for reserves to underpin the growth. Availability of gold could not keep pace. In 1956 gold accounted for about two-thirds of the international reserves; by 1973 it covered under a quarter of the reserves, with two-thirds now provided through foreign exchange.[9] For the United States, many of these apparent liabilities were, if anything, assets. Much of the aid given to other countries was spent on American goods and food, either as a requirement of the aid or quite simply because of the domination of the world economy by the United States. Government spending on defence and the close links between the defence establishment and the military was an important factor in the stability and prosperity of the United States economy, and the centrality of the dollar in international finance gave the financial sector in the United States a vast amount of power.

However, by the late 1960s the cracks were beginning to show in the apparently imposing edifice. 'By 1967 the combination of American stagnation and West European dynamism (with the exception of the United Kingdom) had begun to place intolerable strains on the system.'[10] Both the main reserve currencies, sterling and, of much greater significance, the American dollar, were subject to internal pressures. The United Kingdom had experienced a series of economic and financial crises since the end of the Second World War. In November 1967 a particularly severe sterling crisis led to its devaluation from 2.80 dollars to 2.40 dollars, thus shaking confidence in its role as a reserve currency. As a consequence, in July 1968 the Basle Agreement guaranteed holders of sterling balances the dollar value of their holdings, and in the same year the ten wealthiest members of the IMF set up a new type of monetary reserve to supplement existing reserves of gold and reserve currencies, in the form of Special Drawing Rights, which provided not only a supplementary reserve but also a supplementary line of credit. This was to try to provide sufficient reserves to support expanding trade and international capital flows.

However, sterling was not the only reserve currency to experience problems. In the late 1960s, the United States economy also began to run into difficulties. Although the United States continued to be the strongest industrial economy, by 1970 the extent of its domination was now being challenged by rivals, particularly in the manufacturing sphere. It was also increasingly reliant on imports to meet at least some of the domestic demand for a number of crucial raw materials, including of course petroleum.[11] In 1971 the United States ran a trade deficit for the first time in the twentieth century. Moreover, the United States Government had been engaged for a number of years in a vastly expensive, destructive and unpopular war in Vietnam. At the same time as engaging in war, President Lyndon Johnson's Administration (1963–1968) embarked on a massive reform programme, known as the Great Society. Therefore, the United States Government was trying to pursue policies of both guns and butter. However, it sought to do so without increasing taxes, relying instead upon budget deficits, which led to rising inflation.[12] The Johnson Administration did seek to address the problem of the balance of payments deficit, through a policy of discouraging excessive American overseas investment (which led to an outflow of dollars) while encouraging exports. However, Congress was resistant to proposals for tax increases. This attempt to follow a number of apparently irreconcilable policies could not easily be accomplished within the constraints of a fixed exchange rate for the dollar, because it required a large increase in the money supply.

The United States still remained the world's most powerful economy: in the early 1970s it produced about a third of all the world's goods and services, and was the world's largest trading nation with exports in 1970 totalling 27.5 billion dollars (by 1977 they had climbed to 121.2 billion). The United States was also an important exporter of capital – in 1970 American direct investments abroad represented around half of the world's total of direct foreign investments, standing at 75.5 billion dollars, and this sum virtually doubled within the next seven years,[13] although some of this increase was due to inflation. However, the position of the dollar was less solid. By August 1971 the United States gold reserves could cover less than a third of American gold-convertible liabilities to foreign central banks, and less than a fifth of total liquid liabilities to foreigners, so on 15 August 1971 President Nixon temporarily suspended dollar convertibility and imposed a 10 per cent import surcharge. His intention was to force other currencies to revalue against the dollar and by the Smithsonian Agreement of December 1971 the ten leading trading nations fixed new exchange rates between the major currencies; other currencies were revalued, with a 10 per cent devaluation in the hitherto sacrosanct value of the dollar. Following this, the import surcharge was lifted, and the dollar was made convertible to gold at the new price. However, without action to tackle the underlying problems within the American economy, even these newly negotiated rates were unsustainable. In 1973 the US dollar was again devalued, and by the summer of that year – in other words, well before the oil price was first massively increased in October 1973 – most of the major currencies had abandoned the fixed rates and were floating in value, albeit with some central bank intervention to avoid undue fluctuations. Even so, the effect was increased volatility: during June and July 1973 some European currencies appreciated against the dollar, occasionally at rates of 4 per cent a day.[14]

The immediate response was inflation, which grew at a considerable rate, reaching around 7 to 8 per cent per annum by 1972. Taken together with the uncertainty around the value of the dollar, this had a profoundly destabilizing impact on the world economy. Whereas world import and export prices had risen by less than 1 per cent per annum in the 1960s, from 1970 to 1972 they increased by more than 6 per cent per year, and that rate was further exceeded in the period leading up to the oil price hike.[15] These developments, of course, not only preceded the oil price increase of 1973, they contributed to it. First, since oil was priced in dollars, there was a fall in the revenue received by the host governments, in real terms. Second, the increase in oil posted prices agreed at Teheran and Tripoli, which had in any event presupposed a stable dollar, had allowed for inflation of less than 3 per cent per annum, which was considerably exceeded. In real terms, therefore, the price per barrel received by host governments for their petroleum was falling, while the price of goods they bought from industrialized countries was rising. Since most major oil producers imported the bulk of their manufactured goods, the consequences were profound. Only a couple of years after the Teheran and Tripoli meetings had set out to provide an agreement that would last for several years, its basis was undermined, while host governments argued that further price increases were required, both to compensate for inflation and also to maintain the real value of a commodity priced in dollars.

Meanwhile, the world economy was becoming much more complex. The globalization of the world economy, which had been proceeding apace since the late nineteenth century, entered a new phase, qualitatively different from previous systems. One significant factor in the integration of the world economy was the rapid escalation in the size and power of the multinational firm. The multinational corporation was a company with interests in many countries, whose headquarters might happen to be in one country (usually the United States) rather than another, but whose interests were so vast that they were beyond the control of any one government. If their interests were threatened, it was feasible for the company to move to another jurisdiction, taking with them the employment, capital and prestige that they brought to their parent domicile. The transnational corporation, even more than the multinational corporation, transcended national boundaries, and might well divide even its headquarter operations among a number of different countries. As with the oil companies, in the late 1960s there was a critical literature on the role of the multinational companies. Some of the multinationals had annual turnovers in excess of the annual GNP of the developing countries in which they operated, and while they were a major factor in the transmission of new technologies to LDCs, they were also perceived as the symbol, and even the agent, of American political and economic dominance.[16]

Meanwhile, in part assisted by the development of the multinational corporation, the international division of labour continued apace. As the improvement of technology meant that more and more industry was either requiring only limited skill, or consisted of skills that were easily learnt, it became possible, particularly with the development of the microchip industry and small components, to produce components in several different locations, and assemble them elsewhere as well. This development not only enhanced the international division of labour, but threatened the manufacturing base of traditional industrialized countries, as firms often drew upon the cheap labour of developing countries, such as Japan initially and then other Pacific Rim countries. This contributed to the loss of manufacturing jobs in developed nations and led, even before the 1973 crisis, to calls for protectionism particularly in sectors of the United States economy.[17] Moreover, technological innovations meant that increasingly the same tasks could be accomplished with far less human input, which again contributed to the loss of employment. Communications worldwide became so efficient that trade, supply patterns (stock levels) and above all financial dealings could move across the globe with speed, while currencies could be exchanged very rapidly. Another important factor in the growing complexity of the international economy was the development of a form of currency which was beyond the control of any government – the Eurodollar and Eurocurrency markets. In 1964 the Eurocurrency account amounted to 14 billion dollars, by 1973 it was 170 billion dollars and by 1978, with the added investment of petrodollars, it had reached nearly 500 billion dollars. All these factors combined essentially placed the world's economy beyond any single government's control.

Impact of the 1973 oil crisis

Thus, a number of factors were already destabilizing the world economy by the time of the 1973 crisis and, as we have seen, those forces
were, in part at least, responsible for the decision by OPEC producers
to press for higher prices. However, even if there was already an economic downturn taking place before 1973, the recession which gripped
many of the world's economies in 1974–5 was the most severe since
the end of the Second World War. It is therefore important to consider
the extent to which the oil price crisis in 1973 affected the world economy. Clearly the quadrupling of the price of oil in a matter of a few
months was bound to have an adverse effect on individual national
economies already suffering from the onset of recession, as well as on
the world economy as a whole, not least because demand for oil, at least
in the short term, is fairly inelastic. It certainly led to balance of payments deficits in oil-poor LDCs in particular. Everything cost more to
transport; energy prices rose steeply, particularly as in a number of
countries there were political problems in the coal industry, while there
was a rising tide of protest against the nuclear industry. The flow of
funds turned dramatically towards the oil states, several of which had
only limited ability to absorb this extra funding domestically.
Moreover, traditional patterns of economic management could not
easily deal with the unusual combination of inflation, brought about by
the very rapid increase in energy prices coupled with underlying inflationary tendencies on the one hand, and recession on the other, as
unemployment increased rapidly. In addition, the already floating
exchange rates, coupled with speculation about the likely destination of
surplus petrodollars, led to increased volatility in currency values with
unpredictable and often sharp movements in a currency's value. The
sheer unpredictability of economic changes made planning and coordinated action difficult to undertake. Individual economies had to adjust
to the new situation by reducing demand: in the United Kingdom, for
example, the average annual bank rate, which in 1972 had been a little
over 6 per cent, rose to just over 10 per cent in 1973, and remained
between 10 and 12 per cent throughout 1973–6.[18] Many states which
customarily ran a balance of trade surplus were forced into deficit;
the United States, which had run a trade deficit for the first time in
1971, had, by 1977, experienced a deficit of 26.5 billion dollars.[19] The
additional inflation introduced into the system by the massive increase

in oil prices reinforced the tendency on the part of Western governments to abandon Keynesian economics, and in particular its emphasis
on the goals of economic growth and full employment, both managed
by the governments, towards a greater concern with the rate and
impact of inflation.

There has been considerable discussion as to the precise impact of
the oil crisis upon the world economy. By December 1973 the average annual rate of inflation for industrial goods was over 7 per cent,
and that had increased to 13 per cent by December 1974.[20] Thomas
Enders, who was American Under Secretary of State during the crisis,
suggests that the sharp jump in oil prices accounted for about a quarter of the average inflation rate of around 14 per cent experienced in
industrialized countries, as well as causing industrial dislocation and
subsequent unemployment.[21] Ian Seymour, on the other hand, is of
the opinion that only 2 of the 14 per cent can be attributed to the
increased price of petroleum.[22] Thomas Willett also argued that while
oil prices and exchange rate changes clearly contributed to the
increased rates of inflation, it was essentially of domestic origin as far as
the United States was concerned.[23] There had, after all, been unprece-
dented growth in the world economy in the period 1971–3, which
saw a 17 per cent increase in world production. One consequence was
that in the years 1972–4 there was a rapid increase in the price of not
only petroleum but other key commodities as well, although after 1974
those prices began to drop, indeed followed shortly thereafter by a
decline in the real price of oil. Additional costs were not offset with
productivity gains while, in an era of inflation, pressure for improved
wages to meet or surpass price increases continued in many developed
countries.

On the whole, the impact of the oil price increase was a mixed one.
Foreman-Peck argues that the floating exchange rates actually helped
the major economies to cope with the impact of the oil price increase
and the worsening of the existing economic recession during 1974.
However, the subsequent rise in the rate of inflation encouraged the
main industrial economies to follow deflationary policies, which in turn
exacerbated unemployment.[24] In addition, the OECD combined current account balance of payments surplus of 3 billion dollars in 1973
had turned into a deficit of 35 billion dollars by 1974.[25] The OECD
also saw a drop in what had hitherto been a steady record of economic
growth; the average growth rate was just over 5 per cent in the period
1970–3, but this dropped to only 1.5 per cent between 1974 and 1976,
and some countries even registered a negative growth rate.[26]

It was not just the actual consequences of the oil price increase, on top of the existing problems within the world economy, which affected economic policies however. More difficult to quantify, but significant nonetheless, was the psychological impact of the suddenness and unpredictability of the oil price increase, and the uncertainty it engendered. After nearly three decades of orderly and stable economic growth, the price hike reinforced the changed economic conditions and the collapse of the Bretton Woods system. Moreover, at a time when the United States no longer seemed in a position to exercise world economic leadership, the sudden accretion of wealth to a small number of largely developing countries outside the OECD raised questions about how the world economy was to be managed – if at all – in the future. Articles in the contemporary press were preoccupied with the assumed adverse effects of the shift in economic and financial power to the inexperienced OPEC countries. Many of the concerns voiced at the time about the impact of the oil price increase related to the rapid alteration in the flow of funds, away from the oil consumers to the oil exporters, and the consequences this might have for the stability of the world economy. A new term was coined for these funds: petrodollars. The income that Saudi Arabia received from its oil industry rose from just over 2 billion dollars in 1970 to over 30 billion in 1976. While some of this was as a consequence of increased production, which roughly doubled over the period, most of the increase came as a consequence of the price rise.[27] Taken together, the oil-exporting countries saw a dramatic surge in their foreign exchange surplus, from 6 billion dollars in 1973 to 60 billion in 1974 and 107 billion in 1980.[28] Moreover, as a consequence of budget surpluses, the countries of OPEC built up large foreign assets. By the end of 1978, Saudi Arabia's foreign assets amounted to 60 billion dollars, and in Venezuela the national budget went from 14 billion bolivas in 1973 to 42 billion bolivas in 1974.[29]

Given that, with few exceptions, the recipients of the so-called 'petrodollars' were developing countries with little existing industry, there was considerable concern about the abilities of their economies to absorb the vastly increased oil revenues, and also about the strategies likely to be adopted by their governments, when investing surplus funds that could not be absorbed by their domestic economies.[30] However, this phenomenon did not have as negative an impact as was predicted at the time. Fortunately for the West, many leading oil-producing states had relatively small populations and lacked the necessary resources, labour and skill to develop alternative economic activities. Their funds were therefore in many cases funnelled back into the West, in payment for goods, most of which had to be imported, for services, which the advanced West was in the best position to provide, or through investment – in the very Western institutions which many assumed would be shaken to the core by the impact of the 1973–4 oil crisis, such as the IMF (which set up a special oil fund, mainly contributed by the oil-rich states, to help countries facing particularly severe balance of payments problems as a result of greater oil import bills) or the Eurocurrency markets. Some of the petrodollars were indeed lent to the industrial countries, either directly or through the agency of international institutions such as the International Monetary Fund.[31] The foreign assets of the Gulf states of OPEC, i.e. Iran, Iraq, Kuwait, the UAE, Saudi Arabia and Qatar, increased from seven billion dollars in 1972 to 117 billion dollars in 1977, and these were mainly invested in the United States, European financial centres and offshore Eurocurrency markets.[32] In 1974, 20 per cent of the OPEC financial surplus was invested directly in the United States, another 13 per cent in the United Kingdom, and over 40 per cent in the Eurocurrency markets.[33] However, while this had definite advantages in a period of recession and reduced demand, it also worried the industrialized governments that, in any future use of the 'oil weapon', the Arab oil producers would be able to use their investments in the West to exercise power, for example, by threatening to withdraw all capital. In addition, during the mid-1970s there were considerable fears that OPEC investment in the Eurocurrency market would exacerbate liquidity problems as banks had to reconcile short-term deposits (from OPEC) with long- or medium-term borrowing, but those were relaxed as OPEC funds were placed in longer-term deposits.[34] Although that problem did not manifest itself then, in the 1980s major problems arose as developing nations found themselves unable to service debts undertaken in the 1970s. Instead, the ultimate losers from the recycling of petrodollars were the Third World countries, which ultimately found themselves unable to service the debts that they had incurred in the aftermath of the two oil price shocks.

The economic recession affected each individual economy differently, according to its position in the world economy, existing economic conditions, and the policies adopted by their respective governments in dealing with the problem. It is, of course, impossible to review the impact on each individual economy, even of the most prominent countries in the world economy. As with their energy policies, the major industrial nations followed different economic strategies.

The British economy, for example, had suffered not only from the general worldwide forces of inflation and currency instability, but also had to contend with the legacy of years of successive economic crises, the consequence of over-ambitious imperial and global foreign policy, economic policy swings as a consequence of the electoral cycle, and a determination to retain sterling as a major world currency. Rather than devalue the currency, the preferred policy was to depress demand at home, with an inevitable repressive effect on the domestic economy. As a consequence of continual economic problems, unemployment had been increasing steadily even before 1973, reaching the psychologically significant level of one million as early as January 1971: this had been accompanied by rising inflation. The Conservative Government of Edward Heath had attempted to address these problems through a stringent prices and incomes policy, but was frustrated by successful demands for substantial pay increases on the part of the National Union of Mineworkers (NUM). In 1973, therefore, the Heath Government was already facing serious economic problems; these were exacerbated when, in the aftermath of the oil price hike, the NUM again demanded a substantial wages increase, thus adding a coal crisis to the existing oil crisis. Heath's defeat in the General Election of February 1974, fought as a specific challenge to the miners' claim, hardly strengthened the hand of the incoming Labour Government under Harold Wilson. The economic impact of the dual energy crises was not only further upwards inflationary pressures but also a decrease in output and an increase in unemployment.

Initially the British were optimistic that the traditional role of London as the financial centre through which many of the leading oil producers invested their surpluses, together with the projected revenue from the energy resources of the North Sea, would aid recovery. However, despite these two important factors, the British economy continued to experience difficulties into the mid-1970s, with an inflation rate of nearly 25 per cent in 1975, well above that experienced by its main competitors. The policy of maintaining interest rates at a high level to attract foreign holdings of sterling had a depressing effect, and the attempts to address high inflation rates led to increased unemployment. During 1976 the price of sterling dropped, by an average of 20 per cent compared to a range of other currencies, and eventually Chancellor of the Exchequer Healey approached the IMF in September 1976 for assistance. Thus, although the oil price increase undoubtedly contributed to the British economic problems, not only were those clearly apparent well before 1973, but they continued into the mid-1970s, by which time the real price of oil was in decline, and the United Kingdom's main competitors were showing definite signs of economic recovery. In 1977 the British Government took a significant step by ending the role of sterling as a reserve currency.

Elsewhere in Europe, West Germany's economy remained strong despite the oil crisis, in part because the under-valuation of the Deutsche Mark enhanced its export competitiveness, in keeping with its traditional emphasis on a foreign economic policy directed towards export-led growth. By 1973 West Germany was one of the world's leading trading nations, second only to the United States. After the oil crisis, the West German economy was able to recover quickly; its exports actually tripled between 1971 and 1975,[35] with a particularly strong performance in trade with Eastern Europe. As discussed below, by the late 1970s the strength of the West Germany economy and currency, along with that of Japan, was perceived as a greater global economic problem than any remaining vestiges of the oil crisis. In economic policy, as with their approach to the American energy initiative, the French wished to stress their independence of the United States. Successive French governments had been unhappy with the dominant role of the dollar in the international currency markets, and had preferred, where possible, to keep French reserves in the form of gold. In response to the economic crisis, France continued to encourage state participation in the domestic economy, even in multinational industries such as oil, electronics and steel.[36] The direct state-to-state bilateral deals adopted by the French in the case of energy were also used to promote exports.

Outside Europe, the main industrial state to be affected by the economic consequences of the oil crisis and the subsequent price hike was Japan. Like West Germany, Japanese governments had pursued a policy aimed towards export growth, supported by an under-valued yen, while at the same time rigidly controlling entry into the Japanese domestic economy of foreign capital and firms. Economically it had been one of the major success stories of the postwar period, rising to become the third largest economy in the world by 1974, behind the United States and the Soviet Union. Its GNP rose over sixfold in the period 1952–74, better than any other major industrial democracy.[37] However, its strategic reliance on the United States tended to be reflected in cooperation with the latter's foreign economic and political policies. Nonetheless, as we have seen, it was prepared to challenge the United States in 1973, taking a marked pro-Arab line, a consequence of its extremely heavy reliance upon imports for many key raw materials, including of course petroleum. As with West Germany, Japan was again under considerable pressure to revalue the yen upwards, and reluctantly did so in December 1971, and again subsequently, so that in total it appreciated by about a third. However, intervention was still used to keep the value of the yen high, so Japan continued to be a successful exporter. Although it experienced a sharp downward turn in 1973, its economy was fast to recover, and by the mid-1970s the strength of the yen, along with that of the Deutsche Mark, was regarded by other countries as a cause of imbalances and pressures within the world economy.

In many respects, the importance of the American economy in the global economy was less significant in 1973 than it had been for much of the postwar period. While in 1965 its share of the world GNP was nearly 40 per cent, by 1975 it had fallen to 29 per cent and in 1986 reached 25 per cent. Its share of world merchandise exports also declined between 1973 and 1985.[38] However, the American economy remained the largest in the world, and thus economic trends in the United States clearly had a global impact. The United States was already experiencing high inflation before October 1973, and although increases in oil prices undoubtedly added to that, the federal government continued to control oil prices until 1981, masking some of their impact upon the American economy. I suggested earlier in the chapter that poor American economic management had already had an adverse effect on the world economy even before the 1973 oil price hike. During the 1970s, the United States continued to contribute to the economic difficulties experienced world wide. American Government indebtedness and American banks' liabilities to foreigners continued to grow, more than doubling in five years, from 144 billion dollars in 1972 to 363 billion by the end of 1977. The numbers of dollars held overseas also continued to grow, including Eurodollars which in 1977 accounted for 177 billion dollars, and by the end of 1979 had reached 428 billion.[39] This foreign demand for dollars continued despite the fact that in the new system of floating exchange rates which replaced Bretton Woods, a system managed by a combination of market forces and voluntary central bank intervention, the dollar declined to between half and a third of its previous value. The United States was thus able to export some of its inflation to the rest of the world.

During the 1970s, far from reducing oil consumption, oil imports into the United States, at the new high price, continued to rise. These imports, however, were increasingly paid for by deficit spending as the balance of payments deficits rose, which served only to increase the worldwide inflation; that, in turn, contributed to an increase in the world's money supply, much of which was lent to Third World countries, sowing the seeds for the later debt crisis. However, as American trade and current account balances swung from a substantial surplus in 1975 to a massive deficit in 1977, the impact was clearly to weaken the dollar. By 1978 the current account deficit of the United States, roughly equal to the entire OPEC surplus, was the major cause of imbalances in the world economy. Thus, as in the early 1970s, the United States preferred to export its inflation as far as possible, rather than take tough measures to curb it at home. It was able to do this, to some degree, because of the continued belief not just in the United States but elsewhere in the industrialized world, that the economic problems were the result of OPEC action, thus allowing the oil exporters to be used as scapegoats for the consequences of their own inadequacies and policy failures. Although the real price of petroleum in fact fell in the middle of the 1970s, and despite the apparently successful recycling of the petrodollars, Western industrial countries continued to blame higher oil prices, and by implication OPEC, for the continuing problems in the world economy.[40] Yet, as the price of oil remained fairly static in real terms, the high inflation of the 1970s eroded both its real value and also the wealth of the oil-rich states. The continuation of world economic problems, even after the price of oil stabilized in 1975–6, suggests that the oil crisis was only one factor in creating those problems. By the late 1970s, the strongest economies were seen as those of Japan and West Germany. Yet both of these were major oil importers. This clearly demonstrates that success in the world economy of the 1970s did not rely solely on access to oil revenue, but rather the accumulation of surpluses and the strength of trade and investment.

After 1971–3, the management of the world economy was more anarchic, as the main tenet of the Bretton Woods system – i.e. fixed exchange rates between currencies – was undermined by the collapse of the dollar. No one country had both the will and the economic strength to control it, as the United Kingdom had done before 1914, and the United States from the 1940s to 1971; the question therefore arose as to how decisions were to be taken regarding the future economic direction of the world economy. Existing organizations, such as the OECD, were too large for effective dialogue; there were, as will be discussed in Chapter 6, some discussions on the introduction of a New International Economic Order, which would involve developing countries as well, but these were never really successful. In 1973 there were concerns that the management of the world economy might need to be adjusted to take account of the major transformation in distribution of assets and income towards the oil-rich states. However, a lot of power was still vested in such institutions as the World Bank, the IMF – which baled out the British Government, among others, during the late 1970s – and the large international banks. Fears that the OPEC oil producers would come to dominate the world economy were swiftly put to rest. The oil-rich states, many of which were opposed on religious grounds to banking, did not set up rival institutions. Although a number of governments, including France, Italy, Japan and the United Kingdom, borrowed directly from OPEC, and OPEC funds were invested in the IMF which, in turn, helped to stabilize the industrialized West, it is the case that the most that was proposed by the West in terms of OPEC management of the world economy was that they should be given increased representation in existing institutions.

However, the need for greater coordination of economic policies was certainly recognized by the industrialized countries. In 1975, at the instigation of Chancellor Helmut Schmidt of West Germany and President Valéry Giscard d'Estaing of France, the first of a series of annual summits of the political leaders of the seven largest non-Communist industrialized countries[41] (the so-called Group of Seven) was held in Rambouillet, France. Although the first meeting was intended as an ad hoc response to the economic problems of the early 1970s, it rapidly developed into a regular gathering of heads of state and government along with foreign and finance ministers. The first summit, as was to be expected, was very much concerned with the energy problem, stressing in the end-of-summit declaration the linkage between economic growth and energy and declaring that 'we are determined to secure for our economies the energy sources needed for their growth'.[42] However, by the time of the second G-7 summit in June 1976 energy had already slipped down the agenda and the industrialized countries felt able to declare that economic recovery was 'well under way'.[43] By now, and also in the summit held nearly a year later in May 1977, the clear concerns were inflation and over-expansion, not energy prices. Indeed, at a time when the real price of oil was falling, the 1978 Bonn Summit was more negative in its reading of the world economy. The United States was encouraged to commit itself to expanding exports and reducing inflation, while on the other hand Japan and West Germany agreed to expand domestic demand and, in the case of Japan, to increase imports.

The world economy in the late 1970s

Throughout the 1970s it had been too easy to ascribe blame to the oil producers, but while clearly the massive increase in the price of oil had had a dampening impact on economic activity, there were also major problems of management within the United States and indeed the world economy. Moreover, given that the real price of oil actually began to fall after 1975, and also that much of the OPEC surplus was recycled back to the West either in the form of payments for goods and services or as investment, the economic problems continuing into the 1970s cannot be laid solely at OPEC's door. The smooth functioning of world trade had been assisted by the stable currency exchange rates guaranteed under the Bretton Woods system. After its demise, the world economy had to cope with a number of problems, including United States foreign indebtedness and the marked depreciation of the dollar on the one hand, and the vast and increasing surpluses of West Germany, Japan and Switzerland on the other. Although there had been some adjustments in comparative value after the devaluation of the dollar, West Germany and Japan, with large balance of payments surpluses, preferred to maintain a high exchange rate thus helping to control inflation. In 1978, while the total OPEC surplus was 48 billion dollars, Japan alone had a surplus of over 16 billion dollars and West Germany 9 billion.[44]

West Germany and Japan did begin to take measures to increase domestic demand, thus contributing to a decrease in their surpluses, but their efforts were overtaken by the second oil price shock. While, as discussed below, this second abrupt jump in oil prices undoubtedly had a marked effect on the world economy and helped to trigger the 1980–2 recession, once again OPEC could be used as a scapegoat, allowing the industrialized nations to downplay their own economic problems. This tendency was marked at the Tokyo G-7 summit in June 1979. OPEC was strongly criticized for large increases in the price of oil 'bearing no relation to market conditions'[45] and it was asserted that this had resulted in even higher inflation and the threat of severe recession and unemployment in the industrialized countries. Once again, the situation was portrayed as a confrontation between the OPEC producers and the leading industrial consumers. In keeping with current economic thought, the governments represented at the summit affirmed the importance of reducing inflation by fiscal and monetary restraint and cuts in government spending, and in particular, stressed the importance of breaking the links between economic growth and energy usage. At the same time, the individual governments agreed on objectives for oil imports, which sought to limit 1985 levels to those pertaining in 1978/9.

The Tokyo summit was responding to the likely impact of the second massive increase in oil prices in less than seven years. The rapid increase in oil prices again produced a sudden marked impact on GDP. The growth in real GDP of OECD countries dropped to an annual average of just under 2 per cent in 1979–80, only slightly above that of 1974-6.[46] It also, understandably, had an immediate effect on the inflation rate, which for OECD countries increased from 7.8 per cent at the end of 1978 to 13.6 per cent in the first half of 1980.[47] Although the key cause of the rapid escalation in the price of crude oil was the panic buying by consumers, triggered by the turbulent events in Iran, in some ways there were similarities with the position prevailing in 1973. As had happened between 1971 and 1973, the real price of crude was already in decline by the mid-1970s, and this was exacerbated by the sustained depreciation of the American dollar during 1977-8. OPEC members were already concerned at the double impact of this, first on the exchange value of their oil export earnings and, second, the erosion in the value of their foreign assets, many of them dollar related. There was, therefore, a clear inclination on the part of many OPEC members to take full advantage of rising market prices to push up official prices further. The consequence of the sharp upward movement of oil prices, in conjunction with the policies adopted by the main consumers, was a second sharp recession accompanied by rising inflation.

Already attuned to regarding inflation as a more significant economic indicator than rates of economic growth or levels of unemployment, the main industrialized countries reacted quickly, adopting deflationary policies intended to reduce demand. This tendency was heightened by the coming to power of right wing governments in a number of countries, most notably the Thatcher premiership in the United Kingdom (1979) and the Reagan presidency in the United States (1981). Monetarist policies were accompanied by privatization and deregulation, which reinforced the abandonment of Keynesian economics as the driver of capitalist states' national economic policies. These responses intensified the negative impact upon the world economy of the second major oil price increase in under a decade. However, although the recession was at its height in 1982–3, the decline in first the real and then the actual price of oil did not have a commensurate positive effect, suggesting that, as with the 1973 crisis, other factors than the price of oil both contributed to the initial recession and determined the developments in the world economy once the immediate impact of the oil shock was passed. One consequence of two periods of sharp upward inflation is that even after it was brought under control, which happened in the early 1980s, there was still reluctance on the part of national governments to engage in expansionary policies, which might again release the inflation genie from its bottle. Yet, compared with the levels pertaining in the 1970s, inflationary rates within the OECD countries were well under control during the 1980s, falling to under 3 per cent in 1986, although by the end of the decade it had crept up slightly to 4 per cent.[48]

Faced with economic problems, again the individual governments took action to address the worsening recession. Both the Thatcher Government in the United Kingdom and the Reagan Administration in the United States were committed to monetarism, which in effect premised that changes in the quantity of money determined changes in the general price level, and thus the government, by controlling the quantity of money, could control inflation. Hence, both governments tightened monetary supply, thus triggering a massive slump, In addition, they tried to reduce budget deficits, while also lowering taxes and reducing the role of the state, in an attempt to restore incentives to work, save, and make profits. This approach to economic planning was controversial and complex. In the case of the United Kingdom, in particular, which was already experiencing high levels of sterling exchange rates as a consequence of its oil self-sufficiency, the high interest rates introduced in 1979–80, together with the oil price increase, pushed the value of sterling very high, and this had an adverse effect upon the competitiveness of British manufacturing industry, in particular exports, with a subsequent impact upon unemployment. However, it did succeed in bringing down inflation, which by 1983 had been reduced to below 4 per cent.

The United States economy, already experiencing difficulties, was forced to recognize the impact of the international context upon its own economy, to an extent never before appreciated. In 1981, the United States relied upon imports to meet over half its requirements for 24 of the 42 most important industrial raw materials. 'The United States is no longer a self-contained continent, but rather an integral component of a deeply interdependent global economy.'[49] President Reagan sought to address the increase in inflation through an increase in interest rates, but this not only served to attract massive foreign investments, which played a role in offsetting the enormous United States trade deficit, but also began to change the American role in the world's financial balance. While in 1982 the United States was still the world's largest creditor with an investment surplus of 137 billion dollars, by 1987 it had become the world's largest debtor, owing 368 billion. Although the size of the debt in itself was not necessarily a problem – in 1987 the American public debt was only 31 per cent of GNP, compared with 36 per cent in Canada or 44 per cent in the United Kingdom – the extent of the borrowing from abroad rather than domestically was very marked.[50] This large budget deficit, and the instability in the value of the dollar, clearly had an impact on the world economy, and led to disputes as to whether it was the responsibility of the United States, or of West Germany and Japan, again perceived as having over-strong currencies, to address the West's economic problems.

It should be remembered that while the second oil price shock again forced the developed world to adopt tougher financial measures, it also adversely affected the major Third World debtor nations. Latin American countries, in particular, had borrowed heavily during the 1970s, making full use of the surplus petrodollars, only to find that their ability to repay was drastically undermined after 1979 by a combination of a slump in export earnings, a massive rise in real interest rates as a result of the tight money policies followed in the United States in particular, and a decline in further foreign investment. Domestic American policies reduced demand for imports, which had a further adverse effect upon the economies of developing countries. Ironically it was to be a major oil producer, Mexico, which signalled the problems of Third World debt when it experienced a severe debt crisis in 1982. However, as will be discussed in the next chapter, some OPEC members also had used their oil resources as security for borrowing on the international market, and now found themselves in difficulties. Uncertainty about the impact of Third World debt problems on those international banks which had lent heavily to developing countries, reinforced the mood of uncertainty about economic trends which the turbulent events since 1971 had induced.

The United States did not continue its policies of high interest rates and tight monetary controls, however. President Reagan switched to a policy of tax cuts and increased defence spending, which stimulated a boom but at the cost of a massive federal deficit, described by one writer as 'warfare Keynesianism'.[51] To fund the deficit, interest rates were again raised, thus stimulating upward pressure on the dollar, in turn making American exports less competitive. At the same time the United States (along with Western Europe and the Euromarkets) experienced a fresh influx of OPEC surpluses; within a monetarist framework, this also strengthened already high interest rates. As American exports were undermined by the high value dollar, there was growing trade rivalry with Japan and Western Europe; the huge American budgetary deficit and high interest rates pulled European and Japanese funds to the United States, thus increasing still further its position as an international debtor. As the American trade deficit grew, Japan built up a large trade surplus with the United States, which in turn reinforced American protectionist sentiment. In 1985 the Reagan Administration devalued the dollar, and sought to persuade the Japanese and the West Germans to adopt reflationary policies. Thus, within a very short space of time, and accompanied by falling oil prices, the impact of the second oil price shock was overtaken by imbalances between the industrialized economies, and in particular the problems caused by the massive American deficit. This was again reflected in the deliberations of the G-7 summits; as early as the Ottawa summit in July 1981, while the payments deficits resulting from the 1979–80 oil price increase were mentioned, energy was no longer given the central importance that it had received in 1979 and 1980[52] and by the Versailles summit in June 1982 energy was low on the agenda. Later summits reinforced this point: whereas the first summit had been called largely in response to the interlinked energy and economic crises – which was reflected in its preoccupation with energy matters – they had ceased to be a factor in the economic planning of the leading economies even before the massive drop in oil prices of 1986.

It would be easy to assume that the American role in the world economy was completely undermined by the events of 1973, just as it would be to blame the oil price increase entirely for the gloomy economic picture throughout much of the 1970s, which was marked by recession, high prices, inflation but stagnant growth and high unemployment – stagflation. It is certainly the case that the United States was no longer willing to pay the costs of economic world leadership, the dollar was in decline, and no one country was willing to take on the responsibility and costs of policies needed to lead and direct the world economy. The oil price crisis completed, but did not initiate the process of destroying the Bretton Woods system, which was already in collapse well before October 1973.

However, it posed a number of new challenges to the international economy, and in particular the most powerful industrial countries which had hitherto essentially controlled it: the recycling of petrodollars; the demands from the less developed South for a new international economic order; the need for oil consumers to develop cooperative arrangements to counter the collective power of the oil producers. While in 1973–4 fears were expressed that the West would no longer be able to manage the world economy, in fact the result was a more overt structure for that management through the regular meetings of the heads of government of the main industrialized nations. The problems besetting the world economy in the period from 1971 to 1983 resulted in part from the need to accommodate the unexpected and immense rises in the price of oil, which in both 1973 and 1979 had a marked effect on rates of inflation. However, it also had to address the move from a fixed to a floating currency exchange rate; the comparative weaknesses of the American economy, which affected the role of the dollar as the main reserve currency; the tremendous growth of the Eurocurrency market; and the impact of the two heavily under-valued currencies, the Deutsche Mark and the Japanese yen.

An added concern for the traditional industrial heartlands of the North Atlantic was the rise of the Pacific Rim, as other 'Little Tigers' emulated the path to industrialization followed by Japan in the years after the Second World War. In the early 1990s, attention switched to Japan as the engine house of the world economy: by 1990 the world's ten largest banks had headquarters in Japan, many of the world's largest companies were Japanese and Japan's largest company, NTT, was more than twice the size of the largest American company, IBM.[53] Another pressing problem in the world economy, although this was the legacy of the petrodollar era, was Third World debt. In 1970 only twelve countries had a debt of over 1 billion dollars, and none was over 10 billion; by 1990 Brazil, Mexico and Argentina all owed over 60 billion dollars and a further twenty-eight owed over 10 billion.[54]

Since 1982 the fluctuations and changes in the world economy have occurred as a consequence of factors other than changes in the price of oil. The fears of 1973 notwithstanding, neither OPEC as an organization, nor its individual members, attained any real power in the aftermath of the first dramatic oil crisis; as the power and influence of OPEC has declined, there was no reason for that position to change. In the 1980s, although the world's economy was still grappling with the recycling of OPEC surpluses, it also had to contend with the rescheduling of debts incurred by developing countries, and also the large external imbalances between the dollar and the yen. The 1970s and 1980s saw a structural change in the nature of the world economy, as the massive changes in technology, particularly information technology and communications, had profound effects upon the patterns of employment and investment throughout the world. Advances in communications fostered a liberalization of the financial markets, enabling largely unrestricted capital movements.[55] It is perhaps worth reflecting that in the contemporary world the new fears of monopoly and undue influence centre around the perceived monopoly power of the Microsoft company, not the oil companies, and the information technology and computer organizations have tended to head the lists of the largest companies. It has been too easy to blame a major shake out of the world economy on a small group of oil-producing states, which have themselves experienced considerable instability as the price of oil has risen and fallen.

With the decline in American control and leadership of the world economy, no country has emerged to fill its place, even one such as Japan with its very strong economic performance in the late 1970s and 1980s. It is arguable whether any one country could now control the complex financial structure of the world economy, with its propensity for volatility and rapid change. Multinational corporations continued to contribute to its complexity: by 1996 there were 44,000 such companies world wide: the largest 100 controlled around 20 per cent of global foreign assets, and accounted for between a quarter and a third of the world's output and 70 per cent of the world's trade.[56] The loosening of financial controls, both internationally and nationally, reflects a world economy, and in particular a financial market, vastly different from that prevailing in 1973. In effect, there is now one global stock market, and with controls on the movement of capital largely abolished, one interlocking global financial system.

Earlier in the chapter, I drew an analogy between the 1930s and the 1980s. Charles Kindleberger, in looking at the Great Depression between the two world wars, argues that the Depression was greatly exacerbated, both in severity and duration, by the lack of a single country both able and willing to lead the world economy – if necessary assuming the costs of defending stability.[57] By the 1970s the United States, which in 1945 had been at the forefront of the creation of the new liberal economic world order, was no longer willing to pay the costs of tackling inflation and recession, although it was still the largest economy in the world. So was 1973 a turning point for the world economy? As has been demonstrated above, the problems in the world economy already present before 1973 actually contributed to the oil price crisis, rather than being caused by it. However, the scale of the price increase, irrespective of how much analysts may differ about its precise consequences, inevitably seriously deepened the scale of the recession and had also a psychological impact. In his memoirs, Edward Heath blames the oil crisis for postponing European progress towards a complete free market with a single currency, planned to be in place by 1980. 'After [the oil crisis of 1973], even the most ambitious government could not look far beyond the immediate struggle for survival.'[58] The same was true of the second oil price shock in 1979. The charitable may say that the oil price crisis turned a problem that was mainly appreciated by specialist economic and political analysts into a crisis that was recognized and experienced by everyone. The cynical would say that OPEC provided an ideal scapegoat for governments unwilling to admit their policy failures of the past. Either way, in the space of a few years of crisis, the old Bretton Woods system was jettisoned, traditional ways of managing the world economy were abandoned or modified, and the surge of petrodollars, while not proving to be the calamity predicted by contemporary commentators, contributed to a problem still high on the international agenda: Third World debt. In the same way that 1929, although not a turning point in strictly economic terms, was nonetheless symbolic of the move from prosperity decade to depression decade, 1973 is symbolic of the move from the consensual liberal economic order managed through the Bretton Woods system to a more anarchic international economy, more susceptible to market forces, and largely beyond effective management or control.

Notes

1. A.G. Kenwood and A.L. Lougheed, *The Growth of the International Economy 1820–1990* (3rd edn). Routledge, London, 1992, p. 245.
2. Paul Hirst, 'The Eighty Years' Crisis, 1919–1999 – Power', *Review of International Studies* 24 (1998), pp. 133–48, esp. p. 144.
3. James Foreman-Peck, *A History of the World Economy: International Economic Relations since 1850*. Wheatsheaf Books, Brighton, 1986, pp. 288–339.
4. Foreman-Peck, *World Economy*, p. 270.
5. Charles S. Maier, 'The Politics of Productivity: Foundations of American International Economic Policy after World War II', in Peter J. Katzenstein (ed.), *Between Power and Plenty: Foreign Economic Policies of Advanced Industrial States*. The University of Wisconsin Press, Madison, Wisconsin, 1978, pp. 23–50.

6. Robert Triffin, 'The International Role and Fate of the Dollar', *Foreign Affairs* 57 (1978/9), pp. 269–86.

7. Maier, 'Politics of Productivity', p. 48.

8. Triffin, 'International role of the Dollar', pp. 272-3.

9. Foreman-Peck, *World Economy*, Table 11.1, p. 334.

10. Michael Smith, *Western Europe and the United States: The Uncertain Alliance.* George Allen & Unwin, London, 1984, p. 76

11. Stephen D. Krasner, 'United States Commercial and Monetary Policy : Unravelling the Paradox of External Strength and Internal Weakness', in Katzenstein, *Between Power and Plenty*, pp. 51–88, esp. pp. 66–72.

12. Thomas D. Willett, 'The United States and World Stagflation: The Export and Import of Inflationary Pressures', *Annals of the American Academy of Political and Social Science* 460 (1982), pp. 38–44, esp. p. 41.

13. Thomas G. Paterson and J. Garry Clifford, *America Ascendant: U.S. Foreign Relations Since 1939.* D.C. Heath and Company, Lexington, Massachusetts, 1995, p. 206.

14. Foreman-Peck, *World Economy*, pp. 345–7.

15. Triffin, 'International role of the Dollar', pp. 270–1.

16. See, for example, Raymond Vernon, *Sovereignty at Bay: The Multinational Spread of U.S. Enterprises.* Basic Books, New York, 1971; and Richard J. Barnet, *Global Reach: The Power of the Multinational Corporations.* Simon & Schuster, New York, 1974.

17. Krasner, 'United States Commercial and Monetary Policy', p. 71.

18. Forrest Capie and Alan Webber, *A Monetary History of the United Kingdom, 1870–1982.* George Allen & Unwin, London, 1985, p. 494.

19. Paterson and Clifford, *America Ascendant*, p. 206.

20. Paul Hallwood and Stuart Sinclair, *Oil, Debt and Development: OPEC in the Third World.* George Allen & Unwin, London, 1981, p. 27.

21. Thomas O. Enders, 'OPEC and the Industrial Countries: The Next Ten Years', *Foreign Affairs* 53 (1974–5), pp. 625–37.

22. Seymour, *OPEC*, p. 152.

23. Willett, 'The United States and Stagflation'.

24. Foreman-Peck, *World Economy*, pp. 348–51.

25. Hallwood and Sinclair, *Oil, Debt and Development*, p. 29.

26. Armand Pereira, Alistair Ulph and Wouter Tims, *Socio-Economic and Policy Implications of Energy Price Increases.* Gower, Aldershot, 1987, p. 14.

27. John C. Campbell, 'Oil Power in the Middle East', *Foreign Affairs* 56 (1977–8), pp. 89–110.

28. Marcus, *Controversial Issues*, p. 31.

29. Tim Niblock, *State, Society and Economy in Saudi Arabia.* Croom Helm, London, 1982, p. 215; Gustavo Coronel, *The Nationalization of the Venezuelan Oil Industry: From Technocratic Success to Political Failure.* Lexington Books, Lexington, 1983, p. 165.

30. For example, see J.B. Kelly, *Arabia, the Gulf and the West.* New York, 1980, pp. 427–37.

31. Khodadad Farmanfarmaian *et al.*, 'How can the World Afford OPEC Oil?', *Foreign Affairs* 53 (1974–5), pp 201–22, esp. pp. 216–17.

32. Hallwood and Sinclair, *Oil, Debt and Development*, p. 31.

33. Foreman-Peck, *World Economy*, pp. 352–3.

34. Dankwart A. Rustow and John F. Mugno, *OPEC: Success and Prospects.* New York University Press, New York, 1976, pp. 64–5.

35. Michael Kreile, 'West Germany: The Dynamics of Expansion', in Katzenstein, *Between Power and Plenty*, pp. 191–224, esp. p. 207.

36. John Zyman, 'The French State in the International Economy', in Katzenstein, *Between Power and Plenty*, pp. 255–94, esp. p. 285.
37. T.J. Pempel, 'Japanese Foreign Economic Policy: The Domestic Bases for International Behavior', in Katzenstein, *Between Power and Plenty*, pp. 139–90, esp. p. 169.
38. DeAnne Julius, 'Britain's changing international interests: economic influences on foreign policy priorities', *International Affairs* 63 (1987), pp. 375 —93, esp. pp. 376–7.
39. Triffin, 'International role of the Dollar', p. 272; Scott, 'American Scapegoat', p. 28.
40. A view strongly criticized in Scott, 'American Scapegoat'.
41. France, the United Kingdom, the United States, West Germany, Japan and Italy initially, with Canada added in 1976 and the European Community as a separate participant in 1977.
42. Peter I. Hajnal (compiler and editor), *The Seven Power Summit: Documents from the Summits of Industrialized Countries 1975–1989*. Kraus International Publications, New York, 1989, p. 8.
43. Hajnal, *Seven Power Summit*, p. 15.
44. Hallwood and Sinclair, *Oil, Debt and Development*, pp. 33–4.
45. Hajnal, *Seven Power Summit*, p, 80.
46. Pereira *et al.*, *Energy Price Increases*, p. 14.
47. Marcus, *Controversial Issues*, p. 10.
48. Kenwood and Lougheed, *International Economy*, p. 248.
49. Fred C. Bergsten, 'The United States and the World Economy', *Annals of the American Academy of Political and Social Science* 460 (1982), pp. 11–20, esp. p. 12.
50. Thomas Masefield, 'Co-prosperity and Co-security: Managing the Developed World', *International Affairs* 65 (1988/9), pp. 1–13, esp. pp. 2 and 8.
51. Bromley, *American Hegemony*, p. 210.
52. Hajnal, *Seven Power Summit*, pp. 104–18.
53. Patterson and Clifford, *America Ascendant*, p. 325.
54. Eric Hobsbawm, *Age of Extremes: The Short Twentieth Century 1914–1991*. Michael Joseph, London, 1994, pp. 422–3.
55. John Plender, 'London's Big Bang in International Context', *International Affairs* 63 (1986–7), pp. 39–48.
56. David Held and Anthony McGrew, 'Globalization and the End of the Old Order', *Review of International Studies* 24 (1998), pp. 219–43, esp. pp. 230–1.
57. C.P. Kindleberger, *The World in Depression 1929–1939*. Allen Lane, London, 1973.
58. Heath, *Autobiography*, p. 401.

6

A TURNING POINT FOR THE DEVELOPING WORLD?

While changes in the oil industry, the Middle East and the world economy might have been expected as a consequence of the events of October 1973, at the time many contemporaries assumed that it would also bring about a substantial reordering of the international system to produce a fairer situation for developing countries. OPEC itself claimed that it was acting as a prototype for other primary producers to follow, thus driving up the prices of a wide range of primary commodities: individual members also led the way in calling for a fundamental reappraisal of the relationship between the developed industrial West on the one hand, and the less-developed countries, or LDCs, on the other. In March 1973 OPEC had, for the first time, envisaged a role that went beyond the direct relationship between oil-producing states and the companies, and in June that same year the 34th OPEC conference issued a policy statement in which the member states agreed to take action, first to gain greater access to the technology and markets of the developed countries for their present and future industrial products and, second, to strengthen cooperation with the oil-importing developing nations.[1] In a special United Nations session in spring 1974 the host nation (and OPEC member), Algeria, explicitly presented OPEC's actions as the first step in the fight back of the Third World against their subordination in the world economy. The symbol of this restructuring was the call for a New International Economic Order, or NIEO.

There were also expectations that, as part of the Third World, OPEC collectively and its members individually would assist other developing nations to make the advances that the oil exporters had achieved. Moreover, for the individual oil-producing states, it was assumed that they would realize 'the dream of a Midas-type affluence'[2] through which they would be able not only to finance domestic infrastructure and industrial projects and improve conditions for their populations, but also to invest in Western industrial and financial assets abroad. However, optimistic hopes of a new era of Third World development suffered a setback when the Iranian Revolution threw into doubt the assumption that additional revenues and modernization would automatically lead to political liberalization and stability. This chapter considers whether the 1970s represented a turning point in the history of the developing world, in terms of its relationships with the developed West, its place in the world system and the economic prosperity and political stability of the oil-rich states themselves.

Developing countries in the world economy

There are many different ways of referring to states outside the developed industrialized core. The terms generally applied tend to reflect either political or economic roles, or the position of a particular state within the international economy. Thus 'Third World', often applied generally to the less-developed countries, was initially used with a strongly political meaning. In this approach, the world is divided into three main categories: the 'First World' (the pro-Western industrialized states led by the United States), the 'Second World' of the Communist bloc, and the 'Third World', the non-aligned states. This sense of the 'Third World' as those countries essentially 'left over' after the main Cold War lines of demarcation were drawn is both inaccurate (many of the states, although theoretically non-aligned, nonetheless had strong sympathies and economic ties with one or other side in the Cold War) and also does not fully convey the sense in which the term was first employed. In 1952 Alfred Sauvy, a French economist and demographer, referred to the 'Tiers Monde' as an explicit reflection of the 'Third Estate' or 'common people' in the period before the French Revolution. It was thus meant to convey the economic and political marginalization of, mainly, the post-colonial states which were economically less developed, and politically non-aligned in the Cold War. It also, however, signalled the revolutionary potential of this 'Third World' to rise against and overturn the established order, just as the Third Estate had done 170 years previously.[3]

Economically, the term less-developed countries, or LDCs, is widely used. However, while it is easy to speak of development, it is harder to define what is meant by it, or more specifically how it can be measured. If we use such indicators as the rate of economic growth, per capita income, or the position of state finances, then this raises the difficult issue of how to define the oil-rich, population-poor states along the Persian Gulf, which, during the late 1970s and early 1980s, enjoyed some of the highest per capita incomes in the entire world, yet continued to rely solely upon one natural resource for national income. If, on the other hand, more intangible measures are employed – economic diversification, social structures, value systems – then not only does the task of defining development become more subjective, but there is also the danger of defining 'development' as the economic, social and value systems prevailing in the developed industrial West. The 1970s demonstrated that, despite the vast inflow of petrodollars to the major oil exporters, it was perfectly possible for a country with the highest per capita income in the world, such as the United Arab Emirates, to nonetheless be a developing or semi-peripheral economy because it did not have a developed and diverse industrial economy. In this chapter the term 'Third World', implying the potential for Sauvy's 'Tiers Monde' to overthrow the existing status quo, is generally used when speaking of efforts to reorder the world international order; in looking at the issue of economic development, it is more accurate to refer to less-developed countries, or LDCs, divided further into the oil producers and the oil-poor.

During the late nineteenth and twentieth centuries, more geographical areas than ever before were integrated into the world economy. Many of the countries now regarded as LDCs played a subordinate part in the world economy, contributing cheap labour, primary commodities, and natural resources, and depending upon the industrialized economies for capital and markets. Political, social and economic relationships reinforced that position of dependence; internal elites often played an important role in maintaining the socio-economic structure which, in turn, reinforced the skewed position of the developing country in the world system. The relationship between economic and political domination was a mutual one: political influence helped the development of economic links. It was no coincidence that Great Britain was the mandatory power for Iraq in 1927 when the concession was granted to the IPC, a multinational company whose composition was designed to fit in with British rather than Iraqi interests. Moreover, the developed world, or rather particular countries within it, not only exercised political control or economic influence, but they also reinforced their dominant position through the provision of capital and markets. This relationship was always assisted by formal imperialism; thus, for example, the British Government insisted in the case of the West Indies that any oil company should follow strict rules. However, it could still exist through informal imperialism – a clear example of this is the role of oil companies in Mexico in the early part of the twentieth century.[4] Moreover, even when the direct ties of empire were loosened during the period after 1945, colonialism was replaced with neo-colonialism, imperial governments with the influence of multinational companies.

There have been very few examples of developing countries becoming fully developed in their own right. Certainly there have been exceptions, of which Japan, followed more recently by the other newly industrializing countries of the Pacific Rim, is a key example. However, as the integration of the world economy proceeded apace, as the specialized division of labour tended to develop in the late nineteenth and early twentieth centuries, developing countries found themselves increasingly locked into a subordinate position, both economically and politically, through either formal or informal empire. After the Second World War, however, the rapid collapse of the old empires, urged on in many cases by the ostensibly anti-imperialist United States, loosened existing political ties. In the late 1940s the process of decolonization began in India, Malaysia, Indonesia and Indochina, and proceeded extremely rapidly. In the areas of particular interest for the history of oil, British formal control in the Middle East declined between 1948 and 1971, with the loss of control over Palestine, Jordan, Iraq and the Aden Protectorate. By 1971 the British had also abandoned their protectorates in Kuwait, Bahrain and the United Arab Emirates. In addition, both French and British possessions in North Africa rapidly won independence. In many cases, both in these regions and elsewhere, the withdrawal of imperial influence was accompanied by anti-Western nationalism, as is in part reflected in the formation of OPEC.

Moreover, as more countries gained their independence, this considerably changed the nature of the United Nations. As the number of members of the General Assembly grew – many of them newly independent states from Africa and Asia – a definite Afro-Asian bloc emerged. Symbolically the 1960s was the first UN development decade; the goal was to improve economic growth and, in particular, aim at self-sustaining economic growth.[5] Moreover, many newly independent states also wanted to assert their economic independence, perceived as best achieved through economic nationalism and freedom from extensive penetration by Western companies. Anti-Western economic nationalism was not necessarily the reflection of radical politics, particularly in the oil industry. Although Mexican expropriation of foreign oil interests in 1938 was as a consequence of the Mexican Revolution, in the Middle East, the first major challenge to oil company control came in 1933 from the autocratic regime of Iran's Shah.

By the late 1960s, with only a few exceptions, the formal empires had been dismantled. This process of decolonization was often accompanied by domestic changes, such as mass mobilization, the increased emphasis upon the interests of the indigenous populations, and a middle-class elite, stressing national independence, sovereignty and independence from the West, particularly through economic nationalism. International organizations, such as the International Monetary Fund, and international economic institutions, including the main banks and multinational corporations, were perceived by developing countries as representing Western control and supremacy. For both economic and political reasons their governments were keen to enforce greater control over their national economies. As much of the concern was to reduce or eliminate the level of foreign control over their economies, the mechanisms by which they sought to exercise control often took the form of enlarging the state sector, the development of import substitution industries and, in some cases, outright nationalization of foreign interests.[6]

However, in addition, LDCs wished to see higher prices for their exports, mainly raw materials and food stuffs consumed in the West (in 1960, 86 per cent of all LDCs' foreign exchange was earned by the export of unprocessed raw materials)[7] and, where possible, the increased transfer of advanced technology to the LDCs from the developed West. In this respect, the formation of an organization such as OPEC, determined to make a united stand against Western companies, could be interpreted as heralding a first step in an important realignment of interests and the relationship between developed and developing world. Moreover, during the 1960s there were other indications of a growing assertiveness on the part of developing countries. Particularly after the Cuban Missile Crisis, when there was a diminution in the intensity of the tension between East and West in the Cold War, attention turned slowly towards broader international problems relating to relationships between the developed and developing world, often summarized in terms of North versus South. In 1964 the first meeting was held of the United Nations Conference on Trade and Development, or UNCTAD, which became a permanent organization, seeking to address the situation whereby manufactured goods from LDCs often encountered high tariff barriers to entering developed countries' markets, thus making it very difficult to break through into greater industrialization. What this in effect meant was that developing countries could only hope to earn foreign currency through the sale of primary products, whose prices tended to be comparatively low.

It was not just through such tariffs that the economies of developing countries remained under Western control. For example, when granted food or other aid by the United States, the terms of the aid often demanded that the recipient should buy American goods. Attempts to develop the state sector within the economy often prompted threats of withholding United States or World Bank aid. Where Western companies were already ensconced, it was very difficult to dislodge them without the risk of political or economic sanctions. Although in the period 1960–75 LDC manufacturing output more than trebled, much of this growth was concentrated in a small number of LDCs, including Brazil, South Korea, Mexico, Iran, Hong Kong, Indonesia and Singapore.[8] Some managed to develop a substantial export trade, often encouraged by government policy – for example, Hong Kong, Taiwan, Singapore – but this success was often accompanied by heavy investment from large foreign companies. However, although the success of these newly industrializing countries meant that OPEC nations were not the only developing countries that were claiming and consolidating for themselves a significant role in the world economy, it was to be OPEC, both collectively and as individual states, which overtly tried to redress the balance between developed and developing worlds.

A New International Economic Order?

Given the vast accretion of wealth to the member states of OPEC, it may be questioned to what extent they still remained part of the so-called 'developing world'. Indeed, although the Brandt Commission defined OPEC countries as part of the developing 'South', there was much debate about whether the member states could realistically be described by that term, given the very high rates of per capita GDP and the vast surpluses, generated by both the governments and individual citizens, and invested overseas. However, it is perhaps more accurate in this context to see them rather as a potential part of a 'Third World', whose numerical superiority and potential for revolution might threaten to overthrow, rather than merely reform, the existing system. In the 1973 oil crisis, a group of Third World producers had, for the first time, imposed its own conditions upon the Western world. Traditional mechanisms of control had proved worthless: the West could not realistically use force; there was no ascertainable economic leverage at its disposal; while the withholding of aid was not an effective sanction against the oil-rich states of the Arabian Peninsula. Political pressure, if effective – which was dubious – could not be applied immediately and might have negative consequences, by driving the oil producers towards the Soviet bloc. Might other Third World producers follow OPEC's example in forming cartels to control production and prices?

There were a number of attempts to emulate OPEC's example. However, few countries or commodities could rival the crucial importance of oil, and the small group of countries controlling access to it. Further efforts at cartelization were unsuccessful, either because of market conditions, internal divisions among producers, or the inability to find independent companies with which to deal. The OPEC producers had been able to use the prevailing market conditions to their own advantage, seizing upon the opportunities opened up by the existence of independent companies. In the pursuit of higher prices, even politically diverse nations had been able to cooperate with one another. Elsewhere, however, attempts to follow OPEC's example proved mainly abortive. The copper exporters, comprising Chile, Peru, the Congo and Zambia, proved unsuccessful in their attempt to create an effective organization, due to over-supply and fluctuating prices. The International Coffee Agreement of 1962 had sixty-two signatories, but was also unstable because of differences between its Latin American members on the one hand and its African members on the other; moreover, coffee can be classed as a luxury, with highly elastic demand.

The most successful attempt to emulate the success of OPEC was that of the bauxite producers, the International Bauxite Association, because of the importance of aluminium, but even that did not share the centrality of petroleum to the world economy. Nonetheless, the main producers were able to link their revenue to prices and increase taxes on companies. In 1975 the Jamaican Government imposed a 7.5 per cent export tax on five American companies, and was able to increase its tax revenues almost sevenfold.[9] Even so, this group never obtained the power and status of OPEC, and was unable to formulate a clear cartel-style arrangement. The unique nature of oil meant that it was very difficult for other commodity producers to follow suit.[10] Even such critical commodities as zinc, uranium, plutonium and diamonds were unable to follow the example of petroleum, as both demand and price were relatively elastic. In the case of tin, there was already an international commodity agreement in place, while for a number of crucial commodities, such as iron ore, nickel and manganese, the LDCs were not the sole suppliers. In other words, in most cases the LDCs were still locked into the role of primary producer, and were unable to find a way of breaking free or of obtaining funds sufficient to develop a diversified economy. This was unfortunate, as many countries outside the oil states had a far greater capacity for development in terms of usable land, size of labour force, and alternative resources.

Thus, in one respect at least, OPEC's claim to act on behalf of the Third World as a whole – in other words, by offering a successful example of resource power – lacked substance. Another possibility, however, was that OPEC might act as an important agent to increase awareness of the problems of developing countries within the broader world community. Indeed, this indirect mode of providing leadership for the Third World was perhaps the most hopeful of success. Initiatives in this direction centred upon the possibility of creating a new international economic order acting under the auspices of the United Nations. Since 1964 the Group of 77, a coalition of developing nations which grew in number until in the 1970s it represented more than one hundred nations, had sought to use the United Nations as a forum to present their calls for changes in the structure of the world economy. It was, however, only in the context of the oil price shock of 1973 that calls for international discussions on these proposals fell on receptive ears in the developed North.

The first call for a New International Economic Order (NIEO) came at the Algiers conference of the Non-Aligned Countries in 1973, but it was then given form in a series of official documents accepted by the Group of 77, and finally the United Nations itself. The goals of the NIEO were to bring about major structural changes in the world economy, shifting the balance of power, which was seen as resting decisively with the developed 'North', towards the LDCs of the South. In particular, it called for massive resource transfers, which should be both multilateral, and unconditional, from North to South; increased representation and power of the South in the major international institutions, such as the IMF and the World Bank (which distributed funds for development projects); and preferential terms for the South on matters of trade, investment and technology transfer.[11] The South wanted the

North to charge less for manufactured goods and technology, to pay more for raw imported goods from LDCs , to reduce tariff barriers, and to accept the right of Third World countries to nationalize or otherwise curtail the power of large foreign firms. While the NEIO had a concrete form, as a list of particular demands, it also came to symbolize the negotiating procedure by which the North and the South tried to reach accommodation on the form of the international economic order. As such, it had the potential to touch on a wide range of issues.[12]

In April–May 1974 a special UN General Assembly meeting was held on this issue, and the consequence was the passing of a UN Economic Charter, which tried to set up the right to create cartels, and sought to link the prices of primary producers to those of manufactured goods. It acknowledged the right of nationalization, and suggested mechanisms for the transfer of technology, manufacturing and capital to the less-developed countries.[13] This was passed over the opposition of the core countries by 86 votes to 10. Following the Special Session, OPEC demonstrated its willingness to act as a spokesperson for the Third World generally. Sheikh Yamani of Saudi Arabia called, on a number of occasions, for discussions on the global economy, initially in a small group representing the various groups of countries, and later in a larger forum. It was, however, made plain that OPEC members would not accept any suggestion that prices for oil should be set by any other group. In the event it was a developed country which took the first steps towards setting up such a forum. In October 1974 France, having consulted Saudi Arabia and other producers, suggested that there should be an international conference that would initially deal with oil and energy, and then move on to discuss wider international economic questions.[14]

The following March OPEC Heads of State, meeting in Algiers, also agreed to use their influence to secure a conference between developed and developing countries: however, they stressed that the conference should address a wide spectrum of issues relating to the interchange between developing and developed world, covering primary commodities, reform of the international monetary system, and an active policy to promote development. While resisting all efforts to make this purely a conference on energy, the meeting agreed that OPEC members might consider issues such as price and supply stability in the context of a broad international agreement relating to development.[15] It was made clear in this statement that OPEC was unlikely to accept attempts by the North to turn any such dialogue into a forum in which oil prices themselves might be set. Instead, the members emphasized that the price of oil represented a reasonable readjustment to compensate for previous under-pricing, and that even that readjustment was being eroded by inflation and rising costs of goods bought from the industrialized West.[16] This meeting was highly significant, in that the declaration issued by it made very clear that OPEC had adopted a political position aligning itself with the interests of other LDCs.

Even before the OPEC meeting, France's President Giscard d'Estaing had already sent out invitations to a preparatory conference, to be held in April 1975, in which he suggested that the oil producers should be represented by Saudi Arabia, Iran, Algeria and Venezuela; the United States, the EEC and Japan should speak for the industrialized consumers; while Brazil, Zaire and India were approached on behalf of the developing consumers. However, this preparatory conference was largely unsuccessful: the United States delegate, Under Secretary of State Enders, was attributed with stating that the American Government intended to hasten the demise of OPEC; the industrial consumers wanted to concentrate upon energy issues, while the LDCs were more concerned with the broader policies needed to contribute to development. Despite this disappointing beginning, a second meeting was held in October, and arrangements for the conference, to be known as the Conference on International Economic Cooperation, were put in place, with twenty-seven participants (eight from the OECD and 19 LDCs) and a number of observers, including OPEC and the IEA. However, the CIEC's shaky start was a disappointing, but accurate, reflection of the difficulties it faced, and by the time that the initiative finally came to a halt, in June 1977, it had achieved very little. The developed countries for the most part entered the Conference with the intention of using it to set ground rules that would help secure a stable petroleum regime in the future.[17] In May 1977 the Group of Seven summit in London specifically linked the CIEC with the need for the North to 'secure productive results from negotiations about the stabilization of commodity prices'.[18] There was certainly never any intention of radically rewriting the structure of the international economy, but rather the making of adjustments sufficient to win wider support for the fundamental existing structure.

The creation of the so-called 'Common Fund' was another attempt by the international community to address the problems of underdevelopment. At the fourth UNCTAD meeting in Nairobi during May 1976, a proposal was put forward for an 'Integrated Programme for Commodities', including an integrated commodity price support scheme, financed by a 'Common Fund'. This proposal was an attempt to address the instability of commodity prices, which had been particularly marked since 1973. Volatile patterns of demand and fluctuating price levels for various commodities had hit those countries, usually LDCs, which depended heavily upon one or two commodities for the majority of their export earnings particularly badly. Although this was of immediate concern to the producers, whose economic planning was thus rendered ineffective, it also adversely affected developed countries, not only as consumers but sometimes as producers as well. As the Group of Seven Declaration in May 1977 illustrated, the North wished to see stability (rather than increases) in the prices of key commodities.

The proposed programme included the use of a Common Fund to create 'buffer stocks', which could be created by buying at times of low prices, and then used to reduce high prices through strategic selling. The initial proposal covered eighteen commodities, including food (e.g. bananas, coffee, cocoa, sugar, tea), minerals, metals (such as iron ores, copper and tin), and other key commodities such as bauxite, rubber, tropical timber and vegetable oils. However, there were differences of opinion as to the main goals of the Common Fund: the stability of prices, which would undoubtedly benefit the consumer but would protect the producer from falls in price, or an increase in prices over time to redress the imbalance between developed and developing world. Developing countries proposed that the price of commodities should be linked to an index of manufactured goods, but this was opposed by developed countries. The idea of a Common Fund had been raised before, with little success, and at Nairobi it was opposed by most developed countries, including the United States, the United Kingdom, Japan and West Germany. Edmund Dell sums up the way that the proposals for indexation appeared to the main consumers: 'the Common Fund proposal looked to the developed world like a bid by UNCTAD for power over world trade in commodities'.[19] Nonetheless, it was ultimately decided to hold a negotiating conference, and in November 1977 an UNCTAD conference agreed to put the Common Fund in place. As ever, however, while LDCs hoped to use the agreement as a way of strengthening their position in the management of the international economy and its institutions, the developed world was more concerned with individual commodity agreements. Even after the final details had been put in place, with an agreement on the extent of the buffer stock fund, it was still necessary for the agreement to be ratified by ninety states before it could come into force. This did not happen until January 1986 and, significantly, the United States was not among their number. As with other initiatives to create a new international economic order, the Common Fund raised many hopes, but achieved very little.

The willingness of the developed world to consider progress on commodity prices in part reflected a concern about a general new-found 'commodity power', a fear that, it could be argued, played a major role in winning acceptance for, and participation in, the North–South dialogue. By the early 1980s, with even the price of oil and the power of oil producers in retreat, 'commodity power' was no longer seen as a threat, and the problems of the South were also sidelined. Whereas the developed nations, and particularly the United States, had tended to adopt a conciliatory stance towards development issues in the second half of the 1970s, this approach was not shared by the Reagan Administration (1981–8), which called upon the South to pursue its own development through a programme of trade, and rejected calls for a massive transfer of knowledge and resources from the North to the South.[20]

Thus, despite such apparently hopeful signs as the CIEC and the concept of a 'Common Fund', no concrete action was taken to address the fundamental issues of under-development, which has been the goal of Third World countries. Once the immediate threat of the energy crisis had passed, the West lost interest in trying to address problems of development. In 1980 a major report on the problems of the North–South relationship was produced by the Independent Commission on International Development Issues, under the chairmanship of ex-German Chancellor, Willy Brandt. Of the eighteen members of the commission, ten came from developing countries, including the Kuwaiti Finance Minister, and there were a number of representatives from the developed world, including ex-British Prime Minister Edward Heath. In his memoirs, Heath emphasized the independence of the Commission, and saw the final report as 'the clearest analysis of the problems of the North and South, together with the most constructive and detailed series of proposals for dealing with them, that has ever been published'.[21] It certainly sought to address the causes rather than the symptoms of the problems of development, calling, for example, for sustainable development rather than temporary famine relief. As Heath himself admits, however, little positive action resulted from the report. Overall, despite the various efforts, particularly in the 1970s and early 1980s, to create a programme of action to address the real problems of the LDCs, the income gap between richer and poorer nations has actually increased: while in 1960 the richest 20 per cent of the world controlled 70 per cent of gross global domestic product, by 1989 the richest 20 per cent owned 82.7 per cent.[22]

There was another respect in which OPEC had the potential to affect the situation pertaining in the developing world, this time by the provision of financial assistance, either through direct foreign aid packages, or by the introduction of differential oil price structures for LDCs as opposed to the industrial West. By giving active assistance to other Third World countries OPEC might free them from the need to appeal to the developed world for aid. Many OPEC countries soon developed a massive surplus, despite ambitious development plans and consumer spending. Much of this was invested in Western institutions, some – such as the World Bank and the International Monetary Fund – intended to assist countries facing difficulties. However, even with the investment of petrodollars, management of international institutions still rested very strongly in the hands of the developed world. In particular, the World Bank and other organizations insisted that loans should be contingent upon appropriate behaviour; for example, it would not lend money for state enterprises which had been created by expropriation or inadequately compensated nationalization. The IMF still tended to assume that its role was to assist governments facing short-term, reversible problems rather than longer term structural difficulties. Ironically, even when Third World countries did benefit from extra funds available, for example in the Eurodollar market, it could prove ultimately destructive. Many loans advanced to the developing countries created extra problems; when governments found it impossible to repay the loans, the result was a worsening debt crisis which left many developing countries on the verge of bankruptcy. The world recession of 1974-5 saw Third World debt increase substantially, and the majority of these loans came from international banks rather than aid organizations.[23] In the next recession, in 1980–2, interest rates on those loans rose steeply, with devastating effects.

OPEC members did provide assistance on their own behalf, often in aid programmes, frequently contributing a higher proportion of GNP than many developed countries. A number of states, notably Libya, Kuwait and Saudi Arabia, had either already created special development funds, or gave generously to existing ones. This assistance increased after 1973, and between 1975 and 1979 OPEC members together gave between 4 and 5 billion dollars annually in aid. In 1975, while the industrial countries that were members of the OECD's Development Assistance Committee gave only 0.35 per cent of GNP in official development assistance, OPEC members gave 2.71 per cent, well in excess of the UN official target of 0.7 per cent, and some gave even more.[24] In the aftermath of 1973, a number of special development funds were created, the Arab Fund for Social and Economic Development (1973), the Arab Bank for Economic Development in Africa (1974), the Islamic Development Bank (1973), the Arab Investment Company (1974), the Arab Monetary Fund (1976) and the OPEC Special Fund (1976). However, much of the aid was bilateral and direct, enabling its use for political purposes. Thus, Arab oil producers offered aid to other Arab and Islamic states, particularly front-line states against Israel, such as Egypt. When, in 1979-80 the second massive oil price increase threatened the economic balance of oil-importing countries once more, Mexico (a non–OPEC oil producer) joined forces with Venezuela to provide up to 80,000 barrels per day crude oil to nine nations in the region at concessionary rates, provided that the oil so provided was solely for domestic consumption, and that industries involved in the export business would not have access to the cheaper oil.[25] This, however, was highly unusual in that OPEC members rarely accepted lower prices for their oil, from whatever quarter.

OPEC aid, although generous as a proportion of GNP, was not distributed equally among the many oil poor LDCs suffering severe balance of payments difficulties as a result of steeply rising oil import bills. It was therefore suggested, by both industrial countries and oil-importing LDCs, that OPEC members, either collectively or individually, might offer practical assistance to fellow developing nations by offering discounted prices for petroleum. In 1973, the Organization of African Unity called for special oil prices, a call rejected by OPEC, although it did set up two new agencies, the Arab Fund and the Arab Bank for Economic Development in Africa, and funnelled 200 million dollars through them for development. A similar call was made at the March 1977 Afro-Arab summit in Cairo. In 1979, at a session of UNCTAD in Manila, Costa Rica was responsible for the setting up of a new organization, the Organization of Petroleum Importing Countries, and Colombia pressed for oil to be formally included in the meeting's agenda, but this too was successfully resisted by the oil exporters. The Mexican and Venezuelan initiative mentioned above is highly unusual, in that it provided for a discounted price, and then only subject to stringent conditions. Despite the various aid programmes, the fact nonetheless remains that LDCs suffered as a consequence of the substantial rise in oil prices during the 1970s, and the high levels of inflation in the industrialized countries. The increased oil costs had a major impact on the balance of payments of oil-poor LDCs; during 1974-80 the non-oil LDCs' collective trade deficit with the world was 280 billion dollars, about two-thirds of which was with OPEC members.[26] Increased exports to OPEC countries, which rose by around 10 billion dollars over the same period, could not compensate for the extra oil costs, and in any case, as with aid, did not apply to all oil-poor LDCs. With little alternative in the way of renewable energy sources or other fossil fuels, and with little money to spend on energy conservation programmes, LDCs remained dependent upon oil for energy, while the economic recessions of the 1970s and early 1980s in industrial countries, in part exacerbated by increased oil prices, reduced demand for their own exports.

Thus, even at the peak of their power, OPEC was able to do comparatively little to redress the balance of power in favour of the developing world. In 1973 many commentators believed that one aspect of the international system which would be radically and permanently changed was the relationship between the developing and the developed world. This was reflected in the debates about the New International Economic Order, and also attempts by other primary producer cartels to follow in the footsteps of OPEC. However, for a number of reasons, the challenge to the developed world from the newly assertive Third World proved not to be revolutionary at all. For many oil producers, particularly low absorbers such as Kuwait, Saudi Arabia and the UAE, a stable Western economy was nearly as important as a high price for oil. Moreover, it was not just the rulers of these states who had a vested interest in the stability of the West. The wealth of their citizens also increased dramatically as the price of real estate rocketed, and in view of the legislation that was passed in many states requiring foreign firms to operate in partnership with a national. These wealthy commoners also invested in the Western economies. Moreover, even those states without such foreign investments, still needed access to Western armaments and education, and were reluctant to pose a direct threat to Western stability.

So the oil producers did not use their wealth to lead a radical developing world challenge to the developed world; moreover, while a number of oil-rich states developed aid programmes aimed at other developing countries, they were normally not prepared to offer oil supplies at discount prices. While OPEC support succeeded in bringing debates on the New International Economic Order to the forefront of the international agenda for a short time at the peak of their influence, it achieved very little. There was no diminution in the developed world's monopoly on military predominance, political power and leadership of the world economy. Moreover, far from setting a precedent that would then be followed by other LDCs, the vastly increased oil import bill proved a major economic stumbling block to the oil-poor developing nations: as Hallwood and Sinclair argue, while there are undoubted elements of cooperation in the economic relations between OPEC members and non–oil LDCs, 'it is competition which tends to dominate, a factor that cannot be disguised by "Third World" rhetoric'.[27]

The oil exporters and domestic development

OPEC might have been unable to redress the balance between the Third World and the developed West, but its individual states were themselves developing nations, and the vast accretion of oil resources opened up exciting possibilities for states which, in many instances, had already embarked on plans for their own economic development. In addition to individual programmes, OAPEC pursued joint schemes, intended to promote the economic integration of the oil sector in Arab countries and assist Arab oil producers whose export volume was not high, and who therefore did not benefit from a vast increase in government revenues. It encouraged joint ventures such as the Arab Shipbuilding and Repair Yard and the Arab Maritime Petroleum Transport Company for tankers. In addition, the Arab Petroleum Investment Corporation invested not just in the oil industry or OAPEC's members, but also provided funding for capital projects in oil-poor Arab states.[28] For most oil-exporting states, however, the pursuit of economic development was a national, rather than collective, enterprise. Many producer governments had already embarked upon development plans before 1973, but the dramatic increase in their revenues provided the opportunity for expanded and accelerated programmes. While in some states, such as Libya, a decision was taken to limit production in response to higher prices, the government still saw a tripling of oil revenue in the period from 1972 to 1975; Iraq meanwhile saw a twelve-fold increase in oil revenue, and Saudi Arabia's revenue increased eightfold.[29] A further dramatic increase took place in 1979–80. Even in 1986, when the price of oil dropped sharply, OPEC members were still receiving incomes that were markedly higher than they had received fifteen years earlier. How successful were the oil exporters in pursuing development for their own economies?

It is clear that no one model of development would suit all OPEC members. Apart from the fact that they could all be defined as developing states, and relied upon oil exports as their main source of export and government income, they were a diverse set of states, even in so basic a measure as population: whereas in 1974 Gabon, Kuwait, Qatar and the UAE all had populations of under 1 million, Nigeria had 73 million and Indonesia 132 million.[30] Some had agricultural potential, but others did not: some had other significant minerals and metals (especially Algeria) and others did not. Countries such as Kuwait, Saudi Arabia and the UAE combined high levels of production with small populations and few opportunities to diversify their economies – hence the term 'low absorber' that was often used to describe them. However, other members, such as Algeria, Ecuador, Gabon, Indonesia and Nigeria – whose oil supplies were limited but who had other potential economic activities – and also the large oil producers who had not only good oil reserves but other resources and economic opportunities (Iran, Iraq and Venezuela) had opportunities to diversify their economies. All had to plan for a post oil future, however far distant that might be, which presumed, where possible, the development of non-oil economic activities and the building up of assets and financial reserves at home and abroad. However, to diversify successfully and also meet the rising expectations of their populations, the oil exporters needed to modernize, gain access to the most up-to-date technology and develop an educated indigenous workforce.

As already suggested, in many states development plans were already in place by 1973. During the 1950s, a new 'post-oil' generation of technocrats and government officials emerged, often educated in the West, with clear concepts of the appropriate path towards development.[31] With the dramatic increases in government revenue in the mid-1970s, and again at the end of that decade, the individual governments appeared well placed to invest in productive enterprises capable of providing jobs and infrastructure, which in turn would promote prosperity, rising living standards and hence political stability. Oil revenues going to the state meant that the state was the main engine of economic growth and development: it should, therefore, have been possible to plan and implement coherent development programmes.

Space does not permit a detailed discussion of each of the OPEC member states, but in order to reach some general conclusions as to how far the 1970s provided a watershed in the history of their development it may be worth briefly considering a small number of case studies. That rapid development and modernization does not automatically bring political stability and popular support for the government was graphically illustrated in Iran, as was discussed in Chapter 1. Saudi Arabia was, in many respects, similar to Iran (although of course there remained many substantial differences). It also provides a useful example of the sparsely populated, oil-rich states of the Arabian Peninsula. During the 1970s and early 1980s it received a greater income from its oil exports than any other OPEC member, and had the capacity to increase production if required to obtain more revenue. The effect of the 1973 oil price increase on government revenue was immediate and dramatic: oil revenue rose from 655 million dollars in 1965 to over 4 billion in 1973 and 22.5 billion in 1974.[32] In the decade of highest oil prices, from 1974 to 1984, real GDP grew at 9 per cent per annum on average, while in 1980–1 alone Saudi oil income nearly doubled.[33] It remains to be seen what use the Saudi Government made of this substantial income.

A number of very positive policies were introduced as oil wealth brought radical changes to Saudi Arabia. In purely demographic terms, the percentage of the population living in towns increased from 10 per cent in 1950 to over 50 per cent by the mid-1980s.[34] The Saudi kings, from King Feisal (1962–75) onwards, also followed a policy of allocating most of the country's escalating oil revenue to development, modernization and improvements in the general standard of living of the population. The government invested heavily in public utilities such as electricity, water (including desalination plants) and sewerage, communications systems, transportation networks and facilities. Through development, education and welfare programmes, an infrastructure was constructed, an educated and skilled workforce was created, and most individual Saudis gained directly from government policies without being required to contribute to the costs through taxation. In 1973 taxes were lifted altogether: the per capita GNP, already 12,000 dollars in 1972, reached 17,000 dollars in 1981 (only to slump to just 5,000 by the end of the decade).[35] The dispersal of wealth created a 'multi-layered bourgeoisie' whose incorporation into the government played an important part in retaining the traditional regime, and helps to explain why 'despite the rapid modernization of Saudi Arabia its rulers managed to avoid the socio-political dislocations that often accompanied development in the Arab–Muslim world'.[36] The government also actively promoted education, including sending students to universities overseas.

This meant that in effect the Saudi royal family bought political stability by subsidizing health, education, public services and utilities, as well as acting as the direct employer for many Saudi nationals. However, once oil prices began to drop in the 1980s, the government had to balance its reduced income against the possible political costs of cuts in expenditure. During the first half of the 1980s oil revenues dropped dramatically from 113 billion dollars in 1981 to only 20 billion in 1986.[37] From 1983 onwards the government actually ran at a deficit, meeting the costs by domestic borrowing and drawing on foreign assets, rather than risk the political costs of reducing subsidies. Whereas in 1982 Saudi Arabia's budget was 140 billion dollars in surplus, by the end of the twentieth century it operated with a debt of around 130 billion.[38] Although Saudi Arabia has partially succeeded in diversifying within the oil industry, it lacked the resources to develop other economic activities. Moreover, after the Iranian Revolution, while government spending on welfare, services, and state employment has continued, a marked shift has been discernible, particularly in education. Already strongly religious in content and method, after 1979 the influence of Islamic teaching was heightened. The Saudi Arabian Government remained firmly in the hands of the royal family, and political, social and cultural tradition has prevailed.

Kuwait is another example of a 'low absorber', and in many respects provided a classic example of a rentier state: in 1989, while the Kuwaiti Government received 7.7 billion dollars in oil revenue, it obtained a further 8.8 billion from overseas investment.[39] Although it depleted its international assets during the Gulf War, to contribute towards the costs of the international coalition and also to repair the damage done during the invasion, Kuwait still retained substantial overseas assets. As in Saudi Arabia, with a very small national population it was possible for the government to provide an extensive welfare state for Kuwaiti citizens, including education, health care and housing. Even after the drop in the price of oil, Kuwait's small national population and its overseas investments enabled it to continue its welfare programmes, as well as offering employment to the vast majority of its citizens. These benefits were not, however, offered to foreign workers, who on the eve of the Iraqi invasion numbered over one million, compared to a national population of 650,000.[40] Kuwait followed an ambitious policy of international economic diversification, but this was still based on petroleum, with domestic oil refining and petrochemicals, oil refineries outside its borders, and direct ownership of the Q8 chain which operates thousands of service stations in Europe.[41] As in Saudi Arabia, where the royal family remained firmly in political control, economic benefits were not accompanied by major political gains by the population.

Although Kuwait's constitution provided for a legislative assembly, this was suspended from 1976 until 1982 and then again from 1986 until after the Iraqi invasion. Elections were finally held in 1992, but only 81,000 Kuwaiti males were allowed to vote out of the total national population of 650,000: foreign workers were given no right to participate. The tendency of the first post-Gulf War assembly to criticize the government did not encourage greater freedom, and in the 1996 elections the same highly restricted franchise prevailed.[42]

Kuwait and Saudi Arabia were therefore able to use their oil revenue to provide substantial benefits for their individual citizens, although in the case of Saudi Arabia at the cost of going into deficit. Although their programmes of economic diversification still relied heavily on petroleum, with massive reserves and few other resources, this was a logical policy. However, other more populous and resourced states had more opportunities for rapid development. Venezuela was one of the founding states of OPEC and the leading oil exporter in Latin America; even though its policy was not to increase production, but rather to conserve future supplies while increasing revenue from the higher prices, the country saw a current account deficit turn into a surplus, making it Latin America's wealthiest nation. The Venezuelan Government earned more money from selling its oil between 1973 and 1980 than for the entire period from 1921 to 1973.[43] As a democracy of twenty-five years standing enjoying apparent political stability, Venezuela was, as George Philip points out, ideally placed to benefit from oil wealth.[44] Moreover, it had other natural resources, including iron ore and bauxite, thus opening up a number of industrial opportunities, including steel, aluminium and petrochemicals. Yet this was insufficient to trigger a genuine economic prosperity. With a large population, it could not afford to introduce the kind of welfare state seen in Kuwait and Saudi Arabia. Without sufficient improvements in the standard of living, the unrealized expectations of many of the population led to political instability. Moreover, while manufacturing did expand in Venezuela, the greatest growth tended to be in the urban services sector, and there was a decline in agriculture. Poor administration and planning, over-ambitious projects and waste and corruption all contributed to the failure to diversify. As the international financial community became concerned about the adverse position on Latin American debt after 1982, and oil prices dropped from 1983 onwards, Venezuela found itself in a cycle of inflation and devaluation. By the mid-1990s, Venezuela had the highest inflation and deepest recession in Latin America, and the combined problems of high unemployment, political and economic crisis produced both political and social instability.[45]

The other leading oil exporter in the region, Mexico, also fared less well than might have been expected. It was to have the dubious honour of being the first developing country to experience significant debt problems in the 1980s. Even before the discovery of massive new petroleum reserves, the Mexican Government had pursued a programme of industrialization, and it intended to use the promise of its oil revenues to embark on an ambitious development programme. However, so ambitious were its plans that it chose to anticipate future oil revenues and rely on borrowing in the first instance. The public sector's external debt rose from 22.9 billion dollars in 1977 to 85 billion by 1982.[46] However, in planning for development the Mexican Government made a number of problematic decisions, not least in assuming, after the dramatic price increase of 1979–80, that not only would those high prices remain, but also that they would continue to grow by 6 per cent per year throughout the 1980s. This, however, created considerable problems as the price of oil declined in the 1980s, and with it Mexico's export earnings, which dropped from nearly 17 billion dollars in 1984 to only just over 6 billion dollars in 1986.[47]

The other major oil-exporting area was North and West Africa. In 1973 Nigeria seemed poised to become a major African economic success story, with extensive supplies of high-quality crude oil ideally placed for the European market, and a large labour force. However, with a population of 73 million, it faced the problem of how to use the oil revenue to provide both employment for all its population and plans for the post-oil future. In the period 1974–94 the Nigerian Government received around 237 billion dollars in oil revenues, but the amount per year fluctuated widely. The government was under immense pressure to direct oil revenues towards the relief of poverty, but soon it was spending more than it received on improving education, the infrastructure and the development of import substitution industries (ISI), but often also on large-scale and high-cost projects. As inflation grew, the government tried to introduce drastic fiscal control, and this contributed to the military coup in 1983, after which the new military government introduced stringent fiscal austerity. By 1994 the government faced a domestic public debt of 12 billion dollars and external debt and arrears totaled nearly 34 billion dollars.[48]

Individual case studies, therefore, do not offer a particularly positive picture. Those states with large surpluses tended to have very small populations and few resources other than oil, making economic diversification impossible; those with the resources to support economic diversification found it impossible to sustain development programmes in the wake of the oil price fall from 1983 onwards. One obvious strategy for all oil exporters was to diversify oil activities into refining and distribution, as well as encouraging petrochemical industries and other energy–intensive activities such as aluminium and steel. However, while refineries in particular appeared a sensible route to diversification, there was already over-capacity in the industry, and the overall static demand for petroleum in the period after the price crisis meant that it was difficult for oil-producing states, without the market outlets and transportation facilities, to compete. As Turner and Bedore point out, the international competitiveness of many products of these giant projects was questionable,[49] particularly as many of them could only compensate for capital start-up costs, high costs of transportation and reliance on highly skilled foreign labour by the provision of cheap oil and natural gas and ready access to capital, provided by the governments. Thus, even in the one obvious area of development, the oil exporters could not be sure of an economic return.

Why did the oil-rich states in OPEC, whose oil wealth multiplied severalfold over the space of a few years, generally fail to capitalize upon the opportunity to pursue their own political and economic development as well as that of the Third World more generally? One reason for the lack of sustained development programmes was that the levels of revenue were unpredictable and did not maintain a continuous upward momentum. The political upheaval experienced in a number of oil-producing states, notably Iran, and the wars or fear of wars which affected a number of states – especially those bordering the Persian Gulf – both directly affected political structures but also acted as a warning against too rapid a pace of modernization. Moreover, regional instability prompted large defence expenditure, including advanced Western weaponry.

It is also significant that the added wealth was in the first instance directly channelled to the governments, whose task therefore became one of allocation rather than accumulation. Economic wealth was not accompanied by social transformation, and in particular the formation of a bourgeoisie, which might have led to genuine domestically generated economic growth and development. Instead, the psychology of 'easy money',[50] the wide gulf between the Western educated elites and bureaucracy on the one hand and the rest of the population on the other, the over-reliance on government spending and state intervention and the heavy expenditure on arms all contributed to the disappointing impact of the oil wealth.

Of itself, the oil industry in the various countries did not absorb much labour; not all states were in a position to be able to stimulate alternative economic activities. In many OPEC member nations, the state became the preferred employer. While the oil wealth did trickle down to many, not least in the partnership arrangements imposed by many of the governments on foreign firms operating in their jurisdiction, much of this wealth came as a consequence of soaring land values or over-paid state contracts rather than economic enterprise; moreover, many individuals chose, as did their governments in many instances, to invest overseas. Many OPEC members did invest in refining and petrochemicals at the height of the oil income boom at the beginning of the 1980s, but there was already substantial over-capacity in the world. The use of government money to provide heavily subsidized health and welfare programmes was economically unproductive and raised expectations, which proved difficult to meet in the following period of oil income decline.

Thus there is little evidence, despite what one might assume to the contrary, that oil revenue has had a marked and positive impact on economic development, especially outside the sparsely populated states of the Arabian Peninsula. For example, in 1990 Mexico and Venezuela, both major oil producers, had per capita incomes roughly similar to Brazil, Chile and Argentina, all non-oil exporters. Writing some seven years after the first dramatic increase in price, Jahangir Amuzegar (one-time Finance Minister and Prime Minister of Iran under the Shah) referred to the new oil wealth as 'a very mixed blessing.'[51] George Philip, from a later perspective, concludes that 'the most striking conclusion concerns what oil money did not do'.[52] Oil money did not encourage democracy or liberal politics; in most cases, it did not even achieve sustainable economic development.

If we look at the balance sheet, therefore, should we conclude that the crisis of 1973 was or was not a turning point in relationships between developing and developed countries? As Hallwood and Sinclair point out,[53] OPEC countries themselves certainly used the claim that they were striking a blow for the rest of the developing world when they chose to use their producer power. In the short term, the transfer of financial resources to the developing oil exporters offered a psychological boost to the entire Third World, not just the oil producers. The assertion by the Third World of its ability to take direct action in both the economic and political spheres was certainly crucial.

However, the impact of increased oil prices on many countries in the Third World was mainly negative, contributing to financial problems which, in turn, led to the debt crises of the 1980s and 1990s. The division between oil-rich and oil-poor states became far greater. The impact of the increased oil prices, and the deepening recession in the industrialized world, has been to worsen the position of oil-poor LDCs, while even the newly-rich OPEC states have experienced severe problems when the expectations created by a decade of rapidly increasing oil prices had to be contained within an income reduced by dropping, and at times plummeting, oil prices. Despite the various global conferences at least ostensibly concerned with the problems of development, capitalism and market forces – implemented by international organizations such as the IMF, the World Bank and, since 1994, the World Trade Organization – have, if anything, increased the existing inequalities between states.[54] Writing in 1999, Bruce Cumings commented that 'the least noticed collapse of our time is that of the Third World'. Pointing to the growth of revolutionary nationalism in the first thirty years after the end of the Second World War, culminating in the demands for a New International Economic Order, Cumings concludes that 'Twenty years later we have a collection of failed states ... The Third World moves not up the developmental ladder, but from statehood to catastrophe.'[55] One recent estimate suggests that while the 'Third World' currently is home to about 85 per cent of the world's population, it accounts for only 20 per cent of the world's GDP.[56]

To what can we ascribe this dismal record? In terms of economics, even at the height of their perceived power, the OPEC members never came close to undermining the international order: their calls for a New International Economic Order went largely unheeded, and the political structures of the international order, at least in terms of North–South relations, remained largely unchanged. This mirrored a number of different factors. The West was genuinely concerned by oil prices, to the extent that it was prepared to contemplate a North–South dialogue, for only a short period, which was over even before the first full meeting of the CIEC could be held. The economic influence of OPEC was never as great as some predicted in 1973, and in any case declined within a decade as oil revenues dropped. Even during the height of its powers, many of its individual members wished to ensure the stability of the Western economies in which they had invested their surplus funds. As first alternative sources of supply for oil developed, and then as more and more OPEC members embarked upon ambitious military and development programmes which required all of their available revenue, and in some cases reserves as well, their potential influence declined. In terms of the international economy, OPEC as an organization, and its individual members, were unable to challenge the existing methods of controlling and directing the world economy in any fundamental way. As we saw in the chapter on the world economy, the management of that economy remained very firmly in the hands of the industrial countries.

A major issue divided the West and the LDCs – including the members of OPEC – in the approach to development: the West saw the problem as essentially an economic one, whereas the developing nations saw the issue as essentially political. Much of the debate hinged around the issue of whether the correct approach was to work within the existing system, along with the international presumptions upon the need for a liberal world economy based on the acceptance of capitalism and the primacy of market forces; or whether a fundamental reordering of the world economy was required, to alter the basic relationships between the already developed industrial economies and the predominantly primary producers of the Third World. Developing nations saw their subordinate position in the world economy as a consequence of political and economic intervention by the industrialized world; for the West, the causal factor was a lack of appropriate values and attitudes on the part of the developing nations. The countries of OPEC found themselves in an uncomfortable position in these debates. On the one hand, they had developed a collective consciousness, in part as a consequence of fighting to regain control over their own resources and economic development, but on the other they had become heavily dependent upon the industrialized capitalist world economy for technology, expertise and investment opportunities.

The Third World's demands for a New International Economic Order demonstrated the extent of the division between North and South, and on other issues too there has been considerable disagreement and dissension. Although debates on the NIEO centred around formal economic issues, other problems began to elicit international awareness during the 1970s: problems of food supply, including the provision of fertilizer at affordable prices; and environmental problems such as pollution and climate change, and the rising world population (in 1975 the world population passed 4 billion; in 1994 it reached 6 billion), much of it in the Third World. As environmental problems such as the thinning of the ozone layer, global warming and the depletion of the world's fisheries began to affect the developed world, those countries took a keen interest in issues that they had hitherto regarded as minor. In June 1972 the United Nations sponsored the Conference on the Human Environment in Stockholm, at which 113 nations were represented. However, a problem soon emerged which was to continue to bedevil attempts to construct a global approach to environmental issues. Given that the fastest rates of population growth were in the less-developed countries, it might appear that that would be the best place to address world population: however, in states too poor to create welfare systems and with limited medical facilities, it was (and is) very difficult to provide either the rationale or the practical means to encourage individuals to limit their families. Similarly, while the developed world was concerned that the spread of industrialization to the Third World would spread pollution, not only did the LDCs wish to develop their own industries to reduce their dependence on imports, but they also resented demands that they should use only the most recent technology, which might be more environmentally friendly, but was also often under patent protection and more expensive. Proposals to limit the use of pesticides potentially spelt disaster to countries struggling to maximize their own food output. For the South, the economic costs of the proposed environmental policies have been a considerable disincentive. Even the rapidly industrializing countries within the developing world share the assumption that the problems with the ozone layer and global warming are as a consequence of Northern historical development and high levels of fossil fuel consumption.[57]

OPEC was formed at the height of the period of decolonization: as the newly independent states (most of them developing nations) sought to find a role in the post-colonial world order, the potent success of a small group of developing countries in striking directly at the economic interests of the developed industrial world suggested that a new era in international relations had begun, one in which the interests of the Third World would rise above the conflict between the First and Second. Indeed, it appeared that the Third World, like the Third Estate, had the potential to bring about revolutionary change. Such was not to be. 'Within less than a decade, most OPEC members were plagued by economic chaos, social unrest and political turmoil.'[58] The Third World's hopes of a substantial reordering of the world order – prompted by the dramatic success of OPEC and its willingness to champion the broader cause of developing nations – were rapidly dashed: in this respect, at least, the oil crisis was not the turning point that so many had hoped it would be.

Notes

1. Skeet, *Opec*, p. 87.
2. Amuzegar, *Managing Oil Wealth*, p. ix.
3. Alfred Sauvy, 'Trois mondes, une planete', *l'Observateur* 14 (August 1952), cited in Odd Arne Westad, 'The New International History of the Cold War', *Diplomatic History* 24 (2000), pp. 551–65, esp. p. 561.
4. These various examples of formal and informal oil imperialism are discussed in my earlier book, Venn, *Oil Diplomacy*.
5. Hallwood and Sinclair, *Oil, Debt and Development*, p. 11.
6. Caroline Thomas, 'Where is the Third World Now?', *Review of International Studies* 25 (1999), pp. 225–44.
7. Hallwood and Sinclair, *Oil, Debt and Development*, p. 10.
8. Hallwood and Sinclair, *Oil, Debt and Development*, Table 1.4, p. 14.
9. Foreman-Peck, *World Economy*, p. 372.
10. The reasons for this are explained in Rustow and Mugno, *OPEC*, pp. 70–8.
11. Rachel McCulloch, 'U.S. Relations with Developing Countries: Conflict and Opportunity', *Annals of the American Academy of Political and Social Science* 460 (1982), pp. 118–26, esp. pp. 120–1.
12. Robert W. Cox, 'Ideologies and the New International Economic Order: Reflections on Some Recent Literature', *International Organization* 33 (1979), pp. 257–67.
13. Foreman-Peck, *World Economy*, pp. 371–2.
14. Skeet, *Opec*, pp. 121–2.
15. Seymour, *OPEC*, pp. 258–60.
16. Skeet, *Opec*, pp. 125–7.
17. Statement of John H. Lichtblau, and subsequent discussion, 12 January 1977, United States Congress, Joint Economic Committee, Subcommittee on Energy, *Energy Independence or Interdependence: The Agenda with OPEC*. Washington, DC, 1977, p. 32; Rustow and Mugno, *OPEC*, pp. 76–8.
18. Declaration of the Industrialized Countries, 8 May 1977, Hajnal, *Seven Power Summit*, p. 41.
19. Edmund Dell, 'The Common Fund', *International Affairs* 63 (1986/87), pp. 21–38, p. 24.
20. McCulloch, 'United States Relations with Developing Countries', pp. 118–20.
21. Heath, *Autobiography*, p. 610.
22. Gareth Porter and Janet Welsh Brown, *Global Environmental Politics* (2nd edn). Westview Press, Boulder, Colorado, 1996, p. 110.
23. Foreman-Peck, *World Economy*, pp. 361–2.
24. Seymour, *OPEC*, pp. 238–9.
25. Grayson, *Foreign Policy*, pp. 123–39.
26. Hallwood and Sinclair, 'OPEC's Developing Relationships', pp. 276–8.
27. Hallwood and Sinclair, *Oil, Debt and Development*, p. xiii.
28. Tetreault, *OAPEC*, pp. 58–87.
29. George Philip, *The Political Economy of International Oil*. Edinburgh University Press, Edinburgh, 1994, Table 10.1, p. 173.
30. Amuzegar, *Managing Oil Wealth*, p. 2.
31. On Saudi Arabia, for example, see J.S. Birks and C.A. Sinclair, 'The Domestic Political

Economy of Development in Saudi Arabia', in Tim Niblock, *State, Society and Economy in Saudi Arabia*. Croom Helm, London, 1982, pp. 198–213.

32. Abir, *Saudi Arabia*, Table 5.1, p. 127.
33. Amuzegar, *Managing Oil Wealth*, p. 152.
34. Abir, *Saudi Arabia*, p. xviii.
35. Amuzegar, *Managing Oil Wealth*, p. 154.
36. Abir, *Saudi Arabia*, pp. 212–13.
37. Philip, *International Political Economy*, Table 10.2, p. 174.
38. Amy Myers Jaffe and Robert A. Manning, 'The Shocks of a World of Cheap Oil', *Foreign Affairs* 79 (2000), pp 16–29, esp. p. 23.
39. Bromley, *Middle East*, p. 145.
40. Miriam Joyce, *Kuwait 1945–1996: An Anglo-American Perspective*. Frank Cass, London, 1998, p. 164.
41. Amuzegar, *Managing Oil Wealth*, pp. 79–84.
42. Joyce, *Kuwait*, pp. 159-71.
43. Rabe, *The Road to OPEC*, p. 188.
44. Philip, *International Political Economy*, pp. 181–5.
45. Amuzegar, *Managing Oil Wealth*, pp 185–187.
46. Grayson, *Foreign Policy*, p. 30.
47. Grayson, *Foreign Policy*, p. 41.
48. Amuzegar, *Managing Oil Wealth*, pp. 89–93.
49. Louis Turner and James Bedore, 'The Trade Politics of Middle Eastern Industrialization', *Foreign Affairs* 57 (1978–9), pp. 306–22, p. 309.
50. Philip, *International Political Economy*, p. 139.
51. Jahangir Amuzegar, 'Oil Wealth: A Very Mixed Blessing', *Foreign Affairs* 60 (1981–2), pp. 814–35.
52. Philip, *International Political Economy*, p. 147.
53. Hallwood and Sinclair, 'OPEC's Developing Relationships'.
54. Thomas, 'Where is the Third World?', p. 225.
55. Bruce Cumings, 'The United States: Hegemonic Still?', *Review of International Studies* 25 (1999), pp. 271–99, esp. p. 296.
56. Thomas, 'Where is the Third World?', p. 227.
57. Porter and Brown, *Global Environmental Politics*, p. 112.
58. Amuzegar, *Managing Oil Wealth*, p. x.

7

CONCLUSION

In 1974 Walter Levy, a well-known oil expert, writing in the prestigious *Foreign Affairs* journal, was in no doubt about the significance of the 1973 oil crisis: 'Rarely, if ever, in postwar history has the world been confronted with problems as serious as those caused by recent changes in the supply and price conditions of the world oil trade.' He regarded this turn of events as 'comparable in its potential for economic and political disaster to the Great Depression of the 1930s'.[1] Others shared this gloomy prognostication of economic disaster, a world turned upside down as the developing countries of OPEC challenged the mightiest companies in the world, and prevailed. However, as the previous chapters have shown, the worst financial and economic effects of the crisis were contained, and the power of OPEC, both as an organization of oil exporters and as a representative of Third World interests more generally, was short-lived. In the concurrent Middle Eastern crisis, the Arab oil exporters confidently expected that the use of the 'oil weapon' would succeed in bringing about the withdrawal of Israel from all the territories occupied in the 1967 war. Thirty-five years after the territories were first captured, and nearly thirty years since the oil weapon was brought into play, the fate of the Occupied Territories is still a matter of bitter dispute. The impact of the 1973 crisis proved to be very different from that anticipated by its contemporaries.

Indeed, even before the end of the decade, many of the predictions of contemporaries had been proved erroneous. Although the cash price of petroleum remained high, the escalating rates of inflation in the industrialized world eroded its impact upon their economies, while increasing the prices of manufactured goods to the developing world (including the members of OPEC). Management of the world economy remained firmly in the hands of the developed nations, and attempts to construct a New International Economic Order, even with the support of OPEC members, had failed to come to fruition. Instead, the economies of oil-importing developing countries had been badly hit by the sudden increase in oil prices, and although some attempts were made by the wealthier members of OPEC to address this, aid programmes were carefully directed, often for political reasons, and were insufficient to offset the increased costs of oil imports. By the end of the decade, experts were predicting the demise of OPEC, and complacency replaced the panic which had beset so many in 1973. There was a brief resumption of that panic following the Iranian Revolution of 1978–9, but it was short-lived, and did not return, even in the face of new outbreaks of turmoil in the Middle East. Thoughts of a New International Economic Order faded, and the North–South divide remained as acute as ever.

While the position of oil companies in the international oil industry had been affected by the unilateral decision by OPEC to take total control of oil price and production levels, it did little to affect their profitability. Although the states of OPEC appeared to challenge the existing international petroleum regime,[2] through the continued use of the dollar as the pricing medium for oil, and the need of leading oil producers for American arms and protection, the United States had still been able to maintain hegemony.[3] Many at the time made the mistake of assuming that economic power, in the form claimed by OPEC, implied political power, but although the 'action of OPEC was undoubtedly the greatest forced redistribution of wealth in the history of the world',[4] it could not challenge the existing world order. That was the case even before the decline in OPEC's position in the oil industry after 1983.

In short, the detailed study of virtually every theme allows us to identify clear trends of change emerging before 1973, as well as demonstrating that there was more continuity after 1973 than had been expected at the time. Does this, however, mean that the much vaunted 'oil crisis' is somehow of little real significance, or are we in danger of underestimating its real effect? After all, the 1973 crisis alone increased the price of oil fourfold in under three months, diverted funds to underdeveloped countries and hence changed their pattern of development, accelerated world economic problems and led to the peculiar phenomenon of stagflation, i.e. stagnation accompanied by rapid inflation, which signalled the final death throes of the Breton Woods system. An important precondition for an historical turning point must surely be that the event examined has an impact beyond its own immediate consequences, and that is certainly true of both the 1973 oil crisis and, albeit to a lesser extent, the second crisis in 1979. Their consequences spread beyond the oil industry and the Middle East, where they had their origins, to affect the world economy, trans-Atlantic relationships, and internal European Community politics. The two successive increases in oil prices directly affected the domestic economy of every country in the world, oil producers and consumers alike. Whatever its outcome, the debate on the fairness (or otherwise) of the prevailing international economic order, and the growing international awareness of the problems of development and the North–South divide, was given a new prominence during OPEC's short period of power.

Even if – as has been argued on a number of occasions in this book – the consequences proved to be less permanent or far-reaching than those originally anticipated, in many instances it is the exaggerated nature of those anticipated consequences, rather than their limited impact, which should be highlighted. The outcomes may not have been quite those predicted at the time. Thus, it is Third World debt, rather than a New International Economic Order, which is the main legacy of the oil crises for the Third World. For the leading oil exporters, increased oil revenues led to political instability and in some cases economic difficulties, rather than a new era of prosperity and development. In the Middle East, attention shifted from the security of Israel to the future of the Palestinians, but no solution has yet been found that could reconcile the two. Each of these actual outcomes is, however, highly significant in its own right. When taken together, particularly when combined with the economic changes often associated with 1973, their impact is momentous. The year 1973 has come to be employed as a reference point in time for a shift which, for many, first became apparent in that year, however much it is possible to identify signs of change well before that date. It represents a break point between a postwar era of economic growth, improved standards of living (at least for those in the developed West) and a stable economic regime to one of successive recessions, increasing globalization and the negative impact of unemployment and inflation. For the developing world, the hope of decolonization has given way to mounting debt crises and mounting poverty. This shift is well reflected in the comment by historian Eric Hobsbawm: 'The history of the twenty years after 1973 is that of a world which has lost its bearings and slid into instability and crisis.'[5] Robert Lieber, writing a decade after the crisis, argued that 'In light of the passage of a decade, October 1973 appears as a virtual continental divide, separating a post-World War II generation of economic recovery, prosperity and Western unity from an era of stagflation, lost confidence and disarray.'[6] In both perception and reality, the year 1973 was a powerful symbol of change, and the oil crisis amply warrants inclusion in this series on historical turning points. Whether there will be another oil crisis, with similar consequences, in the future is a moot point.

As a historian, I may draw lessons from the past, but hesitate to apply them to the future. There have been too many instances, some quoted in this book, where experts have found that their confident predictions have been overturned by events. However, as long as the main consumers of petroleum are not its main producers, access to secure and affordable oil supplies will remain a matter of high international and national politics. Although there has been a definite slowing down in the rate of growth of consumption, the world – both developed industrialized countries and also LDCs – remain heavily dependent upon oil. Alternative energy sources may have expanded, but the generation of energy is only one of a myriad of uses for petroleum and its various derivatives. While in many respects the contemporary international oil situation does not appear to suggest that another oil crisis, at least in the foreseeable future, is imminent, nonetheless, it remains the case that a very large proportion of the world's known reserves lie under the Middle East, much of it in the area around the Persian Gulf. Its secure exploitation therefore depends upon political stability in a region notable for its instability. Apart from the Arab–Israeli conflict, the Persian Gulf saw two major wars in a little over ten years, the Iran–Iraq War of 1980-88 and the Gulf War in 1991, while the Iranian Revolution demonstrated that even apparently stable regimes, with advanced weaponry and strong military forces, could be overturned by internal upheaval. As the oil crises of the 1970s conclusively demonstrated, the politics of oil and the politics of the Middle East make a highly explosive combination. The West succeeded in managing the worst consequences then, but it cannot afford to overlook its vulnerability in the future.

Notes

1. Walter J. Levy, 'World Oil Cooperation or International Chaos', *Foreign Affairs* 52 (1973–4), pp. 690–713, pp. 690 and 713.
2. Stephen D. Krasner, *Structural Conflict: The Third World Against Global Liberalism*. University of California Press, Berkley, California, 1985, p. 71.
3. Bromley, *American Hegemony*, pp. 1–7
4. Robert Gilpin, *War and Change in World Politics*. Cambridge University Press, Cambridge, 1983.
5. Hobsbawm, *Age of Extremes*, p. 403.
6. Lieber, *Oil Decade*, p. 1

APPENDIX ONE

OPEC MEMBERS, 1960 TO THE PRESENT

The date of joining OPEC is given in parentheses.
Iran (1960)
Iraq (1960)
Kuwait (1960)
Saudi Arabia (1960)
Venezuela (1960)
Qatar (1961)
Libya (1962)
Indonesia (1962)
Abu Dhabi (1967) – *NB*, after 1971 the United Arab Emirates
Algeria (1969)
Nigeria (1971)
Ecuador (1973 – left 1993)
Gabon (1975 – left 1994)

APPENDIX TWO

OAPEC MEMBERS

The asterisk indicates states that are also members of OPEC:

★Algeria
  Bahrain
  Egypt
★Iraq
★Kuwait
★Libya
★Qatar
★Saudi Arabia
  Syria
  Tunisia (membership was made inactive in 1986)
★United Arab Emirates

APPENDIX THREE

CHRONOLOGY OF A MONTH OF CRISIS: OCTOBER 1973

3 October	Egypt warned Soviets that an attack on Israel was imminent.
4 October	Soviets evacuated their citizens from Egypt.
6 October	Egypt and Syria attacked Israel.
8 October	Talks began between Gulf states of OPEC and oil companies.
9 October	Israeli planes bombed Damascus.
9/10 October	Soviet airlift of supplies to front-line states begins.
10 October	Israel announced that it had recaptured its prewar positions in Golan.
10 October	US Vice President Spiro Agnew resigned.
12 October	Oil companies requested an adjournment of talks.
12 October	Nixon announced that he would nominate Gerald Ford as the new Vice President.
12 October	Nixon ordered to hand over seven Oval Office tapes.
13 October	First American airlift to Israel.
14 October	New Egyptian offensive in the Sinai.
16 October	Persian Gulf producers set oil price unilaterally at 5.12 dollars a barrel.
16 October	King Feisal requested the United States to halt all shipments of arms to Israel.
17 October	OAPEC members met, and agreed selected production cuts, in support of Egypt and Syria.
17 October	Arab Ambassadors asked President Nixon to intervene.
19 October	Sadat agreed to the Soviet proposals for a ceasefire.
19 October	Nixon asked Congress for an appropriation to re-supply Israel.
20 October	Kissinger left for Moscow.
20 October	US Attorney General Elliott Richardson resigned: Nixon fired Special Prosecutor Archibald Cox.

20 October	OAPEC decided to impose an oil embargo on the United States (later extended to the Netherlands and Portugal).
21 October	Superpowers agreed on a joint ceasefire proposal.
22 October	UN Security Council passed Resolution 338, calling for a ceasefire and implementation of Resolution 242.
22 October	Ceasefire went into effect in the Sinai Peninsula, only to break down after a few hours.
23 October	Security Council passed Resolution 339 calling on all parties to return to lines held at first ceasefire.
23 October	21 resolutions for Nixon's impeachment introduced in the House of Representatives.
24 October	Second ceasefire broke down in the Sinai.
24 October	Sadat appealed to Nixon and Brezhnev to send troops to police the ceasefire.
24 October	Brezhnev wrote to Nixon threatening to act unilaterally if the US did not join it in policing ceasefire.
24 October	Ceasefire went into effect on the Golan Heights.
25 October	American troops world wide put on nuclear alert (DEFCON 3).
25 October	Security Council agreed to send a UN force, excluding both superpowers, to police the ceasefire.
26 October	US began to ease off its state of alert.
4 November	OAPEC announced additional production cuts.
11 November	Israel and Egypt agreed a six-point plan to regulate the ceasefire.

GUIDE TO FURTHER READING

There is a considerable literature on each of the topics discussed in this book, much of it contained in specialized contemporary or academic journals. Some of these works are referred to in the references. Two earlier studies on the oil crisis, both written before the major downturn in oil prices, are the volume of essays edited by Raymond Vernon (ed.), *The Oil Crisis* (Norton, New York, 1976) and the work by Robert Lieber, predominantly looking at the reactions of industrialized consumers to each of the oil crises of the decade 1973–83, *The Oil Decade: Conflict and Cooperation in the West* (Praeger, New York, 1983). Daniel Yergin's book, *The Prize: The Epic Quest for Oil, Money and Power* (Pocket Books: New York, 1991), is a very lively and readable account of the history of the oil industry. I have written a broader study of oil diplomacy throughout the twentieth century in *Oil Diplomacy in the Twentieth Century* (Macmillan, London, 1986). The best study of the role of oil companies in international relations, and the decline in that role after 1973, is Louis Turner, *Oil Companies in the International System*, 3rd edn (Allen & Unwin, London, 1983). For a superb company history, looking far beyond the history of just British Petroleum, see James Bamberg, *History of the British Petroleum Company. British Petroleum and Global Oil, 1950–1975: The Challenge of Nationalism* (Cambridge University Press, Cambridge, 2000).

There were, predictably, more studies of OPEC immediately after 1973 than since. Useful surveys include Ian Seymour, *OPEC: Instrument of Change* (Macmillan, London, 1980) and Dankwart A. Rustow and John F. Mugno, OPEC: *Success and Prospects* (New York University Press, New York, 1976). The latter contains very detailed references to contemporary writings on the subject. Ian Skeet has written an exhaustive study of the political and pricing policies of OPEC, in Opec: *Twenty-five Years of Prices and Politics* (Cambridge University Press, Cambridge, 1988), although at times his background as a Shell International executive becomes apparent, both in the level of his expertise on the intricacies of the oil business, and in his sympathy for the problems faced by the companies in the turbulent period from 1970 to the late 1980s. The early history of OAPEC is examined in detail in Mary Ann Tetreault, *The Organization of Arab Petroleum Exporting*

Countries: History, Policies and Prospects (Greenwood Press, Westport, Connecticut, 1981).

Peter Odell has written a useful study of the oil industry's role in international history, organized by geographical region, in *Oil and World Power*, 8th edn (Penguin, Harmondsworth, 1986). There are a number of works which look at the international political economy of the oil industry and the oil crisis, often seeking to locate an empirical account within a theoretical framework. In *American Hegemony and World Oil: The Industry, the State System and the World Economy* (Polity Press, Cambridge, 1991) Stephen Bromley argues that United States control of world oil played a significant role in underpinning its international position and power; the oil crisis of 1973 represented a realignment, rather than a diminution, of both American hegemony in general and the American role in the world oil order. George Philip, *The Political Economy of International Oil* (Edinburgh University Press, Edinburgh, 1994) is an excellent source for those wishing to understand why the vast oil revenue has not brought about substantial economic and social development in the member states of OPEC. This subject is also covered in Paul Hallwood and Stuart Sinclair, *Oil, Debt and Development: OPEC in the Third World* (George Allen & Unwin, London, 1981). Jahangir Amuzegar, *Managing the Oil Wealth: OPEC's Windfalls and Pitfalls* (I.B. Tauris, London, 1999), looks at the oil producers on a country-by-country basis and argues that mismanagement played a significant part.

Two good general histories of the Middle East are William L. Cleveland, *A History of the Modern Middle East* (Westview Press, Boulder, Colorado, 1994) and M.E. Yapp, *The Near East Since the First World War* (Longman, New York, 1991). Rosemarie Said Zahlan, *The Making of the Modern Gulf States: Kuwait, Bahrain, Qatar, the United Arab Emirates and Oman* (Unwin Hyman, London, 1989) is the best study of the sheikhdoms along the Persian Gulf littoral. Nikki R. Keddie has written extensively on the history of Iran and its revolution: see, for example, *Roots of Revolution: An Interpretative History of Modern Iran* (Yale University Press, New Haven, 1981) and the collection of essays edited by Keddie and Eric Hooglund, *The Iranian Revolution and the Islamic Republic* (Syracuse University Press, Syracuse, New York, 1986). The relationship between Iran and the United States is analysed in James A. Bill, *The Eagle and the Lion: The Tragedy of American–Iranian Relations* (Yale University Press, New Haven, 1988).

The literature on the Arab–Israeli conflict is particularly vast. There are two useful general surveys of the conflict: T.G. Fraser, *The*

Arab–Israeli Conflict (Macmillan, London, 1995) and Ritchie Ovendale, *The Origins of the Arab–Israeli Wars* (Longman, London, 1984). The history of the disputed land of Israel/Palestine is discussed in Deborah J. Gerner, *One Land, Two Peoples: The Conflict over Palestine* (Westview Press, Boulder, Colorado, 1994). A noted trend in the history of Israel's foreign policy is the new generation of Israeli revisionist historians, who challenge the defensive account of Israeli policy and do not hesitate to criticize the actions of Israel, particularly in regard of the Occupied Territories. Avi Shlaim, *The Iron Wall: Israel and the Arab World* (Allen Lane, The Penguin Press, 2000), is to be particularly recommended. Galia Golan has written extensively on Soviet policy in the Middle East, including *Yom Kippur and After: The Soviet Union and the Middle East Crisis* (Cambridge University Press, Cambridge, 1977) and *Soviet Policies in the Middle East from World War Two to Gorbachev* (Cambridge University Press, Cambridge, 1990). There is a considerable debate as to whether Soviet policy in the region was offensive or defensive, successful or a failure. Robert O. Freedman takes a critical view of Soviet policy, arguing that it was essentially offensive, if unsuccessful: see, for example, *Soviet Policy towards the Middle East since 1970*, 2nd edn (Praeger Publishers, New York, 1978) and *Moscow and the Middle East: Soviet Policy since the invasion of Afghanistan* (Cambridge University Press, Cambridge 1991).

There are a number of studies of the so-called 'special relationship' between the United States and Israel: recent examples, based on declassified documents, include Abraham Ben-Zvi, *The United States and Israel: The Limits of the Special Relationship* (Columbia University Press, New York, 1993) and Yaacov Bar-Siman-Tov, *Israel, the Superpowers and the War in the Middle East* (Praeger Press, New York, 1987). American relations with other states in the region are covered in Burton I. Kaufman, *The Arab Middle East and the United States: Inter-Arab Rivalry and Superpower Diplomacy* (Twayne Publishers, New York, 1996). Stephen Spiegel has written extensively on the place of the Middle East in international relations and American domestic and foreign policy, including two edited collections, *Conflict Management in the Middle East* (Westview Press, Boulder, Colorado, 1992) and *The Middle East and the Western Alliance* (George Allen & Unwin, London 1982), as well as *The Other Arab–Israeli Conflict: Making America's Middle East Policy, from Truman to Reagan* (The University of Chicago Press, Chicago, 1985). William B. Quandt of the Brookings Institution, who in the Carter Administration assumed particular responsibility for Arab–Israeli affairs, has written a number of studies, including *Decade of*

Decisions: American Foreign Policy Toward the Arab–Israeli Conflict, 1967–1976 (University of California Press, Berkeley, 1977).

Relationships between the consuming nations are discussed in Lieber, *The Oil Decade*, and in numerous books and memoirs covering the 1970s. The difficulties within the trans-Atlantic relationship, captured in Henry Kissinger's memoirs of the time, *White House Years* (Weidenfeld & Nicolson, London, 1979) and *Years of Upheaval* (Weidenfeld & Nicolson, London, 1982), are discussed in Michael Smith, *Western Europe and the United States: The Uncertain Alliance* (George Allen & Unwin, London, 1984). Histories of the individual oil producers are cited in the references. For Saudi Arabia, a useful study is Mordechai Abir, *Saudi Arabia in the Oil Era: Regimes and Elites: Conflict and Collaboration* (Croom Helm, London, 1988). The history of Kuwait is set against British and American policy and influence in the Persian Gulf in Miriam Joyce, *Kuwait 1945–1996: An Anglo-American Perspective* (Frank Cass, London, 1998). George W. Grayson's studies of Mexico are to be recommended, including *The Politics of Mexican Oil* (University of Pittsburgh Press, Pittsburgh, 1980) and *Oil and Mexican Foreign Policy* (University of Pittsburgh Press, Pittsburgh, 1988).

A useful general text on the history of the world economy, particularly strong on the nature and collapse of the Bretton Woods system, is James Foreman-Peck, *A History of the World Economy: International Economic Relations since 1850* (Wheatsheaf Books, Brighton, 1983). The interaction between domestic and foreign economic policies for the six main industrial nations is explored in Peter J. Katzenstein (ed.), *Between Power and Plenty: Foreign Economic Policies of Advanced Industrial States* (The University of Wisconsin Press, Madison, Wisconsin, 1978).

An important source for discussions, not only of the world economy but also the oil industry and the internal economies of OPEC and OECD members, is a wide range of statistics charting significant economic and financial indices. There are a number of international organizations which publish detailed statistics, including the World Bank, the International Monetary Fund, the OPEC Secretariat, the International Energy Agency of the Organization of Economic Cooperation and Development, the United Nations and its various affiliates, as well as national institutions such as the Bureau of the Census (United States); however, figures between the various institutions, and even between different publications of the same organization, are not necessarily compatible. This may reflect different sources, different conversion factors or different definitions of what is meant by a particular term (for example, some sources include natural gas liquids within a calculation of crude oil production, others do not).

Statistics on the oil industry may be obtained, in a user-friendly form, from British Petroleum, *Statistical Review of the World Oil Industry* (British Petroleum London, annual). The annual *Statistical Abstract* of the United States, produced by the US Bureau of the Census, and normally published by the US Government Printing Office, provides encyclopaedic statistics on the United States, but also comparative figures for other countries in some instances. For very recent statistics, it is worth visiting the websites of the International Energy Agency and the Energy Information Agency of the US Department of Energy. Finally, no survey of literature on the contemporary oil industry would be complete without mentioning the authoritative journal, the *Middle East Economic Survey*, which also has an informative website.

INDEX